To

The
Ultimate
Reception

God Bless you

Gerry Lifton

Multiple Blessings Unlimited

Romans 1:16

Printed in Canada
First Edition, 2001
Second Edition 2002

Cover Design by Dwayne Cannan
www.dwaynecannan.com
Edited by John Thompson
Page Layout by Debbie Laprise

The New International Version of the Bible
was used in the quoting of Scriptures.

Photographs are copyrighted by Multiple Blessings Unlimited.

ISBN Number 0-9689881-0-5

Multiple Blessings Unlimited
157 Deer Ridge Dr.
St. Albert, AB T8N 6G8
www.aimcanada.ca
E-mail: aim_canada@shaw.ca
780-460-3943

Contents

Introduction

This autobiography is written in honour of the memory of my father and mother, Oliver and Dorothy (Salisbury) Lefebvre. Although Mom and Dad had their share of personal struggles, by the grace of God they raised six kids, who love and respect one another to this day. In a day when many families are torn apart and struggling to stay together, I am blessed to be part of a family that truly loves each other and sticks together through whatever life throws their way.

Along with my personal agonies and ecstasies, this book tells of the birth of Canada's Circle Square Ranches, in particular the one in Halkirk, Alberta. My sister, Pat, and brothers Bob, Blaine, Murray and Mark all served at the ranch with us during those eight glorious years. Numerous miracles and divine interventions are recorded and testified to with my desire to understate rather than exaggerate the accounts. As to why our family was blessed with these many miracles, only God knows. All I know is that they did happen and they have dramatically contributed to our family's spiritual growth. These stories still remain indelibly printed in my mind to this day, as I have been privileged over the past 30 years to share them from time to time.

My life's story reveals how a dream in one's heart, when pursued with passion, can really come to pass and how simple faith, when acted upon, can bring dramatic results. It is my aim, through the following chapters, to show that grace, faith and the blessings that follow are all undeserved gifts and are given by God to be received by anyone and everyone.

Foreword

Garry Lefebvre did it!

Actually he's done a lifetime of unusual things, but I still can't explain the emotional hit I took in 1973 from this football star as I watched Canada's Super Bowl, known as "The Grey Cup" final. I thrilled to Garry's efforts on the field. Because of injuries to his Edmonton Eskimos team mates, he played both offense and defense, as well as handling the punting duties. This almost never happens in pro ball. He was the star both ways, in my judgment. But the big moment that literally caused my tears to do something I'd never experienced before happened after the game. The veteran TV network sportscaster announced Garry as the Canadian Player of the Grey Cup Game.

Tears literally popped out of my eyes, missed my bottom eyelids and landed at least three inches down my cheeks. To find out what Garry did and said on national TV, check chapter 1 in this book. It was something that had never happened before on Canadian Network TV. The reporter, never stuck for words, was speechless. No, I'm not telling the story here. Read this book if you dare. You'll never be the same.

David Mainse
100 Huntley Street

Acknowledgements

To the following people I owe my deepest gratitude. Without them this book would not have come to print.

David Mainse—who encouraged me to write my story.

Larry Jones—who fanned the flame and helped me to get started.

Shannon Cherry—who helped me with the first rough drafts and encouraged me not to give up. Her faithfulness and commitment have inspired my whole family.

Pastor Don Rousu—who helped with the preliminary editing.

My daughter Jules and Nancy Christianson—who edited the second printing.

Dwayne Cannan—who was inspired with the idea for the book cover.

Lee Nohos—who formatted this book and helped to launch it.

John Thompson—who performed the book's final edit.

Al Jenkins—who brought this work to completion and who was instrumental in its release.

Lil Fletcher—who formatted the final layout of this second edition.

Paul Collins—for being a true friend, who supported and encouraged me for many years, and without whose help this work would never have been completed.

Mac Hyland—my dear friend and fellow soldier, whom I loved and admired, who went to be with his Lord on September 19, 2001.

The staff and volunteers of Canada's nine Circle Square Ranches—who have given much of their lives for the cause of our youth.

My Children (Chéri, Brad, Julie, and Jesse)—who are each special and unique in their own right and whom I love very much.

Dedicated To

Sandy, my loving wife and closest friend, who has hung in there with me through many trials and tribulations.

1973 Eskimos

1970 Alouettes

Chapter 1

GREY CUP GLORY

As the team bus pulled into the stadium parking lot, the excitement intensified with each memory that played across my mind. It was three years ago at this very stadium that I first tasted the incredible thrill of the Grey Cup experience. At that time, I was a member of the Montreal Alouettes, who were entering the 1970 Grey Cup game as Eastern Conference Champions. This event would be altogether different.

Growing up in Edmonton, as a young boy I had dreamed of playing in the Canadian Football League, but in those days there was only one team for me . . . the Mighty Eskimos. Now my dream was a reality and I was about to step into the 1973 Grey Cup game as a member of the Western Conference Champion Edmonton Eskimos.

The players and coaches made slow progress towards the dressing room as they waded through the press of hungry autograph seekers. No one was complaining, though. After all, some players go through their entire career without ever making it to the Grey Cup. Being mobbed by excited fans caught up in Grey Cup fever was just a part of the happening.

We finally reached the locker room and changed into our practice gear. After a short talk from Head Coach Ray Jauch, we all headed out to the field, once more surrounded by the ever-present throng of fans. As I surveyed the huge Toronto Stadium, again my thoughts returned to the 1970 Grey Cup. In that game I had played on this same field as a wide receiver with the Alouettes. Our 23-to-10 win over the Calgary Stampeders was capped off with my first Grey Cup touchdown pass. Now that I was with the Edmonton Eskimos, my strongest hope was that the Esks would be equally successful in our battle with Ottawa this Sunday afternoon, and I would claim my second Grey Cup ring.

As I stepped on to the smooth green turf, the sound of Coach Jauch's voice interrupted my thoughts. "Garry, come over here for a minute," he called as he signalled to me from the visiting team bench. As I turned to walk back to where he stood, I wondered anxiously why the coach had singled me out. Ray was an intense coach, in the same way that he had been an intense player. He usually didn't smile much prior to game time. We all knew the look of his "game face," but as I drew closer, I began to relax a little when I noticed a smile beginning to appear at the corners of his mouth.

"Garry, the coaches and I were going over the depth chart last night, and we realized that we don't have anyone backing up Billy Cooper at defensive right corner back," he explained. "If he should get hurt on Sunday, we would be in deep trouble. Billy has been nursing a tender groin the past couple of weeks, and he seemed to aggravate it some in the Western Final. I know you're playing flanker and punting already, but we really need someone to back up Billy . . . we believe you're the best man for the job."

Suddenly, my level of anxiety was on its way up again. The thought of playing corner and having to cover Ottawa's all-star wide receiver, Rhome Nixon, left me feeling a little less than confident. I knew how fast and sure-handed he was. I had played corner back for a couple of games back in 1969, and I didn't enjoy it at all. One of those games was against these same Roughriders, and I had been burned badly by both their wide receivers. Offense was where I felt comfortable. I didn't like the thought of running backward, or tackling for that matter, especially large fullbacks.

"The defensive coaches want you to attend all their meetings until game time so you can learn all the calls and the defensive sets," Coach Jauch continued, interrupting the flow of my thoughts. "You will pick them up easily enough. We've simplified the corner back's responsibilities, and I'm sure you won't have any trouble comprehending the defensive scheme. You'd better be prepared to go both ways, just in case we need you there. To be honest, I don't think it will come to that, but we have to cover our butts."

He was right. What were the chances of Billy getting hurt anyway, and me having to play his position as well as mine? *Nah! It couldn't happen,* I reassured myself, pushing the troubling thoughts out of my mind. Little did I realize that a plan was being set in motion and I was right smack in the centre of it.

Our Friday and Saturday practices were more intense for me than any I had experienced in my eight years as a professional athlete. In addition to my normal offensive preparations, I had to learn our defensive sets and calls, plus study the films from both sides of the ball. By Saturday evening my mind felt like it was about to explode.

Thankfully, the assistant coaches were very helpful, but it was a lot to learn in just two and a half days. Added to my load was the fact that our defensive coaching staff decided to put in a new method of coverage just for this game. It was totally man on man or "mike" as we called it. The Esks always ran some man-on-man coverage, specifically when we were blitzing. This was usually mixed with zone coverage, which we often tried to disguise, in order to keep the offence off balance. Never before had we run a strict "mike" defence. Should I have to replace Billy at corner, I would be covering Rhome Nixon, one on one, without any line-backer or deep help. The very thought of such a possibility set my nerves on edge.

A Miraculous Turn Around

The Ottawa Roughriders were considered the underdogs for the Grey Cup. From the beginning of the season, no one had picked them even to make the playoffs, let alone be in the Grey Cup. In the early going, the team was zero wins and four losses and appeared destined for the base-ment, when they miraculously turned things around. Their all-star place kicker Gerry Organ relayed the story to me later that winter.

The Roughriders conducted pre-game chapel services, as did all but one of the teams in the CFL at that time. At the end of the 1972 season, five Christian players had formed Athletes In Action Canada, starting the chapel program and Bible Studies on eight of the nine teams. Gerry and his team mate, Wayne Tosh, were part of that group of founders, along with Larry Kerychuk, Bob Kraemer and me. During their zero-and-four stretch, the only Ottawa players who showed up for pre-game chapel service were the three Christians on the team: Rod Woodward, Wayne, and Gerry, along with the guest speaker. After their fourth loss in a row, the three of them prayed earnestly for their team-mates and made a special point to personally invite each player.

"It can't hurt you to give it a try," was the standard plea. "We sure aren't doing very well on our own. Why not come at least this once and see what it's all about?" Their fifth game was against Toronto, and an amazing twelve additional players showed up for chapel!

The speaker was a young man named Paul, a lay minister from Hamilton. After he shared an inspiring message with the players, he closed the meeting in prayer. To his own surprise, Paul heard himself saying, "And thank you, Lord, for Ottawa's victory today, for your glory." *Oh Lord!* he thought, *what did I just say? What if they don't win? What will all these guys think?* In all of his time of ministry to athletes, he had never before prayed for one team's victory over another.

Later that afternoon, Paul sat in Lansdowne Stadium praying and hoping that he had not blown it, and at the same time asking the Lord for forgiveness in case he had.

"If Ottawa loses, many of the players who were there for the first time might never return, and will probably label all of us Christians as kooks. Please, Lord," he prayed, "don't let my mistake ruin it for Gerry, Rod and Wayne. Please forgive me if I stepped out of line."

The game was close, but the Argonauts kicked a field goal with less than three minutes to go and pulled ahead by five points. With only seconds left, the Roughriders got the ball back on their own 40-yard line. Paul sat there in the stands feeling numb and sick to his stomach. "God, please forgive me," he repented again quietly in his heart.

On the last play from scrimmage, Rick Cassata, the Ottawa quarterback, dropped back and threw a desperation "Hail Mary" down the right sideline. The ball deflected off one of the Toronto defender's hands and sailed right into wide receiver Rhome Nixon's hands. With his speed, no one was about to catch him as he out-legged everyone to the end zone. Ottawa had won their first game of the season by two points and young Paul nearly fainted with excitement. At the next game, fifteen men showed up for pre-game chapel, and many of them faithfully attended for the rest of the 1973 season.

Now, three and a half months later, the Ottawa Roughriders were in Toronto as the Eastern Conference Champions to face the favoured Eskimos in the Grey Cup.

More Than A Coincidence

Saturday night I tossed and turned until after 3:00 a.m. The new defensive plays ran over and over in my mind. *What if I really do have to play defense tomorrow?* I fretted. Earlier that evening, I had received a telegram from my neighbourhood Bible Study group in Edmonton. I rolled over, turned on the lamp, and read the message once again:

THERE IS A GOOD FLANKER—NO. 11

WHO KNOWS HE IS GOING TO HEAVEN

WITH TEAM-MATES WON GLORY

IN THE '73 GREY CUP STORY

BUT TO THE LORD GAVE ALL THE GLORY

Norm and Judi Dyer had sent the message on behalf of the whole group. The day before the team left for Toronto, we were all at our regular Tuesday evening study group at John and Marianne Willock's in St. Albert. At the close of the study, we were about to end in prayer, as was our custom, when Norm spoke up.

"Before we start praying, there's something that came to me very strongly this afternoon. Wouldn't it be fantastic if in Sunday's game, Garry would win the Outstanding Canadian Player of the Game award, and then give the glory to the Lord."

I shuddered, and goose bumps appeared on my entire body. My wife, Sandy, and I looked at each other as if to say, *How did he know?* Two hours earlier, as we were standing in our kitchen, Sandy had expressed to me those very same words. We had told the others what we were thinking, and they all prayed together for God to grant me the award so that I would have the opportunity to share my faith with the millions of fans who would be watching.

Could this really happen? As I turned out the light and once more attempted to find sleep, a portion of scripture floated through my mind. *"Everything is possible for him who believes."*

The Game of My Life

Six hours later I awoke, not the least bit fatigued. The adrenaline was already flowing, and the butterflies that usually show up on game day had brought along a contingent of their friends. We met for our pre-game chapel, followed by a meal, and then everyone boarded the awaiting Greyhound, bound for Toronto's CNE Stadium.

We arrived two hours prior to the 2:00 p.m. kick-off. Some of the guys went straight into the training room to get taped. Most of the players liked to arrive early on game day, get dressed up to the waist, and then play card games, or just lie around and conserve as much energy as possible. The two hours went by very quickly, and in no time at all it was time for warm up.

The Western supporters exploded with applause, horns, whistles, and the waving of banners as we ran out onto the field. Many fans had come all the way from Edmonton with hopes that their beloved Esks would bring home the long-awaited cup. It had been thirteen long years since we had won the last one.

After the opening ceremonies, Dave Cutler, who set the CFL record for most points in a season that year with 133, kicked off to the Ottawa 12-yard line. The ball was returned by corner back Al Marcelin to the Ottawa 33, and the game was under way.

After two running plays, the Roughriders were forced to punt. Dick Dupuis took it on our 37 and returned it to the 40. After one first down by fullback Calvin Harrell, Tom Wilkinson handed off to Roy Bell who carried the ball over left tackle. As I came in from my left flanker position, I saw Ottawa's deep back John Krusp flying up to make the hit on Bell, who had just broken through the line. Krusp had a bead on Roy and didn't see me coming. I drove him with my right shoulder just below the waist and he tumbled over me to the turf. My momentum carried me another four yards and I took out their other back, Dick Adams, as well. When I looked up, there was Roy flying down the left hash marks with no one within 30 yards of him. Dave Cutler converted the touchdown, and with just three minutes gone, we were ahead 7-0.

Right then I should have realized that something unusual was taking place. Like most wide receivers, blocking was definitely not one of my strengths. When running backs are learning blocking techniques, wide-outs are usually practising pass routes. On running plays, coaches instruct us to get out of the way and take a defensive back with us or, at worst, to shield a defender off and make him run around us. We were paid to catch the ball and run with it. Most wide receivers lack good blocking skills, and I was right in there with the majority, yet I had just taken out two defenders with one block.

After Cutler's convert and second kickoff, our defence held them again. We exchanged punts, and after two Ottawa first downs they snapped the ball on our 38-yard line. Quarterback Rick Cassata spotted wide receiver Rhome Nixon deep down the left sideline and hit him with a perfect strike for a major. On the touchdown, my greatest fear was realized when Billy Cooper pulled up lame with a torn groin muscle.

Coach Jauch looked at me with an apologetic smile and said, "Well, Garry you've got to take his place. I know you can do the job. We're counting on you."

I felt a sense of apprehension mixed with excitement as I jogged out on to the playing surface. Without help from above, I knew I was in real trouble.

Lord, please give me strength and help me to do the best job I can, I breathed silently, entering the defensive huddle. Dick Dupuis slapped me on the back and tried to encourage me.

"You can do it, Garry. Just keep a good cushion and don't let Nixon get behind you. I'll help you up front all I can."

I was sure I would need all the help he could give me, and then some. Gerry Organ kicked the convert and the game was tied. After the kickoff, I was back on offence. I felt much more comfortable on that side of the ball, and silently hoped we would stay out there the rest of the afternoon. Of course, that would be impossible.

Wilkie marched the offence all the way down to Ottawa's 12-yard line, and on 1st and 10 he scrambled out of the pocket and tried to hoof it to the near right sideline. He was hit and spun around just as Dick Adams came hurling through the air and caught Tom in the right side with his knee. Wilkie was helped off the field with re-injured ribs, so Bruce Lemmerman came in to replace him.

Bruce was in pain himself as he had received twelve stitches in the elbow of his throwing arm just the week before. We were stopped on the next play and had to settle for a Cutler field goal. After the ensuing kickoff, the Roughriders proceeded to drive down field. With 1st and 10 on our 15-yard line, Nixon was called on a quick out and up. I went for the *out*, just as he turned *up* the left sideline.

Oh, Lord! I thought, *I'm dead.*

I swung my head around, expecting to see the ball sailing into Nixon's awaiting hands. I could hardly believe it. The ball was badly under thrown, and I went up into the air and came down with it on the 5-yard line. I had intercepted the first pass tossed my way. As I ran off the field amidst the backslapping and congratulating, all I could say was, "Praise the Lord—I was beaten on the play, but the ball came right to me."

The teams changed ends for the second quarter, and both moved the ball sporadically. We didn't manage a single point, and Ottawa picked up two points on a safety when I mishandled a punt snap and was tackled by Wayne Tosh in our end zone. With three minutes left in the first half, Cassata handed off to their big fullback, Jim Evenson. He carried the ball around their right end, just as Ron Estay came off his block and drove his helmet right into Evenson's stomach. Simultaneously, the Ottawa lead blocker slammed me and knocked me off stride. I stumbled frantically, trying to regain my balance and stay on my feet. The ball squirted out of Evenson's hands, bounced three times and landed in my outstretched arms, a fraction of a second before I stepped out of bounds.

It was unbelievable! The Ottawa back knocked me right into the path of the bouncing ball, which had been drawn to me like a magnet.

A little stunned, I awaited the arrival of the rest of my offensive team mates back on the field. When he stepped into the huddle, Bruce slapped me on the shoulder pad with, "Great play, Garry!"

Once more, all I could say was, "Praise the Lord."

The offense bogged down after two plays and turned the ball over to the Ottawa offense. With just seconds to go, Organ hit a long field goal from our 45-yard line. The half ended with Ottawa in front 13 to 10.

At the opening of the third quarter, Ottawa moved the ball well with Cassata mixing running plays with screens and short passes, and they moved the ball to our 40. I moved up tighter on Nixon, expecting a short pass route. He came off the line hard and gave me a head fake to the inside, but I didn't bite. As I anticipated, he turned out to the left sideline. I closed fast, glancing at the quarterback, looking to pick up the flight of the ball. Just then Nixon turned up the sideline and I was had.

"Oh Lord," I gasped, "I'm toast!"

I scrambled after him, but there was no way for me to catch him. He had a big jump and was inherently faster than I. It was hopeless, but I ran after him anyway. Nixon had a good 15 yards on me as he crossed the goal line. When I glanced over my left shoulder, the ball was already in the air.

There was a 35-mile-an-hour wind behind the pass, and I was the most surprised guy in the stadium when the ball just seemed to slow down and landed softly in my outstretched hands. With a strong tail wind, Cassata had under-thrown their speedy receiver by 20 yards, and I registered my second interception of the day.

The rest of the quarter was a seesaw battle with Jim Evenson finally taking the ball in from our 20-yard line to put Ottawa ahead 20 to 10. By the end of the quarter, they managed 2 more single points and increased their lead to 12 points. Neither team moved the ball with any consistency for the first 10 minutes of the final quarter as we exchanged punts three times.

A Guided Missile

I'll never forget my last punt of the day. Standing on our own 35-yard line, I received the snap from centre Bob Howes, took my usual three steps, and swung through with the same motion as I always did. My mouth dropped open as I watched the ball take off in a perfect spiral. I could hardly believe what I was witnessing. I stood there in absolute amazement, as the pigskin climbed higher and higher, and finally the nose turned over and it started back down to

Garry punting

earth. When the ball left my foot, Ottawa's punt return man had started to back up. By the time it came back down, he had back-pedalled 30 yards. The ball hung up in the air for so long that he became dizzy watching it. As he stood there, 10 yards deep in his end zone, the football smacked him right on the helmet and bounced through the end zone and up into the bleachers. There's no telling how far it would have travelled if the stands hadn't been there.

The punt went into the record books at 85 yards. The ball actually travelled 85 yards in the air from the point of contact. (My average punt that season was less than 42 yards.) It was the first point we had scored in the second half.

Bruce threw the ball well, but we kept making costly mistakes at the wrong times and just couldn't seem to put any more points on the board. Halfway through the fourth quarter, Coach Jauch sent Wilkie back out, in spite of his ribs, just to mix things up a little. We were playing catch-up, so he would have to pass the ball even though his throwing motion was greatly impaired. It would take more than bruised ribs to keep a competitor like Wilkie on the sideline for very long.

He moved us down the field with authority, with short outs, hooks and screens to George McGowan, Tyrone Walls, and Calvin Harrell. With 3rd and 10 on the Ottawa 30, we gambled and Wilkie went to me on a quick slant pattern. The ball was thrown short and low. I knew if I dropped to my knees to make the sure catch, we would come up short of the needed first down. I instinctively swooped down and the ball stuck to my fingers just below knee level. I lost my balance, but somehow managed to stumble forward for 12 yards to keep the drive alive.

Three plays later, Wilkie hit me with a beautiful pass just over the goal line. The ball was high, so I had to leap. Just as the ball touched my outstretched fingertips, three defenders crunched me simultaneously. They drilled me so hard, it took me a few seconds before my head cleared and I realized that I was lying on my back with the ball nestled in my stomach. The referee's arms flew up in the air, the western fans cheered—and again, I was the most surprised individual in the stadium!

A few seconds later, the final gun sounded and the '73 Grey Cup was history. Ottawa had won 22 to 18. We had come so close. The emotional letdown was incredible. One player threw his helmet, while others burst into tears. My heart was heavy as I slowly walked towards our dressing room through a tide of Roughrider supporters pouring on to the field, wild with excitement.

The Surprise of My Life

I watched the Ottawa players being mobbed by their fans. Suddenly my solemn mood was interrupted with a familiar voice shouting, "Garry, Garry! You won, you won!"

I looked up to see my wife, Sandy, running towards me with tears streaming down her cheeks.

"What are you saying—I won?"

"Didn't you hear? They just announced it over the loudspeaker. You've just been voted the Outstanding Canadian Player in the game!"

"Praise God!" I shouted, sweeping her off her feet. "That's exactly what we prayed for! This is incredible. The prayers, the telegram—it has all come true."

Tears began to flow and the goose bumps were back again.

"Sandy, this has got to be a miracle," I interjected.

"What do you mean?" she replied.

"The most valuable player awards are always given to players on the winning team and we just lost. I bet this has never happened before."

"That is amazing," she replied.

Just then, one of the CTV crew stepped through the crowd and took me by the arm.

"Would you come with me, Garry? We would like to interview you."

He led me through the crowd under the stadium and into a room full of bright lights and cameras. The TV sports caster greeted me with microphone in hand. Standing next to him was the President of CP Air, the sponsor of the Dick Suderman Award.

"Garry," the announcer began, "you sure played an outstanding game."

His voice drifted away as my thoughts focused on the Lord.

What do you want me to say?

"*Just say what's in your heart,*" I heard from within. My attention came back to the announcer's voice.

"Is there anything you would like to say?"

He held the microphone in front of me.

"First of all, I want to congratulate Ottawa for winning. They played well and they deserved it. And I also want to congratulate our coaches and my team mates for a great year, but most of all I want to thank someone I promised, My Lord and Saviour Jesus Christ, because without Him I would have nothing."

The CTV announcer literally froze. He was speechless for the first time in his life. In all his years as a sports caster, no one had ever given the glory to Jesus Christ during a post-Grey Cup interview, and it caught him completely off guard. He just looked at me with a blank stare. After a few seconds of silence, he abruptly turned away from me and started another conversation with the person on his other side.

By the grace of God, I had said all I needed to say. We had prayed for the award for that express purpose, and God had granted it to me. Little did I know that those few words would set off a chain reaction that would change the course of my life. Later I found out that Ottawa's Gerry Organ had given a testimony for Christ on the radio at the same time as I had on television. This was an eventful day in Canadian Football.

That same afternoon, television evangelist David Mainse sat together with my good friend Larry Kerychuk, watching the post Grey Cup interviews. When David observed me thanking Jesus Christ with that short testimony, he dropped to his knees on the living room carpet. Huge tears sprang from his eyes. David, a wonderful man of God and an avid football fan, had been deeply touched. For the first time in the history of the Grey Cup an athlete had given the glory to the Lord Jesus Christ, and it had a profound effect upon him.

God would use the events of that one single day in my life to influence my future and the future of many others. David Mainse and his family would play an integral part in the lives of the Lefebvres. Years later we would be joined together in a powerful new ministry to the youth of our nation.

But perhaps I'm getting a little ahead of myself . . .

Sandy, Cheekie & I with Vice President of CP Air

Bob & Garry at Cold Lake

*Our parents with the three of us
at Cold Lake*

Garry at Uncle's farm

*Garry in the snow
at Gibbons*

Chapter 2

NEVER GIVE UP

I was born in a small-town hospital in Cold Lake, Alberta, 150 miles northeast of Edmonton. My parents were Olivier and Dorothy Lefebvre. Since Dad was away on a fishing trip at the time, my last moments before entering this earth were spent in a speeding cab, within minutes of being delivered into this world by a robust, frightened taxi driver. My mother had chosen my given names months earlier: Garry, after her favourite movie star, Gary Cooper, and George, after her father.

I spent my first three years on this earth in that small fishing town near the Alberta-Saskatchewan border. My only real memory of those first years of my life is a picture Dad took of my sister, Pat, brother Bob, and I perched on a 50-pound lake trout that Dad had caught in one of his fishing nets in the winter of 1946. Pat, the eldest, was born in April of 1941, and Bob came along just over two years before me in March of 1942. In 1948 our family moved to a small home on 95 Street and 118 Avenue in Edmonton, where Dad took a job with the Canada Post Office. We stayed there only eight months. During that time, my younger brother, Blaine, was born. Later that year, the family moved to a small farm outside Gibbons, 15 miles northeast of Edmonton. We rented the farm from the Beebo family, who were long time residents of that area. The next fall, the family rented another small farm, which was owned by our Uncle Harvey and Aunt Gladys McWhirter, my mother's sister. Pat, and Bob, and I soon learned to make the best of the bitterly cold Alberta winters.

During the first January on our new farm, a storm that blew through brought so much snow that the roads had to be closed for over a month. We were so completely snowed in that no vehicles could travel until the county graders cleared the roads. Fortunately for us, our neighbour, Mr. Williams, brought us food and supplies by horse and sleigh. The incredibly deep snow may have had us stranded, but it certainly could not keep us adventurous kids indoors. In fact, the three of us spent many exciting hours building tunnels under the huge drifts to the barn, the well, and the woodpile. I secretly hoped the deep snow would stay there till spring, so my brother and sister would have to stay home and play with me all winter.

I vividly recall the day we carved a make-believe airplane under the snowdrift that was seven feet deep in places. We even created an imaginary instrument panel made of cardboard dials cut from a box of Corn Flakes. Many happy hours were spent flying all over the world on imaginary journeys, while sitting on three old wooden boxes. The farmers and townspeople may have been annoyed at being snowed in, but Pat and Bob and I had the time of our lives.

The following year I joined my brother and sister at Gibbons Elementary School. The one thing I clearly remember from that first year of school took place during recess in the spring of 1950. As I was walking out on to the playgrounds, one of my classmates came frantically running up to me.

"Your brother has fallen from a tree!" he screamed. I ran with him around the corner of the school building to see Bob's body hanging limp about 15 feet above the ground with a large pointed branch sticking through his side. He appeared to be unconscious. Every kid in the school was gathered around the tree. Suddenly the branch broke and he plummeted to the ground. I shrieked, as I threw my hands over my face. The next thing I knew, an ambulance had arrived and Bob was lifted aboard and it sped away down the road. We found out later that Bob required 54 stitches to close the huge hole in his side. Thankfully, he wasn't more seriously injured. It didn't stop him from climbing trees. It just slowed him down a little. Bob was the most adventuresome boy I ever knew, and his exploits drew me into trouble on more than one occasion. It didn't take much to encourage me, since I was cut out of the same cloth.

Later that summer Bob thought it would be a great idea if he and I played a serious game of war. We found a large number of jagged-edged tin-can lids in the garbage at the back of the house. I picked one up and flung it at a nearby tree. It stuck in like an arrow. An idea popped into his head, and seconds later Bob talked me into this war game. We positioned ourselves behind two large poplar trees about twenty yards apart. The idea was to fire the lid and stick it into the other guy's tree, which would signify a kill shot. Bob threw first, while I hid behind my tree, then it was my turn to try to hit his. This went on for about five throws each. After my last throw, I jumped behind my cover and waited for Bob to fire next. I heard a rustling sound behind me and figured his lid had missed my tree again. Picking up another lid, I stepped out to hurl it in Bob's direction. Unfortunately, the sound I had heard was not a tin lid, and Bob had just then let it go. I didn't see it coming, as it stuck right between my eyes at a 45-degree angle. Thankfully, it didn't do any real damage next to the few stitches it took to close the wound. When my shaved eyebrows grew back, the scar wasn't even visible.

A month later, after all had been forgotten, our escapades continued. This time we decided we were going to be good little boys and help our dad out, by removing a one-inch metal rod, which was stuck firmly in the ground beside the house. After the both of us tugging together on it and the rod not budging at all, Bob decided that it needed some serious persuasion. He walked over to the woodpile and brought back Dad's axe. It was so heavy he could barely lift it.

"I'll chop the dirt around the peg," he suggested, "and then you pull on it and see if it loosens up." Soon we had a pretty good rhythm going. Bob would chop around the rod four times and then I would reach over and try to pull it out. Suddenly one of us lost count and I reached for the peg at the same moment Bob swung the axe. The blade came thundering down across the first knuckle of my right forefinger. It cut right through the bone and left the end of my finger dangling by the skin. Poor mom and dad had to rush another one of their boys off to the hospital again. Thankfully, the finger grew back together like new and only a small bump and the scar remain as a reminder of the accident. In my later teenage years, when I was a baseball pitcher, Bob often claimed credit for my wicked curve ball.

In the spring of 1952, Dad took a job with the post office in Edmonton, and our family moved again. This time we rented a big old house on the outskirts of North Edmonton, where we settled for the next nine years. During that time, my next brother, Murray, was born. The winters seemed even colder there because of thin walls and poor insulation, but that old place and its surrounding 160 acres of field and trees provided a perfect setting for many childhood adventures.

The Lefebvre boys spent many hours exploring, building tree houses, catching and raising wild pigeons, challenging each other to crazy dares, and inventing exciting new games. Of course, each season of the year brought its own brand of organized sport, such as hockey in winter and baseball and football from spring until fall.

Keeping track of four energetic boys was quite a handful for our mother, and now there were twice as many boisterous brothers to gang up on our softhearted sister, Pat. She spent much of her time trying to keep us boys out of mischief. Mom surely needed all the help she could get.

Three Strikes and You're Out! Oh Yeh?

During that first summer in our new place, Pat and Bob took it upon themselves to teach their little brother how to play the game of baseball. When they took me out to the small field beside the house and began my first lesson, they soon realized that they had bitten off a little more than they could chew. First of all, Bob instructed me in the art of holding a bat. The large bat felt a little awkward in my small hands, but I was sure I could drive the ball over the low fence about 30 yards behind the pitcher's mound. Pat decided that she would be the pitcher, and she appointed Bob as the catcher. It was

Bob, Pat, Blaine & Garry

then explained to me that I would get three chances to hit the ball, and then it would be Bob's turn to bat and I would have to become the pitcher. Needless to say, I took three mean swings at the ball, knocked myself on to my backside each time, and did not come anywhere near the large softball.

"You're out!" Bob yelled. "It's my turn to be up."

"But I didn't hit the ball yet," I pleaded.

"You only get three strikes," Pat piped in from the pitcher's mound. "Those are the rules, so it's Bob's turn now. You get to be the pitcher, and I have to be the catcher."

"But I want to hit the ball," I hollered back a little louder, hoping they would see how serious I was.

"Garry, you've got to play by the rules," Bob scowled, as he reached for the bat. I swung it around my head in a wild frenzy.

"I didn't hit the ball yet!" I screamed, keeping them both at bay.

"Okay! Okay! We'll give you another chance," said Bob. "Just don't do anything crazy with that bat." Pat also reluctantly agreed. Twenty-one strikes later, I finally made contact. After that, I could hit the ball almost at will. I played many years of baseball, beginning with little league, and I owe my start to Bob and Pat.

During my childhood in Edmonton, sports played a major role in my life. In my junior and senior years in high school, I was heavily involved in hockey, baseball, track and field, and football. I enjoyed a measure of success at each, and loved participating in all of them. During my high school years, I broke city and provincial track-and-field records in the long jump, triple jump, discus and 4 x 100 relay. My father's dream was for me to become a professional hockey player, as that was his passion. I loved the game of hockey and would have been thrilled to have the opportunity to play in the National Hockey League, but deep down in my heart my prevailing passion was always football.

I discovered the game of football at the tender age of ten and soon became an ardent fan of the Edmonton Eskimos. Jackie Parker, Rollie Miles, Don Getty, Normie Kwong, Johnny Bright, and the rest of the Eskimo players of the fifties were all my heroes. The Esks were the powerhouse Western team of the mid-fifties, winning three consecutive Grey Cups in 1954, 55 and 56 over the Montreal Alouettes from the East. The great quarterback, Sam "The Rifle" Etchevery, led the Alouette team. A small wall in my bedroom was covered with two huge posters of Sam the Rifle and Jackie Parker, two of the greatest quarterbacks of that era.

Our family couldn't afford tickets to the games in those days, so I did the next best thing. On game day I sat glued to the old radio and listened to every play, visualizing the action through the wonder of my young imagination.

During my grade-five year, the seed was firmly planted. My desire to someday become a professional football player started to grow. To become a wide receiver for the mighty Edmonton Eskimos soon became my consuming passion. I dreamed night and day of catching that long touchdown pass. At school we played football nearly all year round, and all of the guys, and even a few girls, enjoyed the competition. Even so, I think I was the only one of my peers who ate, slept, and lived the game.

Shattered Dreams

My first opportunity to play on an organized team came in the summer of 1955 at the age of 11. The Martin Paper Wildcats announced that they were having tryouts at the practice field next to Clarke Stadium (the home of the Eskimos). I was the first one to show up that Saturday morning, eager to take this first step on the road to my career as a professional football player. Soon there was an enthusiastic crowd of about 80 boys standing in front of the locker room. We were informed that 40 players would be selected for the roster. Undaunted by the challenge, I ran onto the practice field, confident that I would be one of the chosen few.

At the end of the morning's session, Head Coach Joe Hudson called me over to talk to me privately. Pleased to be singled out, I fully expected Coach Joe to congratulate me on my great performance, but instead, with a pat on my back he pulled the rug out from under me.

"Garry, I don't now how to tell you this, except to give it to you straight. Son, you'll never be a football player—you're just not big enough or strong enough."

I could hardly choke back my tears as he spoke. "If I were you, I'd take up a different sport, Son. Football is a tough game and you're just not built for it."

My whole world had suddenly come to a screeching halt. At the age of eleven, I thought I had my future all figured out. I had direction and purpose. And now the dream that had been so real to me was shattered in a single moment. I turned away quickly and hid my face. I didn't want him to see the tears as they gushed from my eyes. I didn't look back as I ran towards home, the tears streaming down my face. The crushing disappointment came in waves as the coach's words echoed again and again through my mind, *"You'll never be a football player."*

That's not fair, I argued silently. *He didn't even give me a chance. I know I could make that team. I know I'm as good as those other kids— and maybe better than most of them!*

I arrived home in despair, convinced that the worst possible thing that could ever happen to a person had just befallen me. Yet when I broke the news to my parents, they failed to recognize its significance. To them, I was just a kid who didn't make the local kids' football team. They tried to console me and encouraged me to broaden my focus. After all, there were things more important in life than the game of football.

It shouldn't have mattered that much, really. I was only eleven years old. I gave it my best shot, and I was turned down. Big deal! I wasn't about to give up my dream that easily. For the next three days, I went to the practice field and tortured myself as I stood outside the fence. With a growing heartache, I watched the players run through their drills. After the third practice had come to an end, Coach Joe strolled across the field to where I stood at the fence and looked at my tear-stained face.

"You really want to play bad don't you, Kid?"

"I'd give anything," I replied, swallowing the huge lump in my throat.

"Okay, you can be on the team," he grinned, "but I can't promise you'll get to play very much."

He was still convinced that I was too small to play this tough game and afraid that I might get hurt.

Coach Hudson kept his word. He did put me on the team and sat me on the bench the entire season. Then, in the last game, with just two minutes left to play, Coach Joe looked over to me where I sat in my usual spot on the end of the bench.

"Lefebvre! Get in there and take out the tight end!"

Surprised, I sprang to my feet and charged out to the huddle. Finally I had a chance to show what I could do! Everything happened in a blur. The quarterback called the play and we broke the huddle. I didn't have the slightest idea what I was supposed to do. Too embarrassed to admit that I didn't know what to do on the play, I just ran up to the line the same as the rest of the guys. When the ball was snapped I stood up and looked around, with one plan in mind: *Don't screw up and get in the way.* The next thing I knew, the game was over and I hadn't even touched the ball. My first football season was over.

Even though I didn't get to handle the ball, I still felt a part of the team, so when the final gun sounded, I walked off the field with my team-mates, feeling like I belonged.

Coach Joe walked over to me and placed his arm over my shoulder and began to apologize to me for not playing me all year.

"I am really sorry, Son. I know it was hard for you just sitting on the bench all season, but honestly, Garry, I was afraid that you might get seriously hurt. Some of those boys out there are 140 to 150 pounds, almost twice your size. You can't be more than 80 pounds soaking wet—with rocks in your pockets! You come back next year, Son. You'll probably put on some meat by then and you could be bigger and stronger and maybe even make first team. Who knows? You could be one of next year's stars."

Those parting words rang in my ears and helped my dream to live again.

The following ten months seemed to drag on forever, while I counted the weeks until next season's football tryouts. Even though I stayed involved in other sports throughout the year, I would often find my thoughts wandering to the football field. Again and again, I visualized myself catching that game-winning touchdown pass.

Finally, the season arrived and bantam football practices commenced. It wasn't long before we realized that Coach Joe's prediction was true. I had grown in size and strength, and my skills had improved. It looked like I was going to be one of the better players on the team. I excelled in the running and catching drills. Even at the age of twelve I could catch just about any ball, if I could get my hands on it. It seemed so natural to me. I felt like I was born to catch footballs.

Practices were exciting and I walked around with a perpetual smile from ear to ear. This was it. This was what I had anticipated for ten long months. I was positioned in the running-back slot, and so far there wasn't a player on the team who could stay with me when I got into the open field. I continued to work hard and to do everything I could to prepare myself mentally and physically for the season ahead.

Two days before our first league game, Coach Joe called me aside, just as the guys were walking onto the practice field.

"Son, we need to take a little walk."

"Oh, no!" I thought to myself. "What did I do wrong?"

"There is something I've got to tell you," Joe began. "I am really sorry, but I have some bad news for you."

The solemn look on his face told me there was something terribly wrong. As we strolled towards the dressing room, he placed his strong arm around my shoulders.

Swallowing hard, he continued, "Garry, I don't know how to tell you this. First, I want you to know that I have done everything I possibly can, but the league refuses to bend the rules."

"What's wrong, Coach? What are you talking about?"

"Son, your birthday is the 12th of November, and the cut-off date for 12-year-olds is the 15th. I can't believe it, Garry, but you are three days too old, and the league won't let you play."

"Three days! You mean I'll miss the opening game?"

"No, Garry, I mean you can't play this year at all. You were born three days too soon. I'm sorry, but there's nothing more I can do."

The door had slammed in my face again. I stood there in shock, not believing what I had just heard. Before I could stop myself, I burst into tears. I felt ashamed and quickly spun around, ran to my bike and peddled blindly for home.

My heart ached from the pain that stabbed me over and over. Once more I was denied the opportunity to play the game I loved so much. Yet with each disappointment, somehow the desire to play football seemed to grow stronger. How many times would I be turned away? How many? I wondered how long it would take me to pick up the pieces this time. Coach Joe called me later that afternoon and tried to encourage me not to give up. I thanked him for his kindness and soon set my sights for high school, still two long years away.

Another Bubble Bursts

The next summer, we moved across town, and I entered Victoria Composite High School in 1958 at the age of 14. I had lived for this moment for two years, playing touch football after school and on weekends, almost year-round. Now I would finally get to play on a real team. Tryouts for the High School Junior Team began the first week of school. After a week of practices, our coach informed me that I made the roster as first team tight end. I could hardly contain my excitement.

Three weeks into our practice sessions, my world came crashing down on me again. I had come home from practice after school, as usual, and Mom was waiting for me in the kitchen.

"Garry," she began, "we are really in financial trouble. Your dad and I are doing the best we can, but there is just not enough money coming in to keep the household going. You and Bob are going to have to find after-school jobs to help pay for the food. Garry, you are going to have to give up the idea of playing football."

"But Mom!" I blurted out, "I've been waiting two years to play on this team."

"I know you have had your heart set on it, but I can't see that we have any other choice. Hopefully, things will turn around for us, and you'll be able to play next year."

I knew there was no use arguing with Mom when her mind was made up. Despondent, I ran to my room and cried it out again.

That's it, I said to myself, *I will never get to play football again.*

Those negative thoughts stayed with me for only a couple of hours before they dissipated. Something inside of me just wouldn't let go. Soon I was thinking about next year's possibilities. The dream continued.

That fall was sheer torture, as the whole school seemed to be talking about the football teams, and I was relieved when the season ended and other things became the topic of conversation. The spring and summer of 1959 dragged on as I longed for football season to come. The last of the Lefebvre boys was born that August. From the time he arrived home, little Mark found a special place in my heart, and I looked after him like he was my own son. I took him everywhere with me, even on an occasional date.

At 15, I was the oldest one of the children still in school and at home every day. With Mom working nights and Dad often not there, the responsibility of running the household after school fell squarely on to my shoulders, since Bob was working his first full-time job and seldom home at night. Blaine was three and a half years younger than I, and Murray had just turned seven. The next July the family moved to a house in the Montrose district of North Edmonton, and I went into grade 11 at Eastglen Composite High School that fall. The month before we moved, my sister Pat married Wally Rutkowski.

The next two years I spent most of my leisure time playing sandlot football on the Santa Rosa Playground with the neighbourhood kids and my brother Bob, until he left to join the navy in the fall of 1963. That field was where I taught myself how to punt a football in my bare feet. Painful at first, my instep soon toughened up and I developed my own punting style. Once in a while, I hit a really good one. That summer of 1960 was the first time in my life that the school holidays were too long.

September finally arrived and with it, football tryouts at Eastglen Composite. That year the school did something unprecedented in their history. They hired two men from outside the school to coach the Junior Team. The school's policy was always to have one of the teachers as coach, usually the head of the Athletic Department. Instead, they hired two brothers. Their names were Joe and Bob Hudson, my coaches from Bantam Football! I could hardly believe it.

I really wanted to play wide receiver, a position I had dreamed of playing for seven years, but the coaches decided to play me at tight end. That season was more frustrating than all the previous ones, as I ran up and down the field, blocking for the other players, and with only two passes thrown way over my head, I never even got my hands on either of them. We had a great running offence and really didn't have to throw the ball that often.

The play I remember most was a double reverse hand off to wing back Gary Carson. I would pull and lead him around right end. We often scored on that play. I would come around the corner looking to block someone, and no one would be there. That was the only thrill I had, when we would scamper the length of the field with Gary's hand on my back and nobody else in sight.

That year we were Edmonton City Champions and written up in *The Journal* as the best High School Junior Football Team of the decade. It was wonderful to be on a championship team, but I didn't feel that I had contributed at all. I vowed that next year I would be a wide receiver on the Senior Team and nothing would stop me.

The following September, Joe and Bob were asked to return and coach the Eastglen Senior Team. I approached Joe during the first practice and begged him to give me an opportunity to play wide out and also to try out for punter. I had been practising my punting all summer and had become much more consistent. Every so often, I could launch a perfect spiral. Thankfully, Joe gave me a chance, and I earned a spot at first string in both positions.

Our first league game was against Queen Elizabeth High. We took the opening kickoff and started 1st and 10 from our own 30-yard line. After a five-yard gain on the 1st play, quarterback Jim Bilsky called my number—a deep post pattern. He hit me right on the fingertips and I out-legged the defenders for a 75-yard major.

Finally it had happened. I could hardly believe it—I was playing the position I had dreamed of for years. The next time we got the ball, we bogged down and I had the opportunity for my first punt. I struck a wobbly spiral and it flew over the deep backs' heads and bounced through the end zone for a 76-yard single point. Once again, I exploded with delight.

We changed ends and Queen Elizabeth began to march down the field under the direction of quarterback, Fred Dunn. Coach Joe hollered at me as I was resting on the bench.

"Garry, go in at safety and pick off one of those passes."

"Yes sir!" I responded and quickly ran out to the defensive huddle.

The first play was a sweep to our right, and we stopped it for a three-yard gain. I knew they would throw on second down, so I was ready for it when their wide out ran a deep post through my zone. I played the receiver close and Dunn was forced out of the pocket. He broke a couple of would-be tackles and skirted down the left side-line. When I saw him break, I left my man and hustled up to try and cut him off.

Just as I was about to hit him, he stepped on the out-of-bounds chalk and the referee blew the whistle. I pulled up, not wanting to be penalized for a late hit. In the heat of the chase, Fred didn't hear the whistle and lowered his shoulder and ran right over me. A terrible pain shot through my left ankle, and then it went completely numb. I knew something was seriously wrong.

Minutes later, I was carried off the field and helped into Dad's car. He quickly drove me to the Royal Alex Hospital. After x-rays, the diagnosis was a fractured ankle, and I was told I was finished for the season. On the way home, Dad tried to offer his sympathy.

"There's always next year," he said, yet something inside me refused to believe I was finished for the season.

"I don't care what the doctor said, Dad, we are going to win the championship this year and I am not going to miss it."

"But Son," he replied, "the doctor was sure that your cast would be on for eight weeks and your season will be over in six."

"I don't know how, Dad, but I will play in that final game."

Four weeks later, I broke the cast almost completely off while playing touch football after school. When I walked in with my cast half removed to see my doctor, he x-rayed it to find the bone perfectly knit in place. I returned just in time to play in the City Championship game against St. Joes and we won 3-2 in a freezing defensive struggle.

The following year, I tried out for the Edmonton Junior Wildcats and made the team at slot back. In my first game, I scored 3 touchdowns of 74, 85 and 91 yards. The 85 yard one was called back for an infraction. I played three seasons for them, and as a result of my play, I was invited to Eskimo Advancement Camp. Picked as one of 20 players from that camp to go to the Eskimo's Rookie Camp, I was then one of five chosen from there to attend their regular camp in June of 1966.

I had moved away from home and was sharing an apartment with my best friend, Fred Dunn. Fred was the one who had broken my ankle two years earlier. He was now the quarterback of the Wildcats. That spring he received a football scholarship to Drake University in Des Moines, Iowa. Fred's plans were to leave for college early that summer.

When I drove into Holy Redeemer College to report for training camp that June afternoon, I was more excited than I could ever remember. Just to stand in the same locker room with the Eskimo veterans and rookies was an awesome feeling. I wasn't quite sure what was expected of me, so I slowly made my way to a locker and stowed my gear. Soon,

Equipment Manager, Ted Allard came in, and we were all outfitted for practice.

The next day we began two-a-day practices, which ran for two weeks, under the direction of Head Coach Neil Armstrong. I was not prepared for it, and after the third day I was so stiff and sore, I could hardly get out of bed. I spent most of that first week laying up in the dorm resting my sore body, and trying to digest the two-inch–thick playbook. Somehow I managed to keep going, and the soreness passed after six or seven days. We cut back to practising just once a day when the exhibition season started.

The Esks played four pre-season games as usual, and I was given the opportunity to run in the flanker spot, along with three other rookies. At least I wouldn't have to beat out a veteran. We played the Winnipeg Blue Bombers in our second game, and I caught my first professional touchdown pass. It was a deep "go" pattern down the left sideline that was under-thrown by rookie quarterback Randy Kerbow. I tipped the ball out of the defender's hand on Winnipeg's 25-yard line, and it popped over my left shoulder. Instinctively I threw up my left hand and felt it strike the ball. It then came flying over to my right side. All this was happening while I was still running. In desperation, my right hand slapped the ball, and it sailed to my left again. By this time, I was crossing the goal line. Somehow, I managed to dive and cradle the elusive pigskin in my anxious arms as I hit the turf.

I was overcome with joy as my team-mates swamped me and knocked me to the ground. When I got back to my feet and made my way to the bench, Coach Armstrong walked onto the field and took my hand.

"What a catch, Son!" he exclaimed. "That was incredible!"

Now maybe I will be chosen over the other three rookies, I thought to myself.

Our fourth exhibition game came and went without any of us doing anything spectacular, and it was time for the dreaded final cuts. Some of the veterans tried to relieve the tension by making jokes.

"Watch out for the Grim Reaper," some of the older veterans would say. "He's lurking around the corner."

It had come down to just one Canadian left to be cut, and I knew it was between me and my old high-school team-mate Ken Sigaty. Just before it was time to go out onto the field, one of the assistant coaches came strolling towards our end of the locker room. Ken and I were sitting together in front of my locker. We both held our breath when he stopped in front of us.

"Ken," he said, "you're wanted down at Coach Armstrong's office."

I silently held the explosion of joy within me. All those years of frustration and disappointment had been worth it. My dream had finally come true. I could not hold back the tears as I ran to the phone to call my new sweetheart, Sandy.

"Honey, I've done it! The last cut was just made. I'm now officially an Edmonton Eskimo Wide Receiver."

"Wow, Garry—that's incredible! I want to call my mom and dad and tell them the good news. I know they've been pulling for you."

"Let's go out tonight and celebrate. See you in a couple of hours."

I could not remember ever feeling this good in my entire life. I had really made it.

When our first home-game ended, I strolled out of the dressing room at the north end of Clarke Stadium. A few autograph seekers were mingling just outside the door, along with Sandy and most of the players' wives and girl friends. While I was signing a young fan's ball cap, I looked up to see a familiar smile breaking through the sea of faces.

"You did it, Son. I've got to hand it to you. You sure proved me wrong."

I grabbed Joe Hudson and gave him a huge bear hug.

"You didn't recognize real talent when you saw it, did you?" I kidded. We both laughed out loud.

"Thanks, Joe, for all you did for me. Thanks for all you taught me, and for giving me a chance. You've helped me more than you will ever know."

Joe turned around to the crowd mingling behind him and caught Sandy's eye.

"I taught him everything he knows," he said, grinning from ear to ear.

"Didn't you once say, 'Take up another sport, Son, you will *never* be a football player'?" I replied. This time, all three of us burst into laughter.

Chapter 3

CLOSE ENCOUNTERS OF THE SPIRITUAL KIND

For much of my youth and young adult life, my main focus was on becoming and remaining a professional football player. It was as if this one dream became a guiding star in an otherwise aimless life filled with peaks and valleys. I was generally content with my life whenever the circumstances seemed to settle into a comfortable, manageable place. Inevitably though, something would come along to shatter my secure little world.

I liked to think that I was in charge of the events in my life and could handle whatever came along. But when something occurred that was out of my control, I was forced to look beyond myself to try to understand the reasons behind it all. It seemed that without fail, my search would eventually lead to questioning God. There were many years of struggle, disappointment, confusion, and heartache before I would come to understand the magnitude of God's presence and purpose in my life.

I have many treasured memories from my childhood, but my family also had their share of problems to overcome. It seems to me that much of the friction in the Lefebvre household was just a small sample of the religious wars that have gone on for centuries in this world. My parents were engaged in just such a conflict, my father being of one religious faith and my mother of another. It wasn't a physical battle as such, but more of a constant cold war.

When I was just two years of age, Dad and some of his family took me to their church to be baptized into their faith, without my mother's knowledge or consent. Needless to say, she was extremely upset when she found out what they had done. That was the main reason that, shortly thereafter, the family moved from Cold Lake to Edmonton. Mom wanted to put some distance between the kids and Dad's devoutly religious family. She wasn't going to have her children raised in the Catholic faith, even if she didn't really practise her own.

Even though my parents didn't see eye to eye on matters of religion, they did love their children and raised us all with a clear understanding of right and wrong. But as a result of the constant religious struggles over the 19 years that I lived at home, I developed a rather distorted view of who God was and how He fit into all of this religion. As a young boy, I kept thoughts of God at a distance, afraid that if He got too close, He would mess up all the fun I thought I was having. During the last year I lived at home, however, I was confronted head-on with a painful tragedy that shook me to the core.

Max and I were best friends. We met during our Grade-11 year at Eastglen Composite High School. The two of us spent most of our evenings and weekends together down at the Highlands Pool Hall on 118 Avenue. The rest of our time was spent playing touch football with the guys over at the Santa Rosa Playground, which was kitty corner to my place. Max possessed a fantastic sense of humour. He and I were always goofing around and spent many hours laughing at each other's dumb jokes. Never once did I suspect that his jovial manner was only a cover for the deep pain he carried inside.

His home life was nothing short of dreadful. Max's parents were much older than mine. Perhaps this is partly why they were less tolerant of him. Neither of his parents, in fact, really showed him any love at all. Home was the last place Max wanted to spend any of his time. I suppose this is why he was constantly over at my house. Not once in the two years that we chummed together did he invite me over to his house.

His father openly showed his dislike of him. When Max was a little boy, his dad would throw him down into the dark, damp cellar under their kitchen floor and sit on a chair over the trap door. One day when he was fourteen, Max couldn't take it any more. Because of his tremendous strength, he was able to lift the trap door with enough force to throw his father off the chair. Needless to say, that was the last time Max made a visit to the cellar.

I remember a summer evening in July of 1964 when the two of us sat together on the front steps of my home. There was nothing unusual about that, except it was the first time we had ever talked about anything of a serious nature.

Max looked up at the sky filled with brightly shining stars and said, "Garry, I wonder if there really is a heaven. If there is, I'll bet it must be a fantastic place to live."

We talked for hours that night, just sitting and staring up at the beautifully lit sky. Three days later, Max picked me up at home after dinner and we headed down to the pool hall to play a few games. He talked most of the evening about a girl he had recently met and with whom he was head-over-heels in love. We finished our last game around 10:30 p.m., and Max dropped me off at home just before 11:00 that night.

"I'll see you later. I'm going to see my girl," he informed me, as I slammed the door of his light green 1950 two-door Ford coupe.

The next morning, I went to the postal station where I worked as a letter carrier. While I sorted the mail, two of my superiors approached me.

"Garry," my supervisor began, "the Edmonton City Police just called, and I have been asked to inform you of some tragic news. I am sorry, but your friend Max was found dead this morning. The police would like you to come down to the station. They want to talk to you."

I was numb. I stood there in shock and total disbelief.

"H-how did it happen?" I stammered.

"We don't know. The constable didn't say. I guess you'll have to find out from the police. Would you like someone to drive you over there?"

"No, thank you. I'll be fine."

I left the office and climbed into my car with my mind reeling. It was all happening so fast that I just couldn't get my head around it.

Oh God! I thought to myself, *maybe it's a mistake. Maybe it was someone else who looked like Max. We were just together last night.*

In spite of my hopes, deep inside me I feared it was true.

When I arrived at the police station, I was ushered in to an office where a lady constable was seated. "Garry, your friend Max was found asphyxiated in his car early this morning in his parents' garage. He addressed this note to you."

She handed a small piece of white paper across the desk to me.

"Would you like to read it and tell me what you think it means?"

I slowly unfolded the piece of paper in my hand and read my friend's last words. Printed in blue ink in large letters I read these six words:

GARRY I THINK I AM CRAZY.

That was it. That was all there was to the note. I sat there staring off into the distance for a long minute. Finally I responded.

"I know Max wasn't crazy. I-I think he meant that he was crazy to be doing this . . . I'm really not sure."

I left the police station in a daze and drove home. It was the first time in my life that I faced the finality of the death of someone close to me. There were so many unanswered questions, and the pain of the loss of my closest friend was almost unbearable. I had never had such a close friend as Max, and now he was gone.

God! Why did you let this happen? This was the only question that demanded to be answered. Yet, I didn't really pursue the matter much further. I was still afraid I might get too close to the One I was trying so hard to avoid. I wasn't ready yet to get serious with God.

After a short investigation, the Homicide Division determined that Max's death was definitely a suicide. I went through a time of blaming myself, wondering if I could have somehow prevented it. A week or so after Max's funeral, the pain had eased somewhat, and my life slowly returned to normal. When I was alone, I often thought of Max and heaven. Could there really be a place where there was finally no more pain?

Later that fall, I moved out of home to share an apartment with my new friend, Fred Dunn. We were playing football on the same team, the Edmonton Junior Wildcats. Our high school battles were long over and we had become great friends. Both of us felt the urge to leave the nest at the same time and strike out on our own.

Living on our own was a great learning experience for both Fred and me. He was an only child and was raised to be meticulously neat and tidy, while I came from a pack of six and was anything but organized. At first, we were in constant disagreement over how the apartment was to be kept. He wanted it to look like a department store display window, and I wanted it to look lived in. We both eventually compromised. Neither of us realized it, but Fred was being used to prepare me for my future wife, who would turn out to be an exquisite housekeeper.

During the year and a half that we shared the apartment, Fred and I spent a lot of time together since we were both athletic and enjoyed most of the same things. We shared some great times, especially when he would date Sandy Selkirk, the pretty five-foot-two blond cheerleader from Jasper Place Composite. A girlfriend of mine, Bonnie, had lined her up as a blind date for Fred.

The first moment I saw her, she captured my heart. It was hard seeing her date my closest friend, but it was the only way I could get to see her. One day in April, I made an astounding announcement to Fred's mother, just after he received a scholarship to Drake University in Des Moines, Iowa.

"When Fred goes away to college, I am going to take out his girlfriend and marry her some day. This may sound crazy, but your son is dating my future wife."

"Well, then, if you're absolutely sure, go for it," Mother Dunn encouraged me. Although Fred and Sandy were dating on a regular basis, he was also seeing other girls, while making plans to go away to college. On June 21, 1966, the day before my first training camp with the Eskimos, she called to talk to me about their dwindling relationship. Fred was not home at the time. I was pleasantly surprised, for I had planned on calling her just as soon as Fred left for school.

After a short conversation, I invited her over to the apartment, but she said she had to study for her Grade-12 biology final. I quickly persuaded her that I could be of great help to her, since biology just happened to be my best subject. In return, I suggested she could iron my clothes for training camp. Sandy agreed and arrived at the apartment a little later that afternoon. It wasn't long until I was certain that she felt the same about me as I did for her. We talked and slow danced to my Righteous Brothers album until that magic moment when we kissed.

This is it, I thought, *I've found the one I've been waiting for. This is my wife.* Needless to say, we didn't get much studying done, and my clothes never did get ironed. The next day, Sandy failed her biology exam and I went to training camp with wrinkled clothes. It didn't seem to matter, though. After all, we were in love. Fred was a little upset when I broke the news to him, but we ironed that out before he left for Des Moines later that summer.

My rookie year as an Eskimo was an outstanding adventure. There were times during that season when I wondered if I wasn't just experiencing some beautiful dream, like the recurring one I had as a young boy, which Mom would interrupt when she came and woke me up for school. The Eskimos made the playoffs for the first time in years but lost out in the semi-final that season. I was blessed to be voted the Rookie of the Year in the Western Conference, and was presented with the Dr. Beatty Martin Trophy at our last home game. I felt I had become a star overnight. Suddenly, reporters wanted to interview me and fans even sought my autograph. Another childhood fantasy was also fulfilled when my kid brother, Mark, showed me a bubble-gum card he had collected, with my picture on it. Now I knew I had arrived.

Those experiences lifted me to an emotional height beyond anything I had ever remotely known, but a couple of months into the off-season I began to experience feelings I couldn't put a handle on. Although I had made it as a star, there was an emptiness inside of me that was unexplainable. The strange thing was that there was no apparent reason for it. I was happily married and fulfilling my life's dream. What could be wrong? It was as if I was striving to reach the top of the ladder, only to find myself at the foot of another one. Something was missing, and I didn't know what it was.

Sandy and I had been were married nine days before my second season training camp on June 17, 1967. She had just turned 20 and I was only 22. After our one-week honeymoon in the Okanagan and Coeur d'Alene, Idaho, we were immediately geographically separated.

Our wedding, June 17, 1967

Football season was underway and training camp began June 26th. It was hard to keep my mind on practice, with my thoughts constantly wandering to Sandy alone at the apartment. Whenever Coach Armstrong would give us the night off, which was about every second day, I would rush through dinner and make a mad dash to the apartment. The time would fly by and I would wait until the last possible second and then drive like a maniac to beat the 11:00 p.m. curfew. During those long two weeks, I always cut it close, often within seconds of not making it. However, I wasn't the only guilty party. It was quite common at two minutes to eleven to see a long row of cars sailing down the dirt road riddled with potholes that led to Holy Redeemer College. It was amazing that one of us didn't hit the ditch or crack up.

After training camp and the exhibition season, the final cuts were over. Again I felt a little more secure in my job. The 1967 regular season flew by quickly, and the Esks once more finished in third place, again losing out in the semi-final.

Heaven's Special Child

Within six months of our wedding, Sandy and I felt ready to start our family. After months of trying, and experimenting with all the advice from our married friends on how to make it happen, we finally just gave up. And, of course, by divine providence, a month later Sandy conceived. The baby was due around the first week in November of 1968. I wanted a girl first, and we were so sure this child was a girl that we didn't even bother to pick out a boy's name. We chose the name Chéri, which was French for "Dear One," and waited patiently for our baby to arrive.

The pregnancy was a difficult time for Sandy. She was very sick for the first three months and then spent most of the seventh month in the Royal Alexandra Hospital, weakened with a severe case of influenza. She could hardly keep anything down and lost ten pounds in one week. She recovered after the much-needed rest and, during the final month, her energy level rose substantially, especially in the last few days.

Chéri made her entrance into this world on November 1, 1968, just as the team entered post-season playoffs once again. Sandy was in hard labour for 13 hours. I spent the whole time beside her bed, massaging her back and encouraging her to breathe the way we had been taught in pre-natal classes. Ever since we first decided to have a family, we had talked and planned and dreamed of this special moment. Neither of us was prepared for the shock wave that was about to slam us in the face.

Chéri was born posterior, or face-up, and consequently her lungs were full of fluid. She was immediately rushed from the delivery room and placed in a respirator, where she spent the first ten days of her life.

The real shock was to follow on the second day, when our pediatrician came in to see us, looking quite disturbed as he walked into the room.

"What's wrong!" Sandy blurted out, "Is there something wrong with the baby?"

"Mr. and Mrs. Lefebvre, we have done numerous tests and are now positive that your baby has a condition called Downs Syndrome. It is caused by a malfunction of the 21st chromosome . . ."

Throughout the doctor's explanation, I fought against the storm of emotions that rose inside of me. I refused to believe what I was hearing.

Not my baby girl! Not Downs Syndrome! This could not be happening to us. After the doctor left the room, Sandy wept, while I stroked her head and tried to comfort her. We were both stunned by the unexpected news. But as Sandy released her grief, I tried to be strong, holding back my tears.

"It's going to be all right, Honey. I know everything will turn out fine. I know we don't understand why this has happened, but I am sure it will all work out in the end."

I tried to remain as positive as I could, for her sake and for my own peace of mind. After about an hour, I left Sandy's bedside and went to the phone in the hall to break the shocking news to our families. I returned in a few minutes and sat with her a while longer until she finally drifted off to sleep.

It was late in the evening. The cold November air hit my face when I stepped through the hospital door and headed for the parking lot. Feelings of hurt and anger flooded my soul as I strode towards my car. Suddenly, I lost control. I shook my fist up at the dark night sky and through clenched teeth I shouted, "God—if you're up there—why me?"

I felt as if we had somehow been cheated. Sandy and I had wanted a baby girl so badly, and now she was mentally challenged. A myriad of thoughts flooded my mind. *How will we handle this? How will our friends handle it? What will our life be like now? What have we done to deserve this? What awful thing have I done to be punished like this? I thought we were good people. There are so many other people who deserve this punishment more than we do. Why does this have to happen to us?*

I slammed the car door and sped out of the lot, wiping away the tears of self-pity as I raced home to our empty apartment. I finally drifted off to sleep around 2:30 a.m., still angry with the God whom I thought had caused all of this to happen.

I awoke at about 11:00 a.m. the next morning and called the coach's office to break the news. I hoped to be excused from practice that day so that I could spend the afternoon with Sandy.

"What can I do for you, Son?" Coach Neil Armstrong's gentle voice greeted me.

"Coach," I swallowed hard. It was so painful to say the words. "My wife, Sandy, had our baby last night. It's a girl . . . and she has Downs Syndrome. Is it okay if I don't come to practice today? I'd like to be at the hospital with Sandy."

"I'm so sorry, Garry. Is there anything I can do? Jane and I would like to help any way we can. I'm sure this is tough on the both of you—especially being your first baby. Jane and I will be praying for you both, as well as for the baby. Do you have a name for her yet?"

"Yes, we named her Chéri, which means 'Dear One' in French."

"You take as much time as you need, Son," Coach Neil reassured me.

As I hung up the receiver, I felt in some way strangely uplifted. I had always known that there was something special about Coach Armstrong and his wife Jane, but I hadn't given it much thought before. There had been some talk about them being "Christians," but that didn't mean much to me at that point in my life. My idea of a Christian was someone living in North America who wasn't Jewish.

Later that evening, while I sat with Sandy, Jane Armstrong walked into the hospital room wearing her usual radiating smile.

"Where's the wee baby?" she asked immediately. "I want to see her."

"She's in a room just down the hall," I replied a bit hesitantly.

"Are you sure you want to see her?" Sandy interjected.

"Of course I want to see her! Show me where she is."

The three of us slowly made our way to the glass window that separated Chéri from the rest of the world. Sandy and I were both tense. Jane would be the first person to see our mentally handicapped baby, outside of Sandy's sister, June, who had come up earlier that afternoon.

The nurse on duty wheeled the small respirator over to the glass window and turned it around so we all could get a look at her face. Our fears quickly vanished as Jane surprised us with her reaction.

"She is beautiful!" she exclaimed. "What a dear little baby."

Sandy burst into tears. "Do you really think so?"

"Oh yes! She's a real darling. Let's go back to the room for a minute," Jane suggested. "I have something especially for you two."

We sat by the bed as Jane opened a brown envelope and pulled out a large red card. "I found this poem in a magazine this morning and I know it was written especially for little Chéri. I believe God led me to it right after Neil and I prayed for you." She began to read:

HEAVEN'S SPECIAL CHILD

A meeting was held quite far from earth.
It's time again for another birth,
Said the Angels to the Lord above.
This Special Child will need much
    love.
Her progress may seem very slow,
Accomplishments she may not show,
And she'll require extra care,
From the folks she meets way down
    there.
She may not run or laugh or play;
Her thoughts may seem quite far
    away.

Chéri, age 6

In many ways she won't adapt,
And she'll be known as "handicapped."
So let's be careful where she's sent;
We want her life to be content.
Please, Lord, find the parents who
Will do a special job for you.

They'll not realize right away
The leading role they're asked to play,
But with this child, sent from above,
Comes stronger Faith and richer Love;
And soon they'll know the privilege given
In caring for this gift from Heaven:

Their precious charge so meek and mild
IS HEAVEN'S VERY SPECIAL CHILD.

—Author Unknown

Chéri at 2 years

Sandy and I sat there speechless. An awesome sense of peace swept over our souls. The room seemed to fill with a sweet, gentle presence. After a long moment of silence, we both finally managed to say a weak, "Thank you, thank you."

Jane got up and excused herself. "I think it best if I leave you two alone. If Neil or I can help in any way, please just call us. I mean it. I'll check back with you later."

Our pediatrician called me at home that evening and asked me to meet him in Sandy's room the following morning, during his rounds. He walked in to the room with a sombre look on his face. I knew that he wasn't bearing good news, but neither Sandy nor I was prepared for what was to come next.

"Mr. and Mrs. Lefebvre, I don't think it is wise to become too attached to this baby. Often these Downs children have many other physical problems, as well as the mental retardation—congenital heart defects, for instance. This child will most likely never progress beyond a three- or four-year-old's capabilities, and she will just be a burden upon your family. I strongly suggest that you place her into a government institution, where she can receive professional care. We can recommend one to you, if you wish. Most of these kids don't live past their twenties anyway. You make the decision," he continued, "and I will make the arrangements."

He coldly turned and walked out of the room, leaving Sandy and me once again in shock.

"Honey, what are we going to do?" Sandy finally managed to ask. "I want you to make the final decision."

"There's only one decision to make. Chéri is our child, and we are not going home without her. We are going to love her and give her the best chance at life we can. She's our own flesh and blood."

Sandy quietly nodded her head in agreement. We both knew what we must do. We also knew that it was not going to be easy. God had sent Jane Armstrong with that poem at exactly the right time, or we might have made a grave mistake.

"I know one thing for sure, Honey," I said.

"What's that?"

"We are going to change doctors. I don't like this guy's attitude, and his bedside manner stinks."

That day we switched over to Dr. Andy Stewart, a kind, caring and humorous man who would remain our children's pediatrician for as long as we lived in Edmonton. Doc Stewart would later play a major role in our family.

Finally, after ten days in the respirator, Chéri's lungs cleared of fluid and we were able to bring her home. We were positive that both of our families would accept Chéri for who she was, but we were apprehensive about how our friends would react. Sadly, a great many of them were a real disappointment to us.

It is a difficult task to know how to handle this kind of news appropriately. Everyone is happy and excited for the parents of a new baby. However, when there is something wrong with the child, many people don't seem to know what to say or do. We seldom, if ever, heard from many of our friends and acquaintances. Fearing that they might say the wrong thing, they said nothing. And fearing that they might do the wrong thing, they did nothing. All we really needed from any of them was to know that their love and support was with us. Instead, we felt deserted.

It was a painful, often lonely time for us. We are thankful to our families for their constant support, and to our wonderful, loving neighbour, Peggy. In time, others came around, as they saw our love and acceptance of Chéri, and as they allowed themselves to get to know our special little girl.

Chéri herself has been our richest blessing and our greatest teacher. She continues to live each day with absolute joy, confidently expecting the best from every situation, and persisting with stubborn determination to learn new things. The most precious gift she possesses, however, is that which wins over even the greatest of adversaries: Chéri receives everyone she meets with absolute, unconditional love.

The day Chéri was born, our lives were irrevocably changed. At first we felt devastated, and we raged against a God we didn't know or understand. Yet somehow we were able to pick up the pieces and continue on. Once more I had sidestepped an opportunity to draw close to God, and He continued to be a mysterious, distant presence in my life.

Sandy's dad, Edward Selkirk.
Died of a sudden heart attack on
Oct. 7, 1980.

Sandy's mom, Doreen Selkirk.
She still resides in Edmonton.

Chapter 4

NEVER SAY NEVER

My fourth training camp with the Eskimos came to a close in July of 1969. There were a few rumours flying around at the time concerning possible trades. I wasn't one of the ones being talked about in the press, although I certainly wasn't having one of my better training camps. Just one week before camp started, I signed my 1969 contract with General Manager Norm Kimball. I tried to hold out as long as I could because I felt I was being grossly underpaid in relation to what the other players were making. Although contracts were not openly discussed between the players, rumours circulated on occasion.

After winning Rookie of the Year in 1966, I received a whopping $1,000 raise the next season, which moved me all the way up to $5,000 per year, and that was pretty small potatoes compared to salaries of other professional athletes. I was sure that many of my team-mates were making three to four times that much. I was considered by many to be the most versatile player on the team, because I started at wide receiver, played some defensive back at times, and even punted when called upon. On a few occasions, I played all three positions in the same game. In my second season, I even returned 10 kickoffs for an average of 31.4 yards, and I also handled the team's offensive kickoffs and converts during one game when our place kicker was down with a bruised ankle.

I felt that I was the lowest-paid player on the team, in spite of the contribution I was being asked to make. And since I was a young, naive "Canuck," management would have had no difficulty in exploiting me.

To be perfectly honest, I most likely would have played that first year for nothing. Just to have my dream fulfilled was reward enough. I changed my tune, however, when I realized what some of the other players were being paid. Of course, this was back when player agents were still unheard of in the CFL.

Well, on that unforgettable afternoon, Norm coerced me into signing on the dotted line by offering me a one-year contract. Included in the package were some nice bonuses for pass receptions. What actually convinced me to sign the contract was Norm's verbal offer for an excellent three-year contract the following season. He promised me that it would come into effect if I finished the regular season in the top five pass receivers of the Western Conference. Along with this lucrative offer, Norm proposed to advance me $5,000 for a down payment on a house, in lieu of the three-year contract.

I could barely contain myself as I rushed home to share the great news with Sandy. She was very excited at the prospect of buying our own home. Later that night, we lay in bed feeling quite contented that my career was finally on track.

"Honey," I whispered as we snuggled closely, "I have a feeling this is going to be our best year yet."

My enthusiasm was short-lived, however. Arriving at training camp the next week, I was shocked to discover that the coaching staff had decided some weeks earlier to play me in the defensive backfield this year. Of course, that automatically nullified the promises that Norm had made to me. I knew I had been shafted.

"Norm, You son of a b----, " I spewed out. "You threw me a sucker punch, and I fell for it."

I had never felt more contempt for anyone than I did at that moment. He had to have known about the switch of positions long before I signed the contract. During the three-week training camp, I saw him a few times, and on each occasion he seemed to deliberately avoid me. I carried a deep-rooted anger and bitterness in my heart for Norm Kimball for many years after that.

The incident of my contract really seemed to take the wind out of my sails during camp. Once or twice, I considered throwing in the towel and looking for a real job, where a person would be treated with some respect. My heart definitely was not in playing defensive back. What Norm had done to me haunted me constantly, on and off the field.

Just three months before training camp I had made a rather rash statement to Sandy one evening.

"If I ever get traded from here, Hon, I would go anywhere but Montreal." The Alouettes were the weakest team in the East, and the big city of Montreal was the last place I wanted to play.

"Garry, don't talk like that," Sandy replied rather fearfully. "They wouldn't trade you. You're a homegrown boy. I don't know what I would do if they ever sent us to some other city."

"Look, I'm just kidding," I said. "I'm not planning on going anywhere, but you never know with this crazy business. They're liable to do anything if it suits their purposes. But I don't think we need to worry. Coach Armstrong seems to like me for some reason. He isn't going to trade me away, so relax. One thing I do know, I would never go to Montreal, and that's for sure."

Just three weeks into the season, I was forced to swallow those words.

A Blessing in Disguise

It was the day after our third league game, and our third straight loss. Assistant Coach Ray Jauch walked up to my locker just before we were about to go out on the field for practice and told me to report to Coach Armstrong in his office. When I walked into the office, Coach Neil was standing with his back to me. As he turned to look at me, tears began to fill his eyes.

"Garry . . . you have been traded to Montreal. Son, I want you to understand that this was not my idea, but my hands are tied. There is nothing I can do about it. This came from above me, an upper management decision. If it were only up to me, Garry, you would still be an Edmonton Eskimo. I think you're a gifted athlete, with a lot of natural talent. The positive side of this is that Montreal really wants you as a wide receiver. They've been trying to make a trade for you for some time. This could prove to be a good career move for you. I know you'll play well for them. Their head coach's name is O.K. Dalton—he'll be calling you sometime today. I want to wish you and your family the very best. God be with you, Son."

I swallowed hard and walked out of the room, stunned. I could hardly believe what I had just heard. My bubble had burst and my dream had come to an abrupt end. I was being cast off like a piece of excess baggage, and I knew why. I guess it must have been getting pretty warm upstairs. *Oh my God*, I thought. *Montreal! Anywhere but Montreal! Dear Lord! How am I going to break this to Sandy?*

It took me about 30 minutes to clean out my locker, while saying goodbyes to many of the guys. Most of them were sympathetic and couldn't believe that I had been traded.

When I walked into the apartment an hour later, Sandy was startled. "What are you doing home so early? I thought practice wasn't over until seven o'clock."

"You're not gonna believe this one, Love," I told her. "I've just been traded, and you'll never guess where."

"Not Montreal!"

"You got it, and we can thank Mr. Kimball for this one."

"Oh, no! What are we going to do?"

"Start packing, Honey, and brush up on your French. I am not ready to retire yet. Montreal's head coach, O.K. Dalton, is supposed to call me later today."

The next evening, I was on a plane for Montreal, leaving Sandy behind with Chéri and all our affairs to look after. I didn't see them again for a whole month. That was the longest 30 days of my entire life.

The move to Montreal eventually proved to be a great blessing in disguise, even though the 1969 season was a total disaster. The Alouettes won only two games and tied two others. Then in the following off-season, Sam Berger bought the team and brought in Red O'Quinn as the

Montreal Alouettes
1970

new General Manager and amazing as it sounds, my boyhood hero, Sam "The Rifle" Etchevery, as the Head Coach.

From the onset of our 1970 training camp, football fever reached a new level in Montreal. Red O'Quinn and Sam Etchevery's return to the city was the talk of the town. It had been 14 long years since the Alouettes were in the Grey Cup and 19 years since they had won it. Sam and Red were the team's stars and household names back in 1954, '55, and '56, when the Eskimos defeated the Alouettes in three straight Grey Cups.

Now the talk was that the heroes were both back in Montreal to bring the Grey Cup home.

The team was sitting at one and one when we flew out to Winnipeg for our third regular game of the season. We lost a close one to the Blue Bombers that Wednesday evening, but even more unfortunately we lost one of our starting wide receivers: me.

It happened in the second quarter. I was flanked wide left and Terry Evanshen was split to the right. Quarterback Sonny Wade dropped back in the pocket and fired a bullet to Peter Dalla Riva over right centre. The pass was too high and sailed into the waiting arms of the Winnipeg defensive back, Ed Ulmer. When I saw the interception, I turned and raced towards that side of the field, hoping to help bring him down. Ulmer dodged a couple of would-be tacklers and headed straight towards me. As I closed on him, I realized that his total attention was on my teammates, who were directly in front of him, and he didn't see me coming at all. Right then I had visions of snatching the unprotected ball from his right hand and taking it all the way to pay dirt.

A split second before I was about to grab for the ball, an undetected body came flying in from my left side and slammed into my left knee just as it was planted in the turf. My momentum carried me ten feet off the ground, my feet awkwardly soaring above my head. Two seconds later my body slammed face first into the hard turf, my hands outstretched to break the fall. I felt a piercing pain shoot through my right wrist, and I knew I had seriously damaged it. When I stood to my feet, a few seconds later, cradling my right arm in my left, I noticed that my left leg was a bit wobbly as well. The Alouette trainer, "Smokey," ran out onto the field and helped me slowly to the sideline. "What's happened to you?" he inquired.

"I think I may have sprained my wrist." I responded. "And I took a pretty good blow to my left knee, and I think something happened to it. It feels a little unsteady, although it doesn't really hurt."

"Do you think you can still go?" Smokey challenged.

"Oh, yeah!" I answered. "It'll take more than this to keep me out of the game. Why don't you wrap my wrist and tape my knee up and get me back in there." Five minutes later I was back in the game. Sonny called me on a deep post pattern. I jogged slowly out to the right and positioned myself for the play. At the snap of the ball, I went to push off my left leg and it collapsed under me. Smokey helped me off the field once again and this time decided it would be wiser for me to stay out for the remainder of the game. Within a few minutes of sitting on the bench, my left knee began to throb and stiffen up. By the time the game was over, I could barely walk. The pain in my wrist was much more intense, so I assured myself that the knee couldn't be very serious.

When the team arrived back home that evening I was taken to the Montreal General Hospital and examined by the club orthopaedic surgeon, Dr. Percy. After x-rays, he informed me that my right wrist was cracked and my left medial lateral ligaments were severely torn. He operated on me immediately, and I awoke the next morning to hear the bad news.

"Son," he began, "I have operated on more than my share of knees, and I have never seen ligaments torn as badly as yours. They were literally shredded and ripped completely away from the bone. What I have done is sutured them the best that I could and anchored them to the bone with a large metal staple, which will remain there forever. Your full leg cast will have to stay on for eight weeks or so and you might only have to have the cast on your wrist for seven weeks. Either way, you are definitely finished for the season."

"Hold on, Doc!" I snapped back. "I am going to play again this season. We are going to win the Grey Cup, and I am not going to miss it."

"That is not possible, Garry," he responded. "You will have your leg cast on for at least eight weeks. Your leg muscles will have seriously atrophied by then, and it will take many months to build them up again."

"Mine won't shrink!" I retorted.

"They all do, Son, and besides, the scar tissue will have formed all around the wound and it will take you months just to be able to fully bend your knee again."

"I know this doesn't make any sense to you, Doc, but I am going to play again this year. I am not going to miss my chance to play in the Grey Cup."

"Well, you believe what you want to, Garry. I am just giving you the honest facts."

"We'll see who's right, won't we," I laughed as he moved to the door.

"We'll see, all right," he responded, closing the door.

Within a week, after the pain had subsided, I was able to tense my thigh muscles and hold my heavy cast in the air for increasing lengths of time. After all, what else was there to do except sit and watch TV? Each time I held my leg up, I would look down at the cast and say, "Muscles, you will not shrink. You will remain strong."

In seven weeks, my wrist cast was removed and I began therapy. The following week my leg cast was cut off, and to Dr. Percy's wonder and

First day out of hospital,
August 18, 1970

First Grey Cup Touchdown

amazement, my left leg muscles were the same size as when they were put in the cast.

The season of 1970 turned out to be the all-time "Cinderella" football story for the Alouettes. Coach Etchevery kept only 10 veterans on the roster and added 22 rookies. With Bob Story filling in for me at wide receiver, we finished one point out of second place and whipped Toronto in the semi-final.

To the amazement of everyone but me, I played in the Eastern Final against Hamilton. Sonny Wade tossed me three receptions, one for our go-ahead touchdown and another long sideline pass, which set up the winning touchdown. We defeated them 32-22 and were on our way to the big one. The Als went on to win the Grey Cup, defeating the Calgary Stampeders 23-10, and just for the icing on the cake, I caught my first Grey Cup touchdown pass. For the first time in 14 years—since the days with Sam the Rifle at quarterback—Montreal had a great football team.

An estimated 10,000 fans were packed like sardines into the Montreal airport to welcome their heroes home. Sandy was seven months pregnant at the time and almost passed out from the congestion, trying to make her way through the incredible crowd. I grabbed on to her hand and tried to lead her through the screaming fans, who kept pressing in just to touch one of us. It was the most electrifying thing I had ever experienced.

Winning the Grey Cup was the biggest thrill of my life up to that point, but it still wasn't like playing in Edmonton. My heart was still out West.

The City of Montreal threw us a Grey Cup Parade, where nearly 2,000,000 residents lined the streets. This was followed by an enormous banquet. That week, the entire city honoured their Grey Cup heroes. We felt really special and were grateful for all the fuss, but Sandy and I could hardly wait until we could get on the plane that would take us back to Edmonton to celebrate with our families and friends.

The Biggest Mistake Of Our Lives

Sandy and I arrived in Edmonton the following weekend. We planned to stay until the day after Christmas and then scoot back. Sandy was due January 14, so we didn't want to cut it too close. I also needed to get back and find some work for the off-season. By Christmas Day, our families had talked us into staying out West until the baby was born. My sister, Pat, and her husband, Wally, graciously offered to have us stay at their home in West Edmonton. The way it eventually turned out, we were to stay a lot longer than any of us had anticipated.

The baby decided to set his own schedule, delaying his arrival by a couple of weeks. Sandy finally had to be induced at the Royal Alexandra Hospital on January 28, 1971. Dr. Crooks, who had brought Chéri into this world, was the attending obstetrician once again. Sandy tried her best to get me into the delivery room with her, but to no avail. I wasn't about to pass out in front of a roomful of people and have them attend to me. To be absolutely honest, I was just plain scared to death.

We had wanted a boy from the moment Sandy began trying to conceive again. She was very apprehensive about having another child, although we knew the possibility of another Downs Syndrome child was very remote. But what if something else went wrong? Would we be able to handle it?

Back in Montreal, Sandy's physician had strongly suggested that she have an amniocentesis done, just for her own peace of mind. If something abnormal showed up, she could have a therapeutic abortion before it was too late. They would also be able to tell us the baby's sex. I felt uneasy about the whole procedure, which was relatively new at the time, but in Sandy's fourth month I had finally agreed to have it done. What a terrible mistake it would turn out to be.

Two young doctors performed this very sensitive procedure at the Montreal General. On their first attempt, they went in too close to the baby and drew a needle full of blood. Sandy informed me later that they had both looked very alarmed when the blood filled the needle. They decided to try once more. During their second attempt, one of the interns pushed the baby over to one side while the other one inserted the needle. This time they drew out the amniotic fluid they were after. They both seemed extremely relieved. The worst part of this whole scenario was that the culture into which they put the fluid didn't grow, so the entire ordeal was for nothing. Furthermore, we still knew nothing about the status of the baby.

Now, months later, we had all but forgotten about the doctors drawing the blood from Sandy's womb. We had never once suspected that it would adversely affect our baby. With Sandy in delivery, I was nervously pacing the waiting room alone when I suddenly had the strong impression that we were about to have a seven-pound, ten-ounce, fair-haired boy. Fifteen minutes later, Dr. Crooks walked into the room carrying a seven-pound, ten-ounce, red-headed boy.

"Congratulations, Garry. You are the proud father of a fine, healthy son, with all his toes and fingers. In fact, he looks perfect to me."

I was overcome with incredible joy and ran to the phone. I could hardly see the numbers to dial amidst the flood of tears. I called my mom and my sister, Pat, and asked them to call the others with the good news. Then I hurried in to see the happy mother. Sandy was exhausted from 12 hours of hard labour, but she was smiling from ear to ear.

"We did it!" I proclaimed. "Or should I say—you did good, Honey. He's just beautiful."

"He is gorgeous." she sighed with relief. "He definitely is a Lefebvre. He's got your round face and large head for sure. Bradley Allan Lefebvre—I think the name we picked suits him very well."

"More important, he's healthy, and thank God for that," I added.

"I'm so happy I could get up and dance," Sandy smiled.

"Don't you dare—you've done enough work for one day, or should I say a few days! You just lie there and rest. I'll go back to the house, and I'll see you in the morning."

I kissed her on the cheek as her eyes slowly closed.

"I love you, Sweetheart," I whispered and then quietly walked out into the hall.

I could hardly wait to get back to Pat and Wally's place, but of course I had to stop on the way out and peek through the window at our cute little bundle. This was to become a familiar pose for me—for some time to come. Although I didn't know it then, I would be looking at baby Brad through a similar window for the next three months.

I arrived at the hospital the next morning to find Sandy in a state of distress.

"What's the matter?" I was almost afraid to ask.

"Honey, there is something wrong with the baby. He can't keep anything down. Every time I feed him, he throws it right back up."

"Oh, is that all? Whew! By the way you were looking at me, I thought it must be real serious. It sounds like something minor. He'll be just fine. You stop your worrying."

"I can't help it—I have this terrible feeling and I'm scared."

I tried my best to reassure her, but it was no use. She was positive that something was seriously wrong. I felt it too, but I didn't let on. *No God, I thought to myself. This couldn't be happening to us again.*

Later that afternoon, Dr. Stewart informed us that Brad would have to undergo surgery immediately. He told us that a large mass at the beginning of his lower bowel had shown up on the x-ray. They were positive that, whatever it was, it was stopping his food from being digested, and that would explain why Brad couldn't keep anything down.

The operation was scheduled for 5:00 p.m. Before little Brad was taken up to surgery, Dr. Stewart asked us if we wanted him to be baptized. We consented, even though we ourselves were not religious. We did believe there was a God—at least we hoped there was. Besides, being baptized wouldn't hurt him. Sandy and I prayed a few prayers of desperation during the five long hours before Dr. Stewart returned with the results.

When the surgeon, Dr. Cox, opened up Bradley's little abdomen, he was totally surprised to find that his small intestine came about two feet off of his duodenum and ended abruptly in a large sack, about the size of a man's fist. The remainder of his intestine then continued on and into the large bowel and appeared to be normal. Dr. Cox had spent hours repairing the damage. At first he thought it would be a simple procedure to cut off the large sack and join the two ends together, but it wasn't that easy. There was an absence of nerve cells in the intestine that ran into the large bowel. After 21 biopsies, about one every inch, they found the presence of one nerve cell. Hoping this indicated that the rest of the bowel was all right, they made a decision to hook him up there. Bradley had already been under the anaesthetic as long as they dared keep him.

Dr. Cox informed us later that mechanically there was a 50-50 chance that everything would work as it should. Because of the missing bowel, though, Brad would probably need vitamin B12 shots as he grew older. Much of the absorption takes place through the wall of the small intestine, and he was missing a significant amount. We would just have to wait and see.

Four days later, another crisis hit. Sandy and I had just crawled into bed when the phone rang. My sister Pat answered it, and moments later we heard a light knock on our bedroom door.

"Garry, you're wanted on the phone. It's Dr. Andy Stewart."

I jumped out of bed as Sandy sat up with a start. I picked up the receiver in the kitchen and heard Dr. Stewart's friendly voice.

"Garry, we need your permission to operate on the baby again. I just dropped by and checked on the little lad and found him in serious trouble. His stomach is greatly distended and his temperature is skyrocketing. The little guy is being rushed to surgery at this moment and we need your consent to operate again. I have a nurse here on the line with me to verify your decision."

"You have our permission, Doctor, but what is it and what are his chances?" I asked.

"We don't know what has caused it or what his chances are, but this is very serious, Garry. There's nothing that you or your wife can do but pray. So don't come all the way down here to the hospital. I will call you as soon as we are done."

When I walked into our bedroom, Sandy was sitting up, wide awake.

"What is it?" she stammered, as her eyes filled with tears. She had heard part of the conversation. "What's wrong with our baby?"

"They're rushing him up to surgery again. They don't know what is wrong, but his temperature is rising rapidly and his stomach is very swollen. Dr. Stewart didn't give me any hope. He just said he would call us as soon as he can. Honey, it doesn't look good."

Sandy burst into tears.

"Garry, I'm scared we're going to lose him."

"Dear, we need to pray," I said.

"Oh God, please don't let him die!" Sandy sobbed.

We both dropped to our knees beside the bed and began to cry out to a God we were not sure was even there, never mind hear us.

"God, if you can hear me," I began, trying to hold back the tears, "please don't take our son away from us. Lord, what have we done to deserve this? Please don't take him. He is so innocent and so beautiful. God, it doesn't make any sense. Why would you bring Bradley into this world and then turn around and take him back so soon? Oh God, please save our little boy!"

As I poured out my heart, Sandy wept uncontrollably. An hour and a half went by so quickly. It seemed like only minutes. Sandy and I were in the middle of the biggest pity party that two people could ever have. I was trying my best to remain strong when, unexpectedly, a flood of emotion erupted from somewhere deep within my being and I burst into tears. I sobbed uncontrollably for a couple of minutes, then suddenly an astounding thought struck me. Instantly, the whole atmosphere in the room changed.

I glanced up from my knees and looked into Sandy's tear-stained face as I struggled to regain control of myself.

"Honey," I said in a calm though somewhat shaky voice, "something just dawned on me. If God really is God, then He has to be perfect, right?" She nodded in agreement.

"Then if God is perfect, that means He couldn't possibly make a mistake, right?"

"What are you saying?"

"Well, if He is perfect and can't make a mistake, then what are we doing down here trying to change His mind? If God is perfect, His mind cannot be changed."

Where all of these thoughts were coming from, I didn't know, but something strange yet incredibly peaceful was settling over my mind and heart. I looked up to the ceiling and began to speak.

"Lord, I don't know if You can hear me or if I'm just talking into the air or to myself. If You decide to take Bradley home, I want You to know that I won't be angry with You or blame You for it. If you are truly God, then You couldn't possibly make a mistake—or You couldn't be God and I am talking to the ceiling. If You are here and You can hear me, all I ask is that some day You will tell us why it had to be like this. And Lord, I want to thank You for the time that we did have him. Amen."

Sandy and I both felt a sense of peace and well-being sweep over us. We rose up together and sat down on the side of the bed. We sat there in silence for a few minutes, and then Sandy quietly laid her weakened body down on her side of the bed. At this point, I had fully accepted that Bradley wouldn't make it, and so I began to plan the funeral in my mind and what I would write in his obituary.

Oh, no! I suddenly thought, *I just put his birth announcement in* The Journal *today.* But then another wave of sweet peace swept through my whole being, and suddenly there in front of me was a woman holding a baby in her arms. She looked so peaceful as she smiled down at the baby. I instantly knew that it was our son. Then, just as quickly as the woman had appeared, she was gone. In my mind's eye, I could see Brad on the operating table. It was apparent that where they had joined him together before had ruptured. I instinctively knew that the doctors had reached him in time and that he was all right. It felt like a 1,000-pound weight lifted from my shoulders and I swung around to say something, only to find Sandy fast asleep. I shook her shoulder and she awoke with a start.

"Sandy, Bradley is going to be all right. He's okay!"

"What?" she gasped. "I didn't hear the phone ring."

"You aren't going to believe what just happened to me." Minutes after I had related my incredible experience to her, the phone abruptly rang. Sandy jumped and grabbed onto my arm with a steel-like grip.

"Relax, Dear," I tried to reassure her. "I told you, he is all right."

I walked into the kitchen and picked up the phone with absolute confidence that I would be greeted with the good news.

"It's Andy Stewart," the warm familiar voice began. "Your little guy is okay. Where we had joined him together in the first operation had come apart. We caught it in time and have cleaned all the poisonous toxins out of his system. We didn't dare stay in there any longer, so we had to bring his small intestine out through the abdominal wall. The medical term is *jejunostomy*. We will have to leave him like this for a few weeks until he regains his strength, and then we'll go back in and check the rest of the bowel and finish the job. For now, he is fine. Garry, it was awfully lucky I checked on him when I did. A couple more minutes and he would have probably been dead, with all that poison pouring into his system."

"Doctor, thank you so very much."

"No problem. I'm just glad the little guy is doing better."

I hung up the phone, rushed to the bedroom and blurted out, "Sandy I know God is real! He has just given us back our son."

We stayed up until 5:30 a.m., unable to sleep, while Sandy and Pat and I discussed the unbelievable events of the evening. The vision, or whatever it was that I had had, kept playing over in my mind. I was sure that somehow God had divinely intervened in our son's life. Dr. Stewart's being there at 2:30 a.m. to check on Bradley was too timely for me to believe that it was just a coincidence.

After a four-hour sleep, Sandy and I drove to the Royal Alex to see little Brad. We found him again in his familiar plastic incubator. It was hard not to be able to hold him or comfort him in any way. He looked so helpless lying there on his back with his hands and feet tied to the corners of the unit, so that he couldn't accidentally pull out the intravenous that was taped securely to the top of his head. His bare little tummy was exposed to the air and an ugly half-inch hole on his left side stared us in the face. Every now and then a greenish liquid would bubble up and spill over onto his delicate white skin. The acidic fluid burned the surface of his stomach and the area around the exposed intestine was already red and inflamed. Our hope was that Brad would not require plastic surgery as suggested by a couple of his attending nurses.

After an hour of just standing there and praying through our tears, I noticed that someone had come into the room and was standing to our right, looking at a baby in the incubator right next to little Brad. I did a double take as I recognized Larry Kerychuk, an old friend of ours. He told us his daughter Shannon had been born two weeks premature and just needed some extra care until she gained a little weight. We then explained to him what we were doing there, and the two operations that Bradley had already undergone. He listened intently and seemed genuinely concerned for all of us.

I had heard a few months earlier that Larry had gone religious and I had even made jokes about him to other friends.

"Stay away from Kerychuk or he will try to convert you," I would say. "I hear he's become a Bible Thumper."

Larry didn't try to lay any religious trip on us that day. He just showed real compassion for us in our time of need. As we parted, Larry turned to Sandy and me and said, "I want you to know that I'll be praying for the baby and for you guys."

Those brief words left a profound impression on me and disturbed me for a long time. Although I knew that there truly was a God in heaven, I wasn't about to get too close to Him. One thing I was sure of—I would never become one of those "Bible Thumpers."

Over the next few weeks, the physicians and nurses tried numerous different creams to try to help Brad's burned skin, but nothing seemed to work. By the end of three weeks, though, they had developed a new combination of creams that worked wonderfully, as well as a new formula that greatly aided in his digestion. That formula is still used today for other babies. As we stood and watched him crying unceasingly, our hearts ached. The only thing that eased our pain was the knowledge that he was alive and that his condition should improve in time.

Six weeks later, on March 22, Brad endured a third operation, which joined the small and large intestines, and that was the end of the jejunostomy. For the first time in his young life, he was able to take food in through his mouth. Now all he needed to do was move his bowels and begin to gain some weight. Easter Sunday, April 11, was a very special day for us. Our tiny baby boy's intravenous came out and he gained half an ounce.

The next morning the excitement continued when Brad's bowels moved for the first time. Needless to say, there was much rejoicing as Brad's nurse ran around showing his diaper to all the staff on the ward. Sandy swore that she would never complain about having to change a dirty diaper as long as she lived. After three more days of steady progress, we were able to take him home for the first time. Two weeks later we were on a flight back to Montreal with our two precious babies.

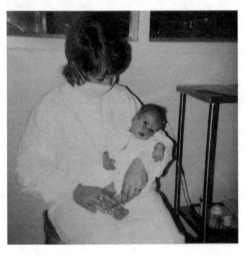

Sandy and Brad in hospital

Brad at 5 months

God bless Mommy and Daddy

Chapter 5

I DON'T WANT NO RELIGION

Our 1971 season in Montreal was a disaster, with the team winding up in last place in the Eastern Conference. That was quite a blow to all of our egos. We'd fallen a long way, after being the Grey Cup Champs the previous year. The season had dragged on and on as the team invented new ways to blow football games. Our team morale had reached an all-time low by the time we faced the Winnipeg Blue Bombers in our last game of the season. It was a "nothing game" for us, and I think most of our team just wanted to get the season over with and head for home with our tails between our legs. Our fan-support had been dropping rapidly, and I couldn't blame them for their lack of enthusiasm. Certainly we as a team had been doing nothing to help the situation.

Actually, I had been looking forward to the game for another reason: Larry Kerychuk played for Winnipeg and was expected to punt and play some defensive back in the game.

The contest turned out to be a defensive struggle with numerous turnovers. The Alouettes—or "All-Wets" as some were calling us—managed to squeak out a 19-17 win. Unfortunately, Larry was slammed hard from the left side on a punt in the third quarter and separated his shoulder. Because it was the last game of the season, the team trainer advised him to stay behind and see a doctor in the morning, while the rest of the team flew back to Winnipeg that night. This was unheard of. Teams always like their players to be attended to by their own team physicians. As I look back on the events of that day, I believe this was providential in the life of the Lefebvres.

When Larry explained the situation to us after the game, we asked him if he would like to stay over at our apartment. We had an extra bedroom, and it didn't seem right that he should have to stay alone, especially with his pain and discomfort. We expected he would want to rest, but that wasn't the case. He kept Sandy and me up until 7:00 a.m. the next morning. Larry shared, from the heart, his testimony of how he had come to know Jesus Christ as his personal Lord and Saviour. He did not talk about religion but about a relationship he had with God. I had known Larry during our high-school days back in Edmonton, and there definitely had been a dramatic change in his life. It was obvious that he had found something that made a profound difference in him.

In spite of his obvious pain, he sat on the couch for eight hours sharing his heart with us. During that evening, he told us about an athletic conference in Dallas, Texas, that he planned to attend in February. A group called Athletes In Action was sponsoring it. Then he totally surprised us when he said, "If you are interested in going, I believe I know a Christian businessman who will cover all your expenses."

This offer sounded very attractive to me, especially on my Canadian salary. Most of the Canadian players played for the love of the game. We were certainly not going to get rich on our football salaries. I always had to work at another job in the off-season in order to make ends meet.

Sandy was excited at once about the possibility of the free trip. I agreed that we would go if Larry were able to make the arrangements, even though I was somewhat reluctant. That old fear that God wanted to take the fun out of my life still haunted me.

If I got too close to Him, what would He require of me?

The only reason I agreed to go was that Sandy was so excited about it and, after all, it was three months away. I knew I would have plenty of time to find a good excuse for missing it. I drove Larry to see a physician that morning, and in the afternoon we saw him off at the airport. He promised to keep in touch about the AIA Conference.

As February 16 drew near, I still did not have a good excuse to avoid the conference, and I was rapidly running out of time. Larry had called in early January to confirm that a Christian businessman had underwritten our expenses. Now we were less than two weeks away, and as far as Sandy was concerned, we were going. In fact, she was very enthused and talked about it constantly. I had to bite my tongue a number of times. The thought of being at a conference with a bunch of Christians frankly scared me to death.

I just wasn't ready to give up all the things that I enjoyed, like smoking and drinking. I was sure that if I got too close to God, that would be the end of my fun. After all, I thought I knew what being a Christian was all about: give up the joys of life, carry a large black Bible around, and preach to everyone you meet on the street. I certainly was not interested in church three times a week, and I did not look forward to walking around with a frown permanently pasted on my face. I knew I needed an excuse fast or I was in deep trouble.

Hockey had always been a sport I loved playing, ever since childhood, so when the Alouettes decided to form a hockey team to play charity exhibition games during the off-season, I was thrilled. The guys travelled all around Quebec and played some fairly good hockey teams that winter. There were some excellent hockey players on our football team, and we were bolstered with a few others, like the late great Doug Harvey. What a privilege it was to play with him. Man, could he handle a puck.

During January and February, our schedule was the heaviest. One morning as I was looking it over, I realized that the Dallas Conference conflicted with one of our hockey games.

I had finally found my way out.

Sandy sat across the room from me and polished her nails while I worked up all the nerve I had to break the disappointing news to her.

"Honey, I was just going over my hockey schedule and can't believe it, but I have a game on the same weekend as the AIA Conference. If it were just for me, there wouldn't be any problem. But posters have been made, and I'm expected to be there. Besides, I can't let my line-mates down—they're counting on me." (I centred the first line, with Terry Evanshen on left wing and Bob Storey on the right.)

"A hockey game! You would pass up an all-expense-paid trip to Dallas for an exhibition hockey game that means nothing? Garry, you can't be serious!"

That took the wind out of my sails in a hurry. She had me, and she knew it.

"Yeah, I guess you're right. I can play hockey another time."

I had tried to duck out, but now my goose was cooked. Just then, the solution to my dilemma popped into my mind. This time I was sure that I could avoid the conference and appease Sandy at the same time.

"Hon, to be perfectly honest with you, I've been having second thoughts about this conference. I'm really not sure if this is something we should be involved in. I'm afraid we might be heading in the wrong direction. I believe in God, but I don't know about all this religious stuff. Do you remember a story from the Bible about a man named Gideon? If I remember correctly, he wanted to know if God was leading him, so he put out a fleece and God answered him."

"He used some kind of sheepskin, didn't he?" Sandy replied.

"I think God could answer us too. We don't have a sheepskin, but maybe I should pray and ask Him to give me some sign if he wants us to go to Dallas."

Sandy's immediate response really surprised me.

"That sounds like a good idea. Why don't you pray right now?"

She fell for it. I had it made. All I had to do was pray, and when there was no audible voice from heaven saying, "YOU MUST GO TO DALLAS," I would be off the hook and I could play hockey next weekend.

"Let's pray together," I suggested. We bowed our heads and I offered a simple prayer. "God, Sandy and I are not sure if we should be going to this conference in Dallas, or even if it would be a good thing for us to do. Could you give me some type of sign if you want us to go? Amen."

We both sat there in silence for a couple of minutes. Neither one of us knew what to expect. Suddenly the fingers of my left hand went numb, and a familiar pulsating pain began throbbing in my shoulder and upper arm. I had slipped a vertebra in my neck about six months earlier. While diving for a low pass, my head had buckled under me, just as the defender pounced on me. I left the field in a total daze, but no one thought I had been seriously hurt, including me. When I awoke the next morning, there was a pulsating pain in my neck and shoulder area. I thought I had probably slept on it wrong and didn't think any more about it. The pain was mild at first, but it gradually worsened over the period of a month, moving down my left shoulder and arm. The fingers of my hand slowly became numb and tingly. The shoulder pain eventually became unbearable. I actually played four games with the pain until finally I complained to our club trainer, and he booked me an emergency appointment with a leading neurologist.

The doctor immediately did a myelogram test and discovered that my seventh vertebra was protruding and putting pressure on my spinal cord. If I had taken a blow on the top of my head, I could have very easily been paralyzed for life. After nine days of traction in the Montreal General, the vertebra worked its way back into place. The neurologist told me that if the disc slipped out again, I would have to undergo surgery. It would probably lay me up for at least six months and my football career would definitely be over. Now, feeling the familiar pulsating pain again, I instantly broke out in a cold sweat and began to shake.

"Oh, no! Sandy, the disc in my neck has just slipped out again. The same pain is back again in my left arm. Remember what the doctor said? My football career is over!"

*Just prior to
traction*

Sandy burst into tears. "Honey, what are we going to do?"

Then it dawned on me that I had just prayed for a sign. I threw both hands into the air and shouted, "Okay God! I've got the message. We will go to Dallas."

Incredible as it may sound, the pain left instantly.

When Sandy and I flew into Dallas the next Thursday, there was no doubt in either of our minds that we were supposed to be there. We went with open hearts and open minds and, as a result, the events that took place there changed our lives forever.

We arrived at the Holiday Inn on the afternoon of February 16, 1972, along with 125 other athletes and their wives. Larry had flown in from Winnipeg an hour before and was waiting for us in the lobby. He introduced Sandy and me to some of the most loving people we had ever had the pleasure of meeting. Most of them were Campus Crusade For Christ staff and a few were with Sports World Chaplaincy, a ministry of Ira "Doc" Eschelman. At that time, Doc, as he was fondly referred to, was the Chaplain of the NFL. He was the individual who first had the vision to reach out to football players. I would soon come to know and love Doc.

After we were settled in our room, it was time for the first session. Doc Eschelman greeted everyone and spoke for roughly 30 minutes about what God was doing in the NFL. I was amazed at the number of famous football players who professed to be born-again Christians. Norm Evans, the captain of the Miami Dolphins, and his beautiful wife, Bobbie, shared a short testimony on how Jesus Christ had come into their lives and dramatically changed their marriage. This was all foreign to Sandy and me, but we were truly impressed with their sincerity. They were so transparent, I could hardly believe it. We didn't quite know what to make of it all, but we certainly were ready to listen.

After dinner, Tom Landry, the Dallas Cowboys coaching legend, spoke to us about what God was doing on the Cowboys team and what it was like to live the Christian life as an NFL coach.

Later that evening, a black preacher named Tom Skinner spoke. I had never in my life heard anyone speak with such authority. I sat spellbound as he preached the Word of God. Even though Tom spoke for over an hour, it seemed like only minutes. The meeting ended just before 11:00 p.m. and everyone headed for their rooms. Sandy and I talked until after 1:00 in the morning. We had so much to digest.

A New Creation

Even though we didn't get much rest, Sandy and I awoke early the next morning. In fact, we didn't get much sleep that whole weekend. After breakfast, the men stayed together and the women moved to a separate room. One of the members of the Athletes In Action weightlifting team spoke for half an hour and then presented a small booklet called "The Four Spiritual Laws." After a brief explanation of the booklet, he asked us to break up into pairs and practise using this "witnessing" tool with each other. We were instructed to familiarize ourselves with its contents, as we would be sharing it with high-school students later that afternoon.

I immediately broke into a cold sweat. I knew nothing about all this stuff, and the very thought of talking to someone else about God left me terrified.The guys at my table responded at once and began to pair up. I wasn't sure what to do, so I just sat where I was and sincerely hoped no one would notice me in the shuffle. After a few seconds, a young AIA weightlifter walked over and introduced himself to me.

"Hi, I'm Jim Stump. Do you need a partner?"

"Yes, I guess I do," I answered. "My name is Garry. I'm pleased to meet you."

"Well, let's get after it. Would you like to go first, Garry?"

Are you kidding? I thought to myself. *I have no idea what this is all about!*

"Uh, no. It's all right. You go ahead first, Jim."

"All right then, just follow along in your booklet. If you have any questions, don't hesitate to stop me. Before we read the booklet, I want to explain something to you. Just as there are natural laws that govern our universe, there are spiritual laws that govern our relationship with God. Keeping that in mind, let's turn to page one."

He began to read, "Garry, did you know that God loves you and has a wonderful plan for your life?"

"Well, no, not really," I responded quite truthfully.

"The Bible says in John 3:16, 'For God so loved the world that he gave his one and only Son, that whoever believes in him shall not perish but have eternal life'."

Something began to happen to me that I could not explain. I had heard most of these Bible verses before, mainly from watching Billy Graham on television, but this was totally different. The words Jim was reading seemed to have some kind of life in them. It felt as if they penetrated right through my being. I hung onto every word.

Jim continued: "Law Two says that the reason you are not experiencing this love and plan is because you are a sinner and separated from God."

Again the words pierced my soul. Something extraordinary was happening to me. Although I didn't understand what it was at the time, I knew inside my heart that it was good. It seemed that my soul had been thirsting for water and I was drinking from a deep, cool wellspring. It just felt . . . right.

"Garry, the Bible says in Romans 3:23, 'For all have sinned and fall short of the glory of God.' Romans 6:23 also says, 'For the wages of sin is death, but the gift of God is eternal life in Christ Jesus our Lord.'"

"The Third Law is that Jesus Christ is God's only provision for man's sin, and only through Him can you know and experience the plan that God has for you. Jesus Himself said, 'I am the way and the truth and the life. No one comes to the Father, except through me.'"

"Wow!" I interrupted, "He cut everybody else out, didn't He?"

"Yes, He did, Garry, and He rose from the dead and proved His words were truth. Let's go on to Law Number Four."

The entire time Jim shared, he never once suspected that I was not yet a Christian. After all, this was a training conference for "Christian

Athletes," and we were being trained in how to share our faith effectively. When I reacted as if all this was something totally new to me, he thought I was just pretending and playing the role of the non-Christian very well. Thank God that he didn't quit part way through and switch the roles.

"Garry, Law Four states, 'It isn't enough to know all this in your head. You must individually *receive* Jesus Christ as your personal Lord and Saviour. Only then can you truly experience the plan that God has for your life. You must ask Christ to come into your heart and *receive* the payment of His Blood for your sin. When you *receive* Christ, you *receive* *eternal life.*' Ephesians 2:8 and 9 says, 'For it is by grace you have been saved, through faith—and this not from yourselves, it is the gift of God—not by works, so that no one can boast.'"

At that moment I knew that Jesus Christ was the Saviour of the world and that I truly wanted Him to be the Lord of my own life. Jesus had revealed Himself to my heart through His Word, and I was ready to surrender my whole life to Him. Jim read the prayer from the tenth page of the booklet, and then he asked me point blank, "Does this prayer express the desire of your heart? If so, then pray it after me and Jesus will come into your life." While he continued to read, I followed along in my heart, meaning every word I breathed. At that moment, I experienced what the Bible calls the new birth. I was "born again." The amazing thing was that Jim had no idea what had transpired in my heart. He looked up from the book and said, "Okay, it's your turn now. I'll be the non-Christian and you read the booklet to me."

I began to read with a new set of eyes. The words on the page were no longer just like other words. They were "Words of Life." Although I didn't understand what had happened to me, I knew I was dramatically different.

An indescribable peace filled my entire being. I finally knew who I really was and why I had been created.

I had made the ultimate reception.

The meeting broke for lunch at 11:45 a.m., and I met Sandy in the hallway. Before I could explain to her what had just happened to me, she began to tell me that she had given her life to Jesus just minutes earlier in the ladies' meeting. We had both been "born again" at the same time.

From that day forward, we have grown together spiritually and have served the Lord as one.

During lunch, it was announced that the buses would be there to pick us up at 1:30 p.m. to take us to the high schools to share the Four Spiritual Laws with some of the students. The thought of having to speak to someone about the Lord petrified me.

What if they asked me a question I didn't have an answer for?

There was just no way I could do it. All my life I had been the proverbial "wallflower." I was an extreme introvert. Back in high school days, if I ever had to get up in front of the class and give a report or something, I would become very ill. Whenever I could, I just stayed home from school at such times.

My palms began to sweat as they always did when I got nervous. As soon as lunch was over, I made a beeline for the sanctuary of our hotel room. I knew I couldn't get on that bus at 1:30. I would just have to play sick once again. Sandy and I had been married for four and a half years and I had never told her of this horrible fear that plagued me. Afraid to admit it even to her, I wore the *I've-got-it-all-together* mask. She never even suspected what I had hidden so well under the surface. I didn't want to be exposed, so I tried to lie to her.

"Honey, I really don't feel very well. I don't think I'm going to be able to go to the high school this afternoon. I think I should just stay in bed and rest."

"Oh no," she said, showing her disappointment. "That's terrible!"

The moment I said it, a gentle voice from somewhere down inside me whispered, *"Garry, that is a lie. You had better tell her the truth."*

Something incredible had taken place in my heart. My conscience had been awakened and I could no longer justify a lie.

I'm sorry Lord, I breathed inside. *I shouldn't have done that.*

"Sandy, I'm sorry, but that isn't true. I'm not sick. I just don't want to go to the high school. I'm afraid to speak to the students. What if they ask me questions that I don't have the answer for? The only thing I know is that Jesus is my Lord. I think I'll just stay here and read, but you can go with the other ladies if you like. Don't worry about me. You go and enjoy yourself."

"Garry, I don't think it would be right for you not to go. We had our way paid to this conference by a Christian businessman. Besides, this is a great opportunity to help some young people. I'm sure you will do just fine. I feel a little scared too, but all we have to do is follow the booklet.

If they ask you a question you can't answer, just tell them you're new at this. I'm sure they'll understand."

"You're right. I really don't have any other choice. I guess I'm going." As the bus rolled along the highway that afternoon, I sat nervously in the back row, my palms sweating excessively. Suddenly, Norm Evans stood to his feet near the front. He turned and looked to the back. I was sure he was staring directly at me.

"I have been sensing that some of you guys are a little uptight about this engagement. There's something you need to know. God doesn't need any of your *ability*. All He wants is your *availability*. So don't worry about what you're going to say. God will put the words in your mouth that He wants you to speak. If you will just make yourself available to God, He will use you."

Those were the timeliest words I had ever heard. A peace settled over my spirit and somehow I knew that it would turn out all right. Norm's words had given me the confidence I needed. That afternoon I shared the Four Spiritual Laws with five teenage boys, and four of them asked Jesus to be their Saviour. The fifth boy said that he was already a Christian. What an awesome experience to see those young men give their lives to God.

It was a day I will never forget—to receive Jesus Christ as my Saviour and Lord in the morning, and then that very afternoon to lead others into that same wonderful experience. It was an exceptional beginning to the ministry for which God had prepared me. Jesus began to reveal His incredible love and grace to us that very week.

The day after we returned to Montreal, my hockey coach called to tell me that the game I had given up to attend the conference had been postponed at the last minute. I hadn't missed it after all.

Chapter 6

I AM NOT ASHAMED

Flying home to Montreal, we were more excited than we had ever been in our lives. The thought of being literally a brand new person on the inside carried all kinds of possibilities for our future. When you know who you are and why you are alive, it can't help but make life exciting. I had tried to find my identity in the game of football and had come up empty. Sandy and I had just begun to really live.

It was thrilling to envision what our loving Heavenly Father might have in store for us in the coming years.

In addition to our inspiring conversation on the plane ride, I read a few chapters of a Christian book we had purchased at the conference: it was called *The Late Great Planet Earth*, by Hal Lindsay. I nearly jumped out of my seat when I got into the chapter entitled "The Ultimate Trip." Lindsay wrote about the fact that the last-day Christians—those alive on earth when Jesus Christ returns—would not see physical death but would be translated instantly into their eternal glorified bodies and never again be subject to pain or death. The author compared Bible prophecies with modern-day events, and it looked very much like the world was just about to enter that final phase of history leading up to and including the "Second Coming of Jesus Christ." This incredible portion of information sent goose bumps up and down my body. It was the most amazing thing I had ever heard. The thought of checking out so soon frightened Sandy at first. She still wanted to have more children and wasn't quite ready to leave this old earth yet. But after she read the chapter for herself, she came to peace with the idea.

Sandy and I arrived back in Montreal truly excited about our newfound faith in Christ. Ten days later, I was asked to my first official speaking engagement. Al and Sue Phaneuf were youth leaders in their church, so they asked me if I would share my new experience with their young people. Al was a defensive back with the Alouettes. I was a little nervous at first, but the butterflies soon departed, and I was able to really enjoy the rest of the meeting, especially the interaction with the youth. I greatly appreciated their honesty and straightforwardness.

I was completely taken by surprise when Al took me aside after the meeting and began to apologize to me.

"Please forgive me," he began. "I shared my faith with nearly every player on the Alouette team . . . except you. To be completely honest, Garry, I didn't think there was any point in it. In fact, I really thought you would laugh in my face."

"Oh, that's all right, Al," I reassured him. "I probably wouldn't have witnessed to me either. I wore a pretty convincing mask, didn't I?"

"That's for sure, but I still feel that at least I should have made an attempt. I just never imagined that God was dealing with you all along."

"I guess that old saying about judging the book by its cover still holds true," I quipped.

That day I understood that you simply cannot judge a person by what they project outwardly. To Al, I was the team clown, the guy with all the dirty jokes, the guy who never took anything too seriously. But the truth was, during that 1971 season, I was a person who was really questioning what life was all about. I just never let on to anyone what was going on inside, especially to Al. I had fooled him completely with a very convincing disguise.

At the Dallas Conference, one of the guest speakers had mentioned that when a person begins to read the Bible for the first time, they should begin in the book of John. Then they should read the other three Gospels, which portray Christ from different perspectives. After that, they should continue to read the rest of the New Testament. When finished, they can begin to read the Old Testament and understand it better in the light of knowing Christ. Then the Old Testament will come alive as it prophetically looks to the coming of the Messiah. Sandy and I heeded this advice and began to read John's Gospel immediately after returning from Dallas.

One evening in early March, we were reading aloud from John chapter 16 when the 24th verse literally leapt off the page and into my heart. The words of Jesus seemed to come alive: "Until now you have not asked for anything in my name. Ask and you will receive, and your joy will be complete." I turned to Sandy sitting across the table and interrupted her thoughts.

"Did you hear what I just read? Jesus said that we can ask for anything in His name and He will give it to us, so that it will give us real joy."

"That is incredible! What do you think we should ask for?" she replied, rather wide-eyed.

"Well," I continued, "what do you think would give us the most joy? I mean, if we could have whatever we wanted? I think I know what I want to ask for. I would like God to trade me back to Edmonton. All of our family and most of the people we know live there, and none of them know the truth about our Saviour."

Then Sandy said, with an astonished look on her face, "I was just thinking that very same thing,"

"Well, let's give it a try!"

"Okay," she said, "you lead."

We bowed our heads before the Lord and I prayed a simple prayer.

"Father, according to Your Word, You say that we can ask for anything in Jesus' name and You'll give it to us. So we ask You in the name of Jesus—please trade us back to Edmonton so we can share Your love and truth with the people we love and care about. Thank You for hearing us. Amen."

At this point in our young Christian lives, we hadn't been given any teaching or theological understanding. Being the young and inexperienced children that we were, we simply believed what God's Word said and didn't try to figure it all out.

The next morning at 10:00 a.m., the telephone rang. When I picked it up, I heard the voice of Coach Sam Etchevery.

"Garry, I have some news to tell you. To be honest, I'm not sure whether you will consider it good or bad."

In my heart I knew what he was about to say.

"I'll bet it's good," I replied.

"We traded you back to the Edmonton Eskimos this morning."

"That's fantastic!" I shouted. "I just knew it would happen. Thank you, Coach. This is an amazing answer to prayer."

From that time on, God has revealed His will to Sandy and me in the same way that He did in this incident: whenever He has spoken His Word to one of us, He has confirmed it through the other.

After I spoke long distance that afternoon with Ray Jauch, who was now the Edmonton head coach, the Eskimo club agreed to pay for our move back to Edmonton. We stayed in Montreal until the first week in June and then drove to Edmonton the week before I was to report for training camp.

Our belongings arrived in a van four days later, and we moved into my dad's place in North Edmonton. We were home again, but things had changed dramatically. We were not the same people who had left for eastern Canada three years earlier. Our lives were radically different, and we were determined that our family and friends would soon know it.

Training camp was as gruelling as ever. It was always the same, no matter at which end of the country it was held. Thankfully, I came through it without any injuries. The team worked out at North American Baptist College now, and we practiced twice a day for the first two weeks, while living in the school dorms. There were many new faces, but there were also a good number of my old team-mates still around. It felt great to be an Eskimo again. Since the number 10 was already being worn by quarterback Bruce Lemmerman, I was issued number 11, which I wore for the remainder of my career.

One evening during the first week of camp, the players were allowed to go into town and, as was the usual case, we were given an 11:00 p.m. curfew. I went straight home to see Sandy, and when I arrived I found an unexpected visitor. An old girl friend of my brother, Murray, had dropped in to see us. She had no idea that we had become Christians. After we had talked and caught up on old news, she began to tell us about a friend of hers who had just married a guy whom she distastefully called a "Jesus Freak."

"Would you believe the guy even gives away much of his hard-earned money? He's got to be a real kook."

I swallowed hard and looked at Sandy out of the corner of my eye, but neither of us said anything. I wanted to stop the conversation right then and there and tell her that we were Christians too, but I couldn't muster up enough courage. Another hour passed as we talked about different things, and all the time I wanted to go back to the comment about the "Jesus Freak." A short time later she left and we never saw her again. When the door closed behind her, I stood in the foyer with a sickening feeling in the pit of my stomach.

"Sandy, we should have said something."

"I was going to, but I left it too long," she admitted sheepishly. "The longer I waited the more difficult it was to go back to it."

"I know, Honey," I said. "I feel sick about it too. I was too embarrassed to tell her that we were followers of Jesus."

"God, please forgive us for being so fearful that we didn't say anything," I prayed. "How could we have just let her go on like that? Forgive us for being ashamed of you, Lord, after all You've done for us. If You give me the chance, Lord, I will tell the whole world that Jesus Christ is my Lord."

"Amen," Sandy added.

We were truly repentant, and God graciously gave us another chance a couple of weeks later. Our long-time friends, Bill and Bunny, joined us for a fun night out at the Klondike Fair Grounds. After we'd strolled along the midway for about an hour, we passed a Youth for Christ tent. Bunny took one look and immediately offered her opinion.

"I wish those Jesus Freaks would stay out of my face. They bug the life out of me."

"Hold it, Bunny," I quickly responded. "We don't want you to say anything you might be sorry for later. Sandy and I have become Christians too, and we're just like those young people. We were born again last February when we lived in Montreal."

"Oh, no!" Bill interrupted me. "Bunny and I don't like to talk about politics or religion, so if you don't mind, I think we had better drop the subject."

The rest of our time together that evening was very tense. Sandy and I knew their hearts were closed. They were not the least bit interested in hearing how Jesus had changed our lives. We didn't bring it up again the rest of the evening, but there was no doubt in their minds as to where we stood. From that day on, Bill and Bunny came up with all kinds of excuses as to why they couldn't come over for a visit, and we sure didn't receive any invitations to their home. They moved to Regina, Saskatchewan, a few months later and never even left us a forwarding address. All we could do was to pray for them from a distance, which we often did. Seven years later, Bill's company moved them to Calgary and, in answer to our prayers, they bought a home next door to a pastor who also began to witness to them. In April of 1980, Sandy and I were privileged to lead them both to Christ after receiving an invitation to visit them in their home.

During the second week of camp, Larry Kerychuk showed up at North American Baptist College. He informed me that Doc Ira Eschelman, the Chaplain of the NFL, was coming up to Canada the next week to begin a chapel program in the CFL. Each team would need a representative player who would act as the team's chapel leader. He would also be responsible for lining up the speakers for each pre-game chapel, and also to coordinate team Bible studies during the week.

When Larry asked me if I would take on the responsibility, I agreed to do it, even though the thought of being a chapel leader sent fear through my heart. I was really a reluctant leader, but there was no one else. I was the only Christian on the team, so I was forced into the role. If there had been someone else, I would have tried my best to pass on the position. As I have said, I was a total introvert, quite content to follow someone else's lead.

At that time, there was at least one Christian on each of eight of the nine CFL teams. So the Sports World Chaplaincy Pro Chapel Program began that summer on all of the teams except the Hamilton Tiger Cats, who came in the following year.

Larry took on the responsibility of the Canadian Directorship and helped Doc Eschelman set up the programs with the eight teams. Larry spent most of that 1972 season lining up chapel speakers and encouraging and working with each of the team representatives. All through that season, God blessed and prospered our efforts, and many CFL players came to know Jesus Christ through a personal experience.

In that first year, there were eight Eskimo players and one coach who prayed to receive Jesus during the pre-game chapels. That was almost one-third of the 33 players, and it had a profound effect on the whole team. From 1973 to 1982 the Eskimos went to the Grey Cup nine times and won it six times (five in a row). Although some may disagree, I believe very strongly that the spiritual revival that began in 1973 was the foundation for the phenomenal success of the team.

From 1972 to 1973, Coach Jauch had either traded or cut many of the players who were heavy drinkers, womanizers, or carousers. They were replaced with good family-types who were there to play football, not to bolster their egos by seeing how many women they could conquer. We slowly began to come together as a real family unit, and our play on the field reflected this spirit. The coaching staff initiated team family picnics and other functions, and the members of the team grew to really love and respect each other.

I believe that we were experiencing the love of God working in our midst, even though many team members to this day still don't know what it was that caused us to become such a close-knit bunch. I suppose it's not necessary to consciously realize that the light is on in order to benefit from it. The Eskimos went to the Grey Cup that 1973 season, and so began a ten-year dynasty and an amazing chapter in my own life.

Chapter 7

CHRISTIANS VS LIONS

In asking the Lord to trade me back to the Edmonton Eskimos, my heart's desire was to share God's love, not only with my family, but with my team-mates and friends as well. It wasn't very long before the word got around that I was a Christian. After that initial experience with Murray's old girl friend, I became very outspoken in my faith, and why shouldn't I? God was answering my prayers and blessing me with opportunities to share His love, along with the boldness to do it.

When the god of this world has spiritually blinded you, and then your eyes are finally opened, there is great cause for rejoicing. Since I had been spiritually bankrupt for 27 years, I wanted to share the Good News with others, especially those closest to me. At first, I naively thought people would want to hear, but I was in for a rude awakening. Not only were some of my close friends not interested, many of them were quite offended when I spoke of my new relationship with Jesus Christ. I later read in the Bible where Jesus prophesied that many would react that way. He said, "If they're offended by Me, don't be surprised when they are offended by you." I soon learned that people who use the Lord's name as a curse word get really uptight when you use His name reverently. Jesus' name truly convicts people of their own condition of sin. A good sports-reporter friend of ours, who was closely involved with the team, immediately disassociated himself from us the moment he found out we had become Christians.

Sandy and I were shocked by his reaction. Years later, his wife made a comitment to Christ. It was then that she shared with us what had been going on in their marriage back then, and then we understood that his response to us was a result of the conviction he was under.

That first year back with the Esks was the most exiting time of our lives to that point. I was the only professing Christian on the team for most of that 1972 season, but God began to work by His spirit in our team and in the other eight CFL teams, and soon a mini-revival began to move across the league.

A young, rookie Canadian linebacker came to camp that summer and was immediately warned to stay away from me if he wanted to have fun. What a lie of the devil! Mike Lambros, from Queens University, tried his best to heed their instructions and steer clear of me, but God providentially placed his locker right next to mine. Sandy and I started to pray for Mike, and God's Holy Spirit began to draw him. Jesus said, "No one can come to Me unless the Father who sent Me draws him."

As we prayed for Mike, the Lord began to set up "divine appointments." On two separate occasions during that summer, I ran into Mike in downtown Edmonton. With over 600,000 people in the city, it was no coincidence, that's for sure. He was the only team-mate I encountered downtown that season, and Mike was the one Sandy and I were constantly praying for. Each time our paths crossed, I would say something like, "Hey, Mike, would you like to go for a coffee?" He would agree, somewhat reluctantly. During those times, I shared the love of Jesus with Mike, and gradually his heart began to soften towards God.

In midsummer, we played the Toronto Argonauts and I invited Mike to our pre-game chapel. As a rookie, he didn't really want to refuse me; my being a veteran had some definite advantages. So he agreed to come this one time. As he sat and heard the Word of God, Mike came under conviction and gave his life to Jesus. That afternoon, he broke his right arm making a tackle on Toronto's quarterback Joe Thiesman. The temptation to quit on the Lord was very strong. The taunting thought was, *"You fool— you just committed your life to Jesus, and now your season is finished, just like that. God didn't even protect you. How could He really love you? You'd better go back to your old life. It was a lot better than this 'born-again' stuff."*

The devil really put the pressure on, just as the Bible warns us, but Mike's conversion was real, for he had truly made Jesus the Lord of his life. As a direct result of that immediate trial, Mike grew rapidly in his faith and became a bold witness for Jesus Christ. There were other players who made what appeared to be similar commitments. Many of them have continued on to serve the Lord. A few of them fell by the wayside as time and peer pressure took their toll. Jesus taught in Mark's gospel, chapter 4, that the seed of God's Word is planted in four different types of soil (the human heart).

Some fall by the wayside, others seeds are prevented from growing by affliction and persecution, while other seeds are choked out by deceitful riches and life's cares. When the Word of God is planted in the good soil of an honest heart, it will always spring up and reproduce itself 30, 60, or even a 100 times.

Between the 1972 and 1973 seasons, ten Eskimo players out of 33 had made some type of profession of faith in the Lord. A number of them became quite bold in their witness. Ron Estay, Stu Lang, Mike Lambros and I were often quoted in the sports pages about our Christian faith in conjunction with the new Athletes in Action Canada Ministry that was formed that year under the leadership of Winnipeg Blue Bomber, Larry Kerychuk.

In mid-season of 1973, we were scheduled to play the B.C. Lions in Edmonton. The day of the game, *The Edmonton Journal* carried a headline in boldface across the front of the sports page. It read **TODAY IN CLARKE STADIUM, CHRISTIANS VS. THE LIONS.** The article spoke of the Athletes in Action movement that was sweeping the CFL and how a good number of the Esks had become "born again Christians." It was a good article and the headline was sensational, but it really wasn't fair to the Lions, as some of them were young Christians as well. "Who will win this one, and who will have God's favour?" was the big question the writer posed.

That evening, just as in the first-century Christian church, we were taking a kicking from the Lions. We were down 13 to 6 with 16 seconds to go in the fourth quarter. The Eskimos had possession of the ball on our own 50-yard line, with time for only two or three plays. The players rushed to the huddle as we were running our "hurry-up" offense. What took place next had to be divinely inspired. In the natural mind, the play Bruce Lemmerman called was ridiculous and would never have succeeded without supernatural help. (Let me say here that I don't believe Almighty God is the least bit concerned about which team wins which football game, but I know He cares about every player on both teams, and every fan watching. I believe God will cause certain things to happen to bring glory to Jesus Christ, and to show people how much He really loves them.) In *The Journal* that day, the reporter had asked the question as to which team's side God was on. When we huddled up, Bruce knelt down on one knee and began to draw with his finger a typical "sand-lot" football play. He called each of the receivers to run a 10-yard hook, and then he looked out of the corner of his eye at me and called me on an individual pattern that didn't have the slightest chance of working.

"Garry, I want you to line up on the right hash marks and run down 10 yards and then head for the far corner as fast as you can. I'll throw the ball as far as I can, and I hope we'll score."

We all looked at him like he was crazy or maybe the heat and pressure of the game were getting to him. But you don't question the quarter-back—he's supposed to be the leader who knows what he's doing. This one was definitely not in the playbook. We all hustled to the ball to run this impossible new pass-play. As we scurried to the line, my thoughts were anything but positive:

I hope we get another chance to run another play. There's no way I am going to get behind their defense. They'll be on me like bees on honey.

The Lions were sitting back in a deep umbrella zone. Their deep backs were already 25 yards down-field. The chances of my getting behind them were zero or less. I knew they would be in a deep zone called a "zeke," as every professional team would be, in that situation. With only seconds to go in a game, you would never play a man on man (mike) defense if you were ahead on the scoreboard. The possibility of one player making a grave mistake was too high.

When I left the huddle and scurried to the hash marks, I was thinking, *How in the world am I supposed to get behind the deep backs?* All of a sudden I saw a quick vision in my spirit. There I was with the ball under my arm, crossing the goal line, and I knew I was going to score. I didn't know exactly how, but I knew I would.

"Praise you, Jesus. You're going to receive glory for this touchdown, alleluia!" I whispered under my breath.

Two seconds later, I heard the Lion's Head Coach, Eagle Keyes, holler frantically from the sideline to his defensive captain, safety Wayne Mathern, "Mike! Mike! Change it to Mike!"

What transpired next I could only describe as mass confusion. Mathern began to shout *"Mike! Mike! Mike!"* while scrambling back towards the line of scrimmage to find the offensive back he was assigned to cover in a man-to-man defense. The other four defensive backs picked up the changed call and did the same; that is, all except the one who was supposed to cover me man to man. His name just happened to be *Mike Wilson.*

While the other deep backs and linebackers responded to the last second change from "zeke" to "mike," all that registered in Mike's mind was the sound of his own name. Incidentally, Mike was a fine Christian brother and a good friend. As he heard the safety calling *"Mike, Mike,"* he just backed up deeper in his zone, making doubly sure that no one was going to get behind him. It didn't dawn on him for a second that they had changed to a man-to-man defense.

At the snap of the ball, I scooted down the field 10 yards and headed for the far corner. I was totally amazed when nobody went with me. Mike just let me go as I left his zone, fully expecting the other four backs to cover me as I entered their zones, but they didn't see me because they were covering their own men. It was incredible! It was as if I was completely invisible.

When Bruce saw me wide open, he was as surprised as anyone. He laid the ball up and it slowly floated into my waiting arms on the B.C. 15-yard line. I was so far in the clear that all I had to do was tuck the ball under my arm and walk over the goal line. I spiked the ball into the end zone and lifted my hands and shouted, "Praise the Lord!"

As I ran to the sideline, my team-mates hugged me and slapped me on the back, and all I could say was, "Thank you, Jesus! Thank you, Jesus!"

Dave Cutler added the extra point and the game was over. We had tied 13 to 13. Now anyone who had read that article could not say that God had favoured one team over the other.

As was our custom, the whole team led by Coach Jauch hit on one knee as soon as we entered the locker room and gave thanks for the game. A couple of minutes later, all the reporters were let in for the post-game interviews. Terry Jones of *The Edmonton Journal* made a beeline for my locker.

"Garry, you've got to tell me about that last play. I have never in my life seen anyone so wide open. What kind of a move did you put on your man? He ended up on the other side of the field."

"I'll tell you what happened, Terry. It was absolutely amazing. Bruce called a crazy desperation play that really shouldn't have worked. Just as I was running out to the hash marks, I said, 'Praise you, Jesus. You are going to receive glory for this touchdown,' and I knew I was going to score. You and everyone else witnessed it, Terry. God parted the Red Sea and I walked through."

The Journal's sports page the next day carried Terry's article, where he quoted much of what I said. It began with, "God parted the Red Sea and Lefebvre walked through." Alleluia! Once again the Lord was glorified through the Eskimo Football Team.

The sports pages in all nine CFL cities often carried articles on the Christian Athletes Movement, and most of them were just excellent. Many of the different players were quoted often, and when pre- and post-game stories were written about us, they usually made some mention of our faith. It was amazing, but God actually used the vehicle of the sports pages to preach the Gospel.

In Edmonton, many of the Christian players became quite bold in their witness for Christ. Ron Estay, the Louisiana "Swamp Dog" as he was affectionately called by all his team-mates, surrendered his life to the Lord in the middle of the 1974 season. His wife, Debbie, had been saved the year before and had tried everything she could to get Ron to a team Bible study, but to no avail. A few of us began to faithfully pray for him, and he finally stopped running from the Lord and ran to Him instead.

Ron was a great, fun-loving guy, and was loved by all of the team, but sometimes he was hard to understand. He had the thickest Cajun accent I had ever heard. One evening in our regular Thursday Bible study, I jokingly said, "Swamp Dog, if you ever receive the Baptism of the Holy Spirit and the gift of tongues, you'll probably speak in real English."

Interestingly enough, the next season he did receive the Baptism with the evidence of speaking in other tongues. Ron became so fired up in the Lord that you couldn't stop him from talking about Jesus even if you tried, and no one dared. He didn't speak in tongues in English (he spoke in a dialect none of us knew) but, over time, his articulation of the Queen's own language did gradually improve.

After Ron received the Baptism of the Holy Spirit, his Christian experience accelerated rapidly. He grew by leaps and bounds and had a hunger for the Word of God like no other person I had ever known. Perhaps the only person who might have surpassed him in quickened growth was my roommate of five years, George McGowan. George was saved after I retired and was also baptized in the Holy Spirit during a team Bible study. At the time, he owned McGowan Trucking. When one of his drivers quit, he had to drive one of his own trucks for six months. During that time, he spent many hours daily reading his Bible and praying in the Spirit, while waiting for loads.

Both Ron and George have been heavily involved in ministry for years. Ron is presently the Defensive Line Coach with the Saskatchewan Roughriders, and George is committed to working with the youth in his church in Salinas, California.

When I retired in 1976, I handed the Team Chapel Leader responsibilities over to Ron, and he did a wonderful job until his retirement in 1985. He then handed off to Ted Milian who carried the ball until his retirement and handed it over to Dan Kearns. Ted is now an Associate

Pastor with Kenneth Hagin Junior in Tulsa, and Dan is the Director of an Ontario youth ranch. I am so thankful to God for those wonderful years and for the fruit that has grown and matured and reproduced again and again.

"You did not choose me, but I chose you and appointed you to go and bear fruit—fruit that will last. (John 15:16).

Chapter 8

THE VOICE OF AN ANGEL

The year of 1973 proved to be an exciting one for me, both as a father and a football player. On February 24th, Sandy gave birth to our second daughter, Julann Renée, who immediately became a precious "Jewel" in my eyes. As a player, there were new and exciting things afoot as well. In the first chapter, I shared about how at the Grey Cup that year, I was given the opportunity to glorify God on national television. My intent was just to be obedient to His will and to tell as many people as I could that Jesus was my Lord. I never dreamed that the Lord would use that testimony in ways that were beyond my wildest notions. Within two weeks of the game, I had received 121 letters from Christians from coast to coast. They came from places from Victoria, B.C., all the way to New-foundland, and without exception, every one of them was extremely posi-tive. People who represented a true cross-section of Canadians wrote these letters of encouragement. They came from politicians, doctors, housewives, schoolteachers, and even young children.

My favourite letter came from a 76-year-old lady Corner Brook, Newfoundland. It began, "Way to put a punch in for Jesus, Sonny!" I was overwhelmed by the national response to a simple testimony. I didn't know it at the time, but no one had ever before given a clear witness for Jesus at a national sporting event in Canada. Sandy and I were misty-eyed as we sat and read the many beautiful words of encouragement.

Little did I know that those few words I had spoken would actually be used by God, not just to change the course of a man's life, but to literally save it. Bob Nelson had sat watching Grey Cup 1973 by himself, a drink clenched tightly in his fist. Drinking alone was something Bob had be-come accustomed to over the years. He had travelled on the road a lot in the last 25 years, usually for his furrier business, and spent many a night comforted by his bottle. Night after lonely night, Bob would fall asleep alone in his motel room with a glass of whisky in one hand and the Gideon's Bible in the other.

This was a pattern that had been going on for as long as he could remember. For some strange reason, Bob was afraid that if he didn't have the Bible in his hand he might not wake up the next morning. As soon as he checked into a new motel for the evening, he would head straight for the bedside table and pull out the Gideon Bible.

Bob Nelson was a very religious man, although he almost never darkened the door of a local church. Somehow religion had built into his tormented, guilt-laden mind the fear of an angry God who was just waiting for the right opportunity to cast him into an eternal hell. Bob was an alcoholic and he knew it, but he felt powerless to overcome the temptation to drink. Liquor had taken hold of him in his late teens, and at 44 years of age, it had taken its toll. He had long since given up on ever having good health again.

The fourth quarter of the Grey Cup was almost over and the outcome was sure. With Ottawa up 22 to 12, there was little doubt that the Cup would stay in the East this year. He was a die-hard Saskatchewan fan, and he was still ticked over the fact that the Eskimos had squeaked out a win over his Roughies earlier in the playoffs; nevertheless, Bob still pulled for the West.

There were two groups of people that Bob Nelson hated with a passion: Frenchmen from the east, and Edmontonians—in that order—and he made sure that everyone who knew him was aware of it. The Eskies were being heralded as the new dynasty in the West, so Bob hated them all the more, but when it came to East versus West, there was no option but to root for the lesser of two evils.

The final seconds were ticking off on the scoreboard clock when suddenly Bob's attention was arrested by the sound of the telephone ringing on the desk. He finally picked it up, on the fourth ring, and was greeted by a familiar deep voice. It was the landlord of the building where his furrier store was located.

"Bob, get down here as fast as you can. The building is on fire, and I know that you don't carry any fire insurance."

"What are you talking about?" Bob managed to slur. "You can't be serious. The Grey Cup game is on now. Man, what great timing."

"You'd better hurry, Bob, or there won't be anything left of your business. If the flames don't get your fur coats, the smoke damage will."

"Okay, okay, keep your shirt on. I'll be there right away."

Bob hung up the receiver and sat back down in front of the television. "Oh, what the @##@##!!" he stammered to himself. "Let her burn! I want to watch the post-game interviews."

He slumped down in the big chair and reached for the empty glass. As his eyes once again focused on the set, his thoughts were interrupted by the voice of the interviewer.

"Garry, you sure played an outstanding game. Is there anything that you would like to say?"

"Thank you," the young man responded. "First of all, I want to congratulate Ottawa for winning. They played well, and they deserved it, and I also want to congratulate our coaches and my team-mates for a great year . . . but most of all, I want to thank Someone I promised, my Lord and Saviour Jesus Christ, because without Him I would have nothing."

The announcer froze and after a few seconds of deafening silence, whirled around and began talking to the person on his right.

Bob felt a deep anger rise up on the inside as he stumbled to his feet.

"What do you know about God, Lafeb? You're no priest. This is no place for religion. You ignorant Frenchman, I hate your guts."

Twenty minutes later, slumped in the chair in a drunken stupor, the anger still boiled inside.

"You @##@##!!"

Bob slowly sank into unconsciousness, his mouth spewing forth the hatred of his troubled heart. He continued to be disturbed for the next week as fans talked of the West losing the Grey Cup. His mind would continually go back to that interview. Bob was more upset about what he had heard after the game than the fact that he had lost $25,000 worth of furs due to smoke damage from the fire. He was rapidly losing touch with reality.

The following April, four months after Grey Cup day, Bob found himself in a hotel in Winnipeg. He had not thought about the interview for months, and football was the farthest thing from his mind. Business problems had been piling up lately, and life's pressures seemed too heavy to bear any longer. The bottle had become an even closer companion.

As he sat alone in the empty room, he downed the last of the whisky glass. Thoughts of taking his life began to flood his tormented mind. *What's the use of living? Nobody cares if I'm around, and anyway I can't take it any more. Life isn't worth it. Who needs it? I'd be better off dead. I should do the world a favour and end it here and now.*

Bob rose from the chair and staggered towards the third-story balcony French window. Sliding the glass door open, he stared at the pavement below.

"All I need to do is dive off this balcony and crush my head, and it'll all be over. But what if I don't die? . . . I'll ruin my suit."

Go ahead, Bob, do it now. The voice inside his head urged him on.

In a second there will be no more pain, and those who have mistreated you will be sorry for the rest of their lives.

"That's it—I'm going to do it."

Bob took one step forward and suddenly a large television screen opened before his mind's eye. There standing before him, large as life, was a familiar sports caster with a microphone in his hand. Then Bob recognized Number Eleven from the Eskimos standing next to the announcer. Out of the young man's mouth came the words, "Without Jesus I would have nothing . . ." And a glimmer of hope sprang up within Bob's heart.

"Could Jesus Christ be the answer to my problems? I've got to talk to that football player."

Bob scrambled over to the telephone and swung it to his ear, quickly dialling "8" for the hotel operator.

"Operator," he slurred, "get me long-distance information in Edmonton."

In a few seconds, a friendly female voice came on the line.

"Hello, can I help you?"

"Yesh, Operator. I gotta talk to Garry Lafeber."

"How do you spell that, and what city does he live in?"

"I don't know—it's a French name . . . and he plays for the Edmonton Eskimos. He probably lives in Edmonton."

"Do you have an address or street number?" the operator asked.

"No, Lady, but I've got to talk to him right now!"

Bob was stone drunk, and his words were harsh and difficult to understand. He grew more and more belligerent as his temper got the best of him.

"What kind of an operator are you?" he stammered. "Can't you find a simple number?"

The operator tried her best, but the task was impossible. I did not live in Edmonton. By that time we had moved to St. Albert, a small city adjacent to Edmonton, which was a separate exchange and directory. Finally the operator gave up and patiently tried to explain, "I'm sorry, sir, but without more information, I cannot make a connection for you."

Bob's heart sank, and with a curse he pulled the phone from his ear. Then just as he raised it above his head to fire it at the wall, a different female voice spoke out of the receiver.

"I know Garry. His number is 459-5830."

Bob was stunned. So was the operator.

"I'll give it a try . . ." she said with a doubtful tone. "What have we got to lose?"

The phone began to ring once, twice, four times. Bob waited, wondering where that second voice had come from.

Sandy and I had just climbed into the car to go grocery shopping, and I was closing the door when we heard the phone ringing in the house. Answering the telephone had been a problem for me as long as I could remember. If I was outside in the yard, for instance, and the phone rang, I would never go in to answer it. "If it's important, they'll call back," I would say. Being a terribly introverted person, I avoided conversations with others like the plague.

When the phone began to ring that day, my first thought was to ignore it as usual, but this time something inside me compelled me to answer it. I argued with the thought and then gave in, as Sandy seemed positive that I should respond to it. The phone was about to ring for the seventh time when I finally picked up the receiver.

"Hello. Garry here."

"Are you the football player with the Eskimos?" the strong, bold voice slurred on the other end of the line.

"Yes, who am I speaking to?"

"My name is Bob Nelson, and I'm calling from Winnipeg. Look—I need some answers, so I'll get straight to the point. I watched your interview after the Grey Cup last fall, and I wanna know jus' one thing. When you talked about Jesus Christ being your Lord . . . did ya really mean it, or were you jus' blow'n smoke? Can Jesus help me?"

"I sure did, Bob. Yes, Jesus can, and He truly does want to help you."

"Well, if He doesn't, I'm finished. I mean—it's all over . . . . By the way, what church are you with anyway?"

"That's not important right now, Bob. What you need to know is that God loves you and Jesus was crucified and shed His blood for you personally . . ."

Bob slowly began to open his heart to God, and one hour later he had committed his life to the Lord. He was instantly saved—and delivered from alcohol, a three-pack-a-day cigarette habit and, by his own admission, the foulest mouth in all of Regina.

Bob Nelson immediately became a bold witness for the Lord Jesus Christ, and in no time at all led a great number of men to God, most of whom were alcoholic friends that he had accumulated over the years. One of his early converts was Bud McAllister, who himself led

John Sissens of Saskatoon to the Lord. Bud and John both later served as presidents of the Full Gospel Business Men's Fellowship, and I was blessed to fellowship with them both.

I was privileged to meet Bob and his wife, Sandy, two months later in Regina, while making a short commercial for Athletes In Action. That turned out to be a very momentous trip for me. Not only did I meet Bob for the first time, but Jesus also baptized me with the Holy Spirit in the stands of Taylor Field. Why God chose to give me that experience while I was there, I am not sure. It seemed fitting though, as I had played some of my best games as an Eskimo on that very field.

I had been confused for quite a while as to the validity of this experience in the present-day church. Different books I read were the main cause for my turmoil. One author said that the Baptism was definitely an experience subsequent to salvation and that God was still releasing this "gift" today. He supported his position with many Scriptures.

The next author denied the experience, claimed it was of the devil, and tried to support his claims with the Bible. No wonder I was confused. I finally wised up and decided to read only the Bible and ask God what He thought about it. After all, the two opposing views couldn't both be right. It is amazing how the Bible sheds a lot of light on man's commentaries. That's where I was at when I walked into Taylor Field on June 4, 1974.

While I paced up and down the stands, trying to gather my thoughts for the upcoming commercial, I was suddenly overwhelmed with the awesome responsibility that was before me. I had been asked to share a short testimony for 30 seconds. It would be played across Western Canada on CBC as a public service for the next few months. It was an incredible opportunity that had been offered to us, and I did not want to blow it. I suddenly realized that God must have had faith in me to trust me with this responsibility.

As I walked up the stadium steps, I began to praise the Lord for His goodness to me.

"Lord, You are so wonderful; You are so great; Lord, You are magnificent, and glorious . . ." Suddenly my words seemed so inadequate to describe this awesome God.

Without any warning, a river seemed to bubble forth from somewhere deep within me, as out of my mouth flowed a beautiful language that I had never even heard, let alone learned before. God's presence enveloped me like a warm blanket, and I began to weep for joy.

While we walked together for the next 20 minutes, I sensed the Lord's arm around my shoulder. Three or four times I actually heard Him say to me, *"You are my son and in you I am well pleased."*

Each time I heard those words, my heart would burst with joy and the tears would flood down my cheeks. It felt as if years of accumulated guilt and shame were pouring out of me. This was the beginning of a whole new walk for me. This gift of tongues that Jesus gave me was the first of many more gifts He had in store for me, just as He has for all of His children who will open their hearts to receive. Almost three years later, as I was reading Matthew, chapter 3, I noticed those same words that God had spoken to me: "You are my beloved son, and in you I am well pleased." God the Father spoke those words to Jesus just after the Holy Spirit had descended upon him like a dove.

"Lord," I said, "that's exactly what you said to me that day in Taylor Field, when I was baptized with the Holy Spirit."

"I say that to all My children, all the time," was the response I heard within. *"I had been saying that to you for over two years, since you had been born again into My eternal family. When the Holy Spirit came upon you that day, you heard it within your spirit for the first time. I am as pleased as I will ever be with you, because you are in Christ my Son, and in Him I am and always will be well pleased."*

We all need to be constantly reminded of this truth or we will fall into the trap of trying to please God through performance. As a wise man once said, "God loves me so much just the way I am that He won't leave me this way."

Chapter 9

PRAISE GOD THROUGH MY TEETH

After losing the Grey Cup for the second year in a row, the whole team looked forward to the 1975 season, hoping to repeat as Western champs, and this time, to win it all. As exciting as it is to be in a Grey Cup, there is no substitute for being number one. We won three of our four exhibition games without any serious injuries, so we entered the regular season in a very positive mode.

The first league game was against the Winnipeg Blue Bombers, and this team had always been a tough opponent for me. I had sustained a number of injuries, such as torn knee ligaments, two concussions, a broken finger, and a slipped disk in my neck, and with the exception of the broken baby finger, which happened against Ottawa, they had all, for some unexplained reason, happened while playing the Bombers. However, the thought of being injured again was the furthest thing from my mind. I had had my fill of emergency wards and felt confident that I had done more than my share of hospital time. This was going to be our season, and I anticipated an excellent one personally.

The pre-season had gone extremely well for me. During the inter-squad game, I was fortunate enough to catch two touchdown passes, and I played some of my best ball in the other three pre-season games.

Winnipeg won the toss and elected to receive. Dave Cutler booted his usual deep kickoff and we pinned their return man on their 28-yard line. After one first down, our defence forced them to punt. Larry Highbaugh took the ball on our 10 and returned it to the 25. On our first play from scrimmage, Tom Wilkinson called me on a deep corner pattern. He laid the ball into my outstretched arms perfectly, and I took it on my fingertips on the dead run, out-legging the defender 80 yards to the end zone. As I scampered over the goal line, I held the ball high above my head and shouted, "Praise the Lord!!" Somehow, I just knew this was going to be my year.

The teams changed ends at the quarter, and we began to move the ball at will. Wilkie called me on a 12-yard out pattern, on 2nd down and 6. I snagged the ball on my outstretched fingertips near the left sideline, tucked it under my arm and turned up-field. Just then, Winnipeg outside linebacker, Bob Togood, latched on to my jersey. I tried to shake him off, but he held on tenaciously. A second later, he was rocked by one of his own players, stumbled backwards, and landed with all of his 220-pounds on the heel of my left foot, just as it was planted in the firm ground. As I slammed into the turf, an excruciating pain surged through my left ankle. The pain came in waves, and while I lay on the field, I looked over my left shoulder to see my foot in a very unnatural position. It was pointing cockeyed and almost straight up in the air, while the rest of my 200-pound body was facing down. For a brief moment, it didn't even look as though it belonged to me. Intense nausea swept over me, and I began to wretch. My ankle had literally been torn from its socket.

"Praise the Lord! Praise the Lord! Thank you, Jesus! Thank you, Jesus!" I screamed through tightly clenched teeth.

Praising the Lord had begun to become a habit for me lately, especially in the face of adversity. About a year earlier, an amazing book by Merlin Carothers called *Power In Praise* had been given to me by a brother in the Lord. It was one of a series of Carothers' books on releasing God's power through praise, especially in trying situations. This was definitely one of those times, and by the grace of God I had been prepared for it. That book had truly revolutionized my thinking and attitude concerning trials and afflictions.

The Eskimo trainer and Doc Cherry were on the field in moments and immediately called for the ambulance and stretcher. Minutes later, I was in the vehicle, on the way to the University Hospital, a twenty-minute ride from the Stadium. That was the longest twenty minutes of my life. The pain was so unbearable that I began to hyperventilate. Sandy had come down from the stands and was right there with me, holding my hand and trying her best to reassure me that everything would be okay, in between fervently praying for God's intervention.

It seemed to take forever to get to the hospital, but when we finally arrived I was wheeled in quickly. The intern on duty took one look at my foot and rushed me into a small room and, with the help of the two ambulance attendants, quickly rolled me onto a bed.

"Grab on to the railing behind your head!" he shouted, "I've got to reduce this immediately. Here, bite the bullet," I thought I heard him say, as he stuffed a small towel into my mouth and grabbed my foot.

Hey, this kind of treatment only happens in the old western movies, I thought. I was in so much pain, I didn't even think of not cooperating. Nothing could be worse than what I was already feeling. A second later,

I watched in horror and amazement as the young doctor pulled, twisted, and snapped my foot back into its proper place. I felt instant relief.

Our team's orthopaedic surgeon, Dr. Gordon Cameron, arrived at the hospital two hours later and operated on me that night. I came to a couple of hours later with Sandy sitting next to my bed.

"How am I?" I moaned.

"You're going to be all right, Honey," she said as she stroked my forehead. "The Lord is looking after you. You'll bounce right back, just wait and see."

She sat with me for the next three hours, while I drifted in and out of consciousness.

I awoke the next morning feeling very weak, but there was no pain in my foot. As my eyes focused I saw the familiar smile of Reverend Manley Hodges, a man of God and a true friend whom I highly respected.

"How you doing, Son? I would like to pray for you if I could," he said in his familiar, gentle manner. "I feel led to specifically pray that God would give you a miraculous recovery that will bring glory and honour to Him."

"Thank you, Brother," I responded rather weakly. "Please pray."

As soon as Manley began to pray, I felt a calm assurance flow over my spirit, and I knew that God had somehow answered that prayer of faith. The Lord was working through his obedient servant, and I was blessed to be the "receiver."

Within the hour, two more minister friends came in one after the other, and both prayed a very similar prayer to Manley's, asking God for a quick recovery.

An hour and a half later, Doctor Cameron came in to see me on his rounds. As he approached the bed, he managed a weak smile.

"How did it go?" I asked.

"Well, Garry," he answered, "I'd better give it to you straight. Your ankle ligaments were not only torn, they were completely shredded. In all my years of practising sports medicine, I have never operated on an ankle as torn up as yours. In addition to the shredded ligaments, you also fractured the small fibula bone. I have sewn all the ligaments back as well as I could, and then I inserted a two-inch metal screw through your anklebone to immobilize it. Hopefully, everything will knit together in time. We will go in and remove the screw in about seven or eight weeks and then put on another cast for another three or four weeks, then you will have to begin therapy."

"What do you think, Doc?" I queried. "How long am I going to be out for?"

"Garry, I wish I could give you some hope—but I can't. If you walk without a limp, Son, that will be a miracle. I'm sorry to have to say this, but your football career is finished. There's no possible way that you'll ever play again."

This terrible prognosis did not seem to penetrate my heart at all. Instead, an amazing confidence rose up within me.

"I really don't believe you, Doc. We are going to win the Grey Cup this fall, and I am not going miss it. I'll be back, just you wait and see."

"It's good to have a positive attitude," he said smiling, "but that's just not possible, Son."

"I don't want to sound disrespectful, Doc, but I am depending on a higher authority than you, and I believe in miracles. Besides, three minister friends were just here to pray for me, and they all asked God to grant me a speedy recovery. And I believe He answered."

"Don't set your expectations too high, Son, or you'll be in for a real fall." He left the room shaking his head, but I understood what he was trying to do. He just didn't know or understand the faith the Lord had placed in my heart.

Seven weeks later, Dr. Cameron operated on me again and removed the two-inch screw. Dr. MacInnis, our third team physician, instructed me to come to the hospital two weeks later to have the last cast removed.

"Make sure you bring your crutches," he instructed. "You won't be able to put any weight on that ankle for quite awhile."

"I won't need them," I replied. "I'll walk without them." We argued back and forth until I finally agreed to bring them along.

When the cast was removed, Dr. MacInnis was totally amazed, as I immediately began to flex my ankle up and down.

"You shouldn't be able to do that," he blurted out with a surprised look. He stood there with his mouth open while I slid down from the table and walked cautiously out of the room, carrying the crutches over my shoulder.

"See you later," I chuckled, smiling from ear to ear, as I slowly strolled around the corner and out to my car. The ankle was stiff and painful, but at least there was some movement in it. I knew it would take a lot of work, and I would have to endure much pain before it would be good enough to play on again. I remembered the pain I'd had to go through in the rehabilitation of my knee in 1970, and I realized what was ahead of me.

The Esks were still in first place, and the prospects of another Grey Cup appearance looked great. I was willing to pay whatever price was necessary to be there when we won the "Big One." Doctors Cameron, Cherry, and MacInnis put together a rigid physio program for me, which involved four solid hours of therapy per day, seven days a week. The pain was sometimes almost unbearable, but the thought of missing the playoffs kept me pressing on.

As soon as the ankle could take the weight, I began to exercise in the hospital swimming pool. Because of the buoyancy of the water, I was able to jog ever so lightly, and within three weeks I could run hard. Not only did the exercise strengthen my ankle, but it did wonders for my overall conditioning. My physiotherapist was amazed at the speed of my recovery and told me that my ankle had rehabilitated faster in six weeks than most ankles would in six months.

Within another week, I could jog on the hard gym floor, and by the next week, I ran nearly full-out at practice. That same week, the Esks clinched first place and received the coveted "bye" into the Western Final with home-field advantage.

The real test for my ankle came when I began to punt the ball again. Since I was a right-footed punter, my left foot had to take the full weight of all my 200 pounds while I bounced on it. Coach Jauch told me that if I were able to punt well, he would put me back on the active roster for the final. It had been twelve weeks since the injury when I finally tested the ankle in practice. The first time I punted the ball, I felt a slight twinge of pain in my foot, but no more than I could tolerate.

"How does it feel?" asked Coach Jauch. "You seem to be punting quite well."

"It feels a little stiff, but I'm sure it will be all right," I answered.

The next day, I was taken off the injury reserve list. That weekend, Saskatchewan defeated Winnipeg in the Western semi-final, so we began to prepare to meet them in the final.

The Edmonton Journal sports page carried the story of my comeback that following week. The opening line of the article read, "This is not on a par with the parting of the Red Sea, or the dividing of the fishes and loaves, but this is a definite miracle."

All three of our club doctors were quoted on their diagnosis of my ankle, and on the fact that they were almost certain that I'd never play again, especially that year. They agreed that it certainly wasn't any of their doing, and that I believed in the power of prayer. The Lord was truly glorified. The evidence was the fact that I was playing again so soon and, in their professional opinion, I should not have been walking properly, let alone running and kicking.

The Western Final was traditionally a hard-fought battle, especially when it was between Saskatchewan and Edmonton. And once again the game was decided in the last minute, when Larry Highbaugh caught a long pass down the left sideline. A half-time interview by sports caster Ernie Afaghanis gave me another wonderful opportunity to testify for the Lord. Ernie held up the two-inch screw that had held my ankle together only two months before and marvelled at how quickly I had recovered from what should have been a career-ending injury. I was thankful that God had answered our prayers and that He had given me another opportunity to give the glory to Jesus, the Great Physician. We won the game on a great team effort, led by All-Star middle linebacker Dan Kepley, and headed to Calgary for our third Grey Cup appearance in a row.

Grey Cup day in "Cow Town" was the coldest one on record, as the thermometer dropped to -35° F. Twenty-five players showed up for pre-game chapel service, which was an unusually large number. We normally had 12 to 15 of the 33 players attend the services. It amazes me how often people think about God when the pressure is on, and yet never give Him a second thought at any other time. Thankfully, some of my team-mates had come for the very first time and would be exposed to the light of the Gospel.

Our chapel speaker did something very unusual that day, something no speaker had ever done in previous meetings. After he spoke, he presented Gospel records to three of us. He gave one to Coach Jauch, one to Charlie Turner, who had just won the Schenley Outstanding Offensive Lineman Award, and one to me, the team chapel leader. As he presented these records to us, he read the inscription that he had written on the front jackets, *"Congratulations Grey Cup Champs."*

Then he looked up and said, "When I was praying this morning concerning the chapel, God told me that you guys were going to win today. You men will be Grey Cup Champs for 1975."

Most of the team members thought he was a bit strange but hoped that he was right. I knew better than to doubt Sam Benvenutti when he said, "God told me."

My first encounter with Sam was back at the beginning of the 1973 season. He had been the chapel speaker at our first game in Calgary that year. A couple of weeks later, he called me on the phone. It was three days before our home game against Saskatchewan. He announced boldly to me that God had told him he was to come up to our game and sit in on our pre-game chapel service. He also said he was to bring his son and a young rookie who was practising with the Stamps. Then Sam asked me if I would round up three game tickets for them. I told him I had just checked for myself and there wasn't a ticket left. His response blew me away.

"There will be three tickets for me," he replied. "God wouldn't have told me to come if there weren't. You just keep looking, and He'll show them to you. I'll see you on Saturday."

He hung up before I could object any further.

The next day, I asked around the locker room, hoping that by some miracle one of the guys had put some tickets away, but it was all to no avail. I also checked with the ticket office twice more, but there wasn't a single ticket available in all of Edmonton, let alone three together. Sam and the others were coming up on the weekend, and I had no tickets for them.

It's his own fault, I thought. *I told him there wasn't a seat left in the house.*

Saturday morning, as I prepared to leave for our pre-game chapel and meal, Sandy suggested that I call the Eskimo office once more. At least I could tell Sam I had tried right up to the very last possible moment. Our ticket rep, Shona Wards, had already told me twice that there were no tickets to be found anywhere. I didn't want to call and ask her again, so I put off doing it for another fifteen or twenty minutes. Finally, just before I had to leave for the pre-game meal at the Steak Loft, I made the call. I was shocked when Shona said, "Boy, is this your lucky day! A man just walked in here five minutes ago and turned back three tickets, all together." When I handed them to Sam later, he wasn't even the least bit surprised. After that day, I held a lot of respect for the man. So when Sam announced that God had told him we were going to win the Grey Cup, I didn't doubt it for a moment.

The game that day was a defensive struggle from start to finish, and neither team scored a touchdown all afternoon. When the offense was on the sidelines, I spent the whole time standing in front of one of the hot blowers behind the bench trying to keep my hands from freezing. We were ahead 9 to 7 with less than one minute to go in the game. On third down, I unleashed my best punt of the day. It was a 48-yarder into the strong wind. The Montreal back returned the ball only five yards and we were in great shape. With Montreal scrimmaging on their 30-yard line, it looked like we had wrapped it up.

The partisan Western crowd stood to their feet with a roar. Seconds later, they all gasped in disbelief as Montreal quarterback Sonny Wade threw a long bomb down the right sideline. It was caught by their wide receiver and taken all the way to the Eskimo 12. I could feel disappointment sweep over the whole stadium. All Montreal had to do for the win was to kick a field goal. The game would be over for us, and we would go down to defeat 10-9.

Their place kicker, Don Sweet, an active member of Athletes In Action, was known throughout the league as "Mr. Automatic." From inside the 35, he never missed. This would be a simple chip shot from the 19-yard line. As I stood on the sideline watching, one of my team-mates let out a choice expletive and then he screamed, "I can't believe it—we've come all this way and now we lose it on the last play of the game!"

I turned to him and responded with calm assurance, "We haven't lost it yet. We're going to win it."

He looked at me as if I was off my rocker and snarled back at me, "What are you talking about, man? Sweet can't miss from that close."

I answered again, "He hasn't made it—yet."

While I spoke those words, I saw the ball, in my spirit, hooking to the left and missing the outside of the post by about a foot.

"He'll hook the ball and miss it to the left by a foot," I shouted above the screaming crowd.

Everyone in the stadium was on their feet. The entire season had come down to a single field goal. Moments later, our bench went wild as Don Sweet hooked the badly placed ball to the left and missed the uprights by a foot. The stands emptied onto the field in wild excitement. We had won the Grey Cup 9 to 8. The 15-year drought was over; the Esks had finally done it.

And my ankle had never felt better. After the presentation of the Grey Cup and a few minutes of shouting and jubilation, the players headed for the safety of the dressing room, where the usual post-game festivities took place. A few of us Christians were interviewed and were able to thank God for the victory. Ron Estay kept shouting "Praise the Lord, God was with us today," while other players poured champagne over everyone, even the press. It was an exhilarating and emotional time for us all.

Across the hall in the Montreal dressing room, the scene was entirely different. Some players just sat quietly in disbelief, their heads slumped in their hands. Others walked around cursing their luck, a couple even firing their helmets across the room. A few just quietly undressed and headed for the shower. As a few of the press began to make their way into the losing team's dressing room, they noticed something that seemed totally out of place. There in front of his locker sat Don Sweet, smiling ever so sweetly as if nothing at all had happened. A couple of reporters immediately were attracted to him and went for the scoop.

"How can you just sit there smiling when you've just lost a Grey Cup you should have won and you're the guy who missed a 19-yard field goal attempt?" one inquisitive reporter asked.

"Well," Don began, "I gave it my best shot and I missed. All I can do is my very best and nothing more. I am at peace because God still loves me just the same and Jesus is still Lord."

Don Sweet truly gave God glory that day in the midst of defeat. That's when you know if your relationship with God is real and one of trust. It's easy to praise the Lord when everything goes right; it takes real faith to thank Him and give Him glory when everything has gone wrong.

FORECAST: SCATTERED SHOWERS   EDMONTON, ALBERTA, WEDNESDAY, JULY 30, 1975

Before the fall

The agony and the ecstasy, only reversed. Garry Lefebvre salutes the sellout crowd Tuesday at Clarke Stadium with a touchdown (left) as he raced past Winnipeg defenders. Later the fallen Eskimo hero was carried away, his left leg shattered in a sideline tackle.

Chapter 10

A BRAND NEW CHAPTER

The first time I met David Mainse, President of Crossroads Communications, I was overwhelmed with the man's incredible zeal and boundless energy. He was travelling across Canada at the time, recording the Crossroads Programs in various television studios. He and some members of his team had just arrived in Edmonton to begin taping at CITV. I was just four months old in my Christian walk then, and to this point I had not met anyone quite like David. He impressed me as a man with an insatiable thirst for God and an amazing storehouse of energy.

His personality was quite the opposite of mine. I was the quiet type, introverted and shy, having been bound up most of my life by "the fear of man." David Mainse was a man sent from God to me. He was full of the Holy Spirit and the compassion of the Lord. Just being in his presence encouraged and challenged me in my walk with God. This is how our first meeting came about.

Sandy and I were spending a quiet evening at home in June of 1972 when the phone rang. As usual, my first thoughts were, *I hope that isn't for me.* Once again, that familiar twinge of uneasiness invaded my mind, as Sandy handed me the receiver. Telephones had become my enemy, for I was plagued with such a terrible inferiority complex that I had trouble carrying on a simple conversation, even on the end of a receiver in the privacy of my own home.

The person on the other end of the line introduced himself as Glen Rutledge, the producer of *Crossroads*. He explained that he was calling on behalf of his brother-in-law, David, and asked me if I would consider appearing on the program the next day. I felt my palms begin to sweat.

Oh Lord! I thought, *I can't go on television. I don't even know how to speak. What if he asks me questions that I don't know the answers for? I will look like a fool. Besides, I'm too young a Christian. There must be others who would do much better than I would!*

Because of this paralysing fear that plagued me, I had run from interviews ever since I had turned professional. As soon as the football games were through, I was the first guy to hit the showers, hoping to get dressed and out of the locker room before the reporters showed their inquisitive faces.

I wanted to say "no" to Glen right then and there, but instead I told him I would pray about it. That was often a cop-out for me, because I was afraid to say no. It was just a way of stalling. I knew I probably would call him back later and tell him I didn't sense the Lord leading me to go. I took Glen's number and promised to call him that night, since the program was being taped the next afternoon.

Now that I was born again and had been trying to keep a clear conscience before the Lord, I couldn't just call him back without really praying first. "Once you give your life to the Lord, you are ruined for sinning," my brother Murray used to say. You can't just ignore the voice of your conscience the way you used to. So I was caught in a dilemma. There was no way I wanted to appear on that program. As we discussed the situation that evening, Sandy sensed my reluctance even though I hadn't verbalized it.

"You had better go and talk to God about this one," she said. Sandy often gave me that same advice, whenever I was in a quandary over something. Jesus' mother, Mary, also gave us all some wise advice when she said, as recorded in John's gospel, "Whatever He says, do it."

"You're absolutely right, Honey," I responded. "I've got to get alone with the Lord."

I picked up my King James Bible from the coffee table and headed for the bedroom. "Pray for me, Dear," I called over my shoulder, closing the door behind me. I sat down on the side of our bed, took the brown leather-bound Bible, and placed it in my lap. I closed my eyes and began to pray.

"Lord, you know how I hate to speak in public, and going on this TV program scares me to death. God, I know I should take every opportunity given me, but I don't think I can do this. Please show me what to do. You know I want to do Your will. Guide my hands and clearly show me the way."

With my eyes tightly closed, I opened the Bible, and then glanced at the left-hand page. My eyes fell upon the red-lettered words of Jesus.

"Whoever acknowledges me before men, I will also acknowledge him before my Father in heaven. But whoever disowns me before men, I will disown him before my Father in heaven."

I felt a rush go through my body as the force of the words penetrated my heart. I was afraid to appear on this interview and, in essence, was denying the opportunity God was giving me to witness for Jesus. I was caught between the Rock and a hard place.

Oh Lord! I thought, *I don't want to deny You, but I'm afraid of being on TV.*

Inferiority is a terrible bondage to live with. "Please help me, Jesus," I breathed, subconsciously turning the pages of the Bible lying on my lap. All of a sudden, my eyes focussed once more on the red letters, and again I began to read the words of Jesus:

"When you are brought up before men, do not worry about what to say or how to say it. At that time you will be given what to say, for it will not be you speaking, but the Spirit of your Father speaking through you."

The presence of God filled the room, and a tranquil peace invaded me. There was no doubt in my mind whether I was going to accept Glen's invitation or not. This is not the recommended way to seek an answer from God, but I was a young Christian, desperately in need of an immediate answer, so God honoured my simple faith and gave me specific direction. The Lord in His mercy enabled me to receive a very clear and direct word.

The interview the next day went very well and I really enjoyed it, despite my sweaty palms. That was my first introduction to Reverend David Mainse. Over the succeeding years, Sandy and I became close friends with David and Norma-Jean, as we served in ministry together. Even though they were our bosses and spiritual authority for many years, Sandy and I have always felt a special bond with the Mainses, a family of real integrity.

The spring of 1976 proved to be the beginning of some dramatic changes in the life of the Lefebvre family. In mid-March, the Lord began to speak to my heart concerning our future and where we would go from here. Suddenly the thought of my football career ending loomed very large. What did God have in store for us? In the natural view of things, it didn't make sense, since we had just won the Grey Cup and the prospects for the coming season looked fantastic. I was in a position to receive a healthy raise in salary.

I talked to the Lord a lot in the next two weeks about leaving football and going into the ministry. I would usually wait until I was alone in the car to contemplate the possibility, as Sandy had no idea that I was thinking along these lines. I didn't want to burden her with it until I was certain, so I kept it between the Lord and myself.

After this had been going on for a couple of weeks, some members of my family met at our home one evening for a prayer meeting. We had just concluded our time of prayer, when Sandy, right out of the blue, turned to me and said, "You know, Dear, I was thinking about our future today, and I realize that you're not going to play football forever. Wouldn't it be wonderful if the Lord would lead us into some type of full-time ministry where we could serve Him together as a family?"

"That's amazing," I replied. "For the last couple of weeks, I've been talking to God about the same thing. I should've known He'd be talking to you about it too. I'm beginning to sense that the Lord is going to call us out of football in the very near future. What keeps going around in my heart is a farm or a ranch of some type for kids. I've been seeing in my mind's eye a place where children could get away from their normal life's pressures and be introduced to the love of Jesus."

"That's incredible," my brother Blaine, piped in. "I've had the same thing going around in my heart for quite some time. I keep seeing a ranch filled with young people."

An excitement surged through my soul like I had never experienced before, and I knew in my heart that God was about to do something new and fresh in our lives.

"I think we should submit this to the Lord right now," I suggested, and we all agreed.

"Father in Heaven," I began, "if it is Your will for us to leave football and begin a ranch-type ministry for children, Lord, I am willing to hang up my cleats and lay down my football career tomorrow—but I have got to know for sure. Lord, we need a confirmation that we can't miss. We only want to follow Your will, wherever You lead us, but we have to be absolutely positive that this is Your direction for us."

Sandy and I talked and prayed some more until after 1:00 a.m. and finally fell asleep, confident that God had everything under control. I awoke at 8:00 a.m. to the sound of the phone ringing next to my ear. The familiar voice of David Mainse greeted my sleep-fogged mind.

"Hi, Garry! Norma-Jean and I are in Edmonton, down here at the Imperial Hotel. We're here to do a telethon for World Vision at the CITV studios. There's something I would like to talk to you about. Could you come down and have breakfast with us at 9:00, or is that too rushed?"

"No, not at all, David." I tried not to sound like I'd just woken up. "Just give me a few minutes to get dressed, and I'll be right down."

"Who was that?" questioned a tiny, raspy voice from under the pillow.

"Would you believe David Mainse? He's here in town doing a telethon."

"David! Is Norma-Jean with him?"

"Yes, she is. They're at the Imperial Hotel."

"What did he want?"

"He wants to have breakfast with me in about an hour. There's something he wants to ask me, or tell me. I'm not quite sure. He wasn't really specific."

"Maybe he wants you to appear on the telethon?"

"If that was it, I think he would have just come right out and asked. No, I think it must be something else. Who knows? Go back to sleep, Dear. I'll call you from the hotel when I know what it's all about."

When I walked into the coffee shop, David and Norma-Jean were already sipping their coffee. They both greeted me with their familiar bright smiles and bear hugs. In the few short years that our family had come to know the Mainses, we had grown to love them a great deal. We sat down and ordered our food, and then David immediately got down to business.

"Garry, God has given me a vision for a new ministry to reach the young people of our nation. I believe it is to be called Circle Square Ranches. I also believe that God wants us to build ranches right across Canada from coast to coast. They will be places where children can come for a week to get away from all their peer pressures, and where they can be introduced to the love of Jesus."

"We have received over 30,000 letters to our Circle Square children's telecast, from kids all over this country, and we believe that God wants to use this vehicle to meet this desperate need. Garry, as I have been praying for the last couple of weeks concerning the direction the Lord would have us go, your name and face keep coming before me. I believe that God wants to build the first ranch right here in Alberta. Would you consider being the first director of the first ranch?"

"Praise God, David—I'll do it!" I blurted out.

"Wait a minute. Not so fast, Garry. I think you should seriously pray about this decision for at least a little while."

"I have been, David—would you believe for the past two weeks? Last night Sandy and my brother Blaine and I asked God that if he wanted me out of football to pursue a ranch for children, which He had been putting on my heart, we needed a positive confirmation. I actually told the Lord that if He gave me a clear confirmation that I couldn't miss, I would hang up my cleats and go for it. David, it couldn't be any clearer if God wrote it in the sky. When do we start?"

"Wouldn't you know that the Lord would be working on this end at the same time?" smiled Norma-Jean. "Our God is so faithful."

"Praise the Lord!" David chimed in. "This is a real confirmation to me also, that this is truly His will. I don't know exactly how soon God wants us to get going on this. What I think we should do is to put an ad in our next Crossroads newsletter to see if someone might offer some land cheaply, or even donate it for this purpose. Maybe we could title it something like, 'Does Canada Need Circle Square Ranches?' If someone responds to the ad, we'll pursue it from there."

"Well, you know I am ready to go, David. You just say the word, and I'll hand in my uniform and jump in with both feet. Sandy is ready for it too. This is exciting! We're willing to obey the Lord in whatever or wherever He leads."

"Let's not rush on this, Garry. It might not begin for months or even a year. We'll move on it as soon as God provides the land and the funds."

"Praise the Lord," I grinned, "this is the most exciting thing that has ever happened to me."

I left David and Norma-Jean at their hotel, fully expecting to hear from them in the very near future.

Little did any of us know that a Christian cowboy, World Steer Wrestling Champ and All-Around Cowboy Champion Phil Doan, was being prepared by God for this very purpose.

The 1975 football season had been the most memorable of my 10 years in the CFL. Tearing my ankle and coming back in that year to play on the winning Grey Cup team was, without question, the highlight of my career. Not only had we won the Grey Cup, but Jesus had been glorified through the miraculous healing of my foot and the testimonies of Ron Estay, Stu Lang, and other team members as well, not to mention Montreal's Don Sweet. The Grey Cup was a great temporal reward, but the real eternal rewards are yet to be awarded, and soon, at the return of Jesus Christ to this earth.

The 1976 spring training camp was tough and gruelling as usual, especially the two-a-day practices, and I looked forward to the 1976 season with great anticipation. My ankle felt as good as new, and I expected to start once again at first-string wide receiver. I was completely surprised and taken aback when Coach Jauch moved me back to second string for our first exhibition game against Calgary. To make matters even worse, I didn't punt well and averaged only 38.6 yards per kick, far below my usual 42-plus yards. The second game against Ottawa was almost a replay of the first, and my punting average slipped to 37.9.

We arrived home from Ottawa late Sunday night, and none of us looked forward to seeing the team films the next morning, since the eastern Roughriders had humiliated us in almost every department.

Coach Jauch was visibly upset that morning, and everyone tried to sit in the back while the game films rolled. Missed assignments and poor blocking and tackling were generally and frequently pointed out during the gruelling hour, which seemed to go on forever. We all sat in silence, each hoping that his blown assignments somehow wouldn't show up on film. As the projector rolled through one of our third-down punts, Coach Jauch yelled over his shoulder to the back of the room, "Lefebvre, if you can't punt any better than that, we'll have to bring in someone who can!"

I felt my face flush as the sting of those words cut deep into my heart. In ten years of pro football, I had never had a coach criticize me in front of all my team-mates like that.

As soon as the meeting ended, I scooted out of the room and headed for the semi-private room I shared with my young Christian brother, Mike Lambros. I was sitting on the side of the bed with my Bible in hand, still smarting from the coach's cutting tongue, when Mike walked into the room.

"Boy, he really gave you a shot," Mike began somewhat apologetically. "There were a lot of guys who screwed up, including me. I don't know why he decided to single you out."

"I don't know either, Mike. I thought I deserved better than that after ten years. Maybe the Lord is talking to me. Do you remember the story of when King David was criticized and even had stones thrown at him by one of his subjects? Instead of having the man's head removed, he took it as a word from the Lord. Maybe it's time for me to retire. Maybe this is the Lord's way of telling me it's time to hang up my cleats. I don't want to quit unless it's God's will, especially since I've just been raked over the coals. That sure wouldn't be glorifying to the Lord. Mike, I've got to hear from God. Should I go in and retire, or does God want me to keep on playing? I've got to have an answer right now. I believe God will show me from his Word."

I closed my eyes and again asked God to guide my hands. The Bible on my lap fell open to the 52nd chapter of Jeremiah. I didn't even know there were that many chapters in that book. The first thing that grabbed my attention was the large number 52 in the middle of the left-hand page, and I began to read the words of the prophet: "Zedekiah was twenty-one years old when he became king, and reigned in Jerusalem eleven years." I knew I wasn't King Zedekiah and this wasn't Jerusalem, but I instantly understood what God was saying to me. I had begun my career at the age of 21 and I was heading into my 11th year in the CFL. The answer I had asked for was very clear, and there was no doubt in my mind as to what I was to do.

"This is incredible, Mike. Listen to this verse God just gave me."

I read it to him slowly, and his face lit up.

"God has just made it very clear to me that I am to play this one more year and then my football career will be over. Thank you, Lord, for 11 wonderful years."

"Praise the Lord!" Mike chimed in. "The Lord couldn't make it much clearer, could He?"

We both bowed our heads and thanked God for his faithfulness.

"Father," I asked, "please allow me to finish this last season playing as well as or even better than I have in the past, so that when I retire at the end of the year the press won't say that I am going to serve You full-time because I can't play ball anymore. I want them to know that I am leaving football because You told me to, and not because I have to. Let this last year glorify You in every way."

"Amen!" Mike resounded.

"Yes! Amen!" I repeated.

When the pre-season came to a close I was still running at back-up flanker behind my friend and brother in the Lord, Stu Lang. My punting had improved somewhat, although I was still averaging just under 40 yards per kick. Stu was playing well, and the prospects of my returning to first string didn't look very good. I was the only punter on the roster, so my job seemed to be secure, although no position in professional football is ever really secure.

Nine of the sixteen games of the regular season came and went without any change in my status. Stu continued to run at first-team flanker, with me carrying in the odd play from the sidelines. I managed to keep my punting average just above 39, but I could see that Coach Jauch was not satisfied with my performance and constantly chided me about my play. In practices, I kicked the stripes off the ball, averaging over 45 yards per punt, but in the games I was very inconsistent and I was upset with myself. I would even stay out after practices were over, just to work on my timing.

The first day back to practice after the ninth game, a new face showed up in the locker room, punter Gerald Kunyk. Nothing was said to me all week by any of the coaches, but everyone knew that my job was on the line. You don't bring a kicker into town unless you plan on making a change. As the tenth game all too quickly approached, I waited for that dreaded call into the coach's office, signalling the end of my career, but it never came. Finally it was game day, and I knew I had survived at least another week.

An hour before we were to go out onto the field for warmups, Coach Jauch approached my locker. "Garry, I am going to give you just one more chance. If you don't average at least 40 yards tonight, I am going to have to replace you with someone who can."

As he turned and walked away, I buried my head in my hands and began to pray, "Lord, please help me kick to the best of my ability. If I don't average 40 yards tonight, I will take it as a sign from you and retire before Coach has to cut me. If I can't punt better than I have been doing, I'm not being a help to the team or myself, and the only right thing to do is to hang up my cleats graciously and give the job to someone else."

At that moment, I knew I had sealed my future with my own mouth, and by the end of the game I would know whether or not I still had a football career left. *Maybe this is the last game for me,* I thought. *Maybe the ranch ministry is closer than we think.*

Throughout the game I was very conscious of the commitment I had made, and I concentrated intensely on every punt. I hit a couple of pretty good ones in the third quarter with the wind at my back, and when the final gun sounded I breathed a sigh of relief. I was sure my average had exceeded the critical 40 yards. It had been the worst game the Eskimos had played in the 8 years I had been involved with the team. Saskatchewan outplayed us in every department and waxed us 40 to zip.

The custom after every home game was for the players and wives and team personnel to meet in the director's room under the stadium for a buffet. When I walked through the door, I noticed the familiar yellow statistics sheet lying on the counter across the room. Sandy was over in the corner talking with her best friend, Brigitte Lemmerman, and Brigitte's husband, Bruce, one of our quarterbacks. Bruce and I had become close friends during the 1972 season, and since he and Brigitte had become Christians, we had spent a lot of time together as families. None of them had noticed me coming in, so I made a beeline for the counter and scooped up the sheet.

My eyes quickly ran down the paper until they focused on the punting stats. I read *"Edmonton—number of punts: 7; average punt: 39.7 yards."*

I swallowed hard. It was over! *Oh God, I didn't want it to end like this—this isn't glorifying to You!*

My football career had come to an abrupt end and all for the sake of just three-tenths of a yard. I knew what I had to do.

Oh Jesus, I thought, *why did it have to end like this? Lord, I know I promised you and I can't go back on it, but first I have to break the news to Sandy before I talk to Coach Jauch.*

As I approached the three of them, Sandy looked up.

"What's wrong with you? You look like you lost the game all by yourself, Dear. You didn't get hurt, did you? Are you feeling all right?"

"You okay, Bud?" Bruce piped in.

"No, I'm not. I promised the Lord before the game that if I didn't average at least 40 yards a punt tonight, I would hang it up . . . and my average was 39.7. Can you believe it? I missed by three-tenths of a yard."

"Well that's close enough for me," Sandy interrupted. "If you round it off to the nearest number, it's still 40 yards."

"You don't understand, Dear. I made a promise to God, and if I had averaged 39.999, it still wouldn't have been enough. I said it had to be 40 yards or better. It's over, Honey. I've got to tell the coach tonight."

Just then Bruce spoke up.

"Look, Garry, why don't you sleep on it tonight, and if you still feel the same in the morning, then go see the coach. This is too big a decision to be made in haste."

"I agree with Bruce, you'd better sleep on this one," Mike Lambros added.

I hadn't noticed that he had joined our little circle. Sandy and Brigitte were in complete agreement as well.

Mike continued, "Didn't God tell you back in training camp that you would play for eleven years?"

"Yes, but maybe He didn't mean a whole eleven years."

"One question, Garry. When you heard the Word, what did you think He meant?"

"Well, I thought it was eleven complete years."

"Then that is what it will be. Wait and see."

"I'll sleep on it, but I still have to retire in the morning. I made a promise, and I have to carry it out."

We left the party early, and I fully expected it to be my last one as an Eskimo.

Sandy and I talked until the wee hours of the morning about our future, for she knew I had no choice but to honour my word to God. Our main concern was what I would do now. We were not sure if we were to pursue the vision of the youth ranch ministry with Crossroads or to attempt something on our own.

The only money we had was about $50,000 in equity in our St. Albert home. We decided in prayer that night that if God asked us to, we were willing to sell the house and put the money into the youth ministry we both knew we were being called to. Football had been my life for 20 years, since Bantam Football days, and Sandy's for over 10. We both knew that it wouldn't be easy leaving this major part of our lives behind. We took comfort in knowing that God had a plan and that He would reveal it to us when He chose.

I awoke around 9:00 a.m., showered and shaved, and headed for what I thought would be my last meeting with Ray Jauch. He was already watching the game film when I walked into his office. It didn't take a genius to see that he wasn't in a very good mood. He motioned for me to sit down as he came to the end of the first reel. My palms felt hot and sweaty. I had planned on making this one short and sweet. I just wanted to get it over with and get out of there, before any of the other players showed up.

"Hi, Coach," I began, "I would like you to accept my resignation. I have not been much help to the team as a punter. So I think it would be better for everyone concerned if I retired."

Right then, I expected the gracious handshake and the nice parting words, but instead, he began to question me.

"Garry, what has happened to your punting ability? You kicked well for us last year, and you've punted excellently in practices. What has changed to cause you to be so inconsistent? You kicked so well for us in the playoffs last season, and that was after an incredible recovery with your ankle. Is there a problem with your ankle? What is the real problem here?"

"I'm not sure, Coach. The only thing different from the past years is that you're not playing me very much at the receiver position."

As I spoke those words, it suddenly dawned on me what the problem was.

"I guess my legs are not as young as they used to be and I'm just not warm enough. It's somewhat like being on the first tee in golf, but not having a mulligan. I think the reason I punt well in practice is that I am constantly running and keeping my leg warm."

"Well, Garry, I think I owe you one last chance. I'll tell you what I'll do. Next Sunday in Regina, I'll play you at flanker on second-down plays so that your leg will be warmed up in the event we have to punt on third. This is your last and final opportunity to prove to me that you still have what it takes to play in this league."

"Thank you, Coach. I'll give it my best shot."

"I don't know if that is the real reason for your poor performance, but we will know this weekend, won't we?"

"Yes, Sir, and thank you, Sir. You will not regret your decision."

I shook Ray's hand and almost ran out of the office. I couldn't wait to tell Sandy the great news.

On Tuesday of that week there appeared on the sports page an article by Ray Turchansky revealing Coach Jauch's and my private conversation. I don't know who leaked the information. I know it wasn't me. The article mentioned that this was my last chance and the coach thought that my excuse for not punting well was pretty feeble, but we would see. I knew for sure that this time it was definitely do or die.

The team responded amazingly from our 40-0 drubbing and played inspired football that afternoon. With just a minute and a half to go, I caught a long pass and took it to the Saskatchewan 2-yard line. Roy Bell took it over on the next play and we won the game 25 to 22. My punting average was 48.7 yards per punt on 10 attempts, my highest average ever. Included in the high average was an 87-yard single, the longest punt of my entire career.

I punted well the rest of the season and averaged an all-time high 49.3 yards against Winnipeg in the Western semifinal. Although we lost out to Saskatchewan, the final days of my football career ended on a high note just as I had hoped, and I was ready for a new challenge. Football had been my life for over 20 years, but that chapter was definitely over, and a new exciting one was just beginning.

Chapter 11

YOU'VE GOT TO BE KIDDING!

The day after my final game against Winnipeg, sports writer Terry Jones from *The Edmonton Journal* wrote an extremely uplifting article announcing my pending retirement and my new pursuit of the Circle Square Ranch ministry. This was the answer to the prayer Mike and I had prayed at training camp that spring. Jones' final line was, "Football's loss is society's gain." I wouldn't go so far as to say that, but it was a very positive article and God was glorified, and that's what I had prayed and believed for.

With football now behind me, I officially accepted the position as Director of Circle Square Ranch. The ministry did not yet have an actual plot of land on which to build the first ranch in Alberta, but we were confident that God would supply a suitable property in the near future. Although we were not receiving any remuneration at that time, our hearts were definitely with the vision of the ranches. All we could do for those first few months following my retirement was to pray and wait.

The winter of 1977 was awfully cold. As I mused on the weather one day, my memory took me back to the coldest Alberta winter on record. At that time, I was just out of high school and had secured a well-paying letter carrier's job with Canada Post. One day that winter, the temperature, calculated with the wind chill, dropped to $-90°$ F. What a day to remember! It was so bitterly cold that at least four people in Edmonton froze to death, waiting for buses that never came. But in spite of the weather, the mail still had to be delivered. I had never been so cold in all my life. The people on my mail route were very kind, and dozens of concerned folks invited me in for coffee. I must have consumed 20 cups of coffee that day and borrowed almost as many washrooms.

I was just wondering if we were in for a spell like that when Glen Rutledge called from Crossroads in Toronto.

"Garry, the ministry has just been offered a 160-acre parcel of land about 125 miles southeast of Edmonton, near a small town called Halkirk. Have you ever heard of it?"

"No, I can't say I have. Is that in Alberta?"

"Apparently. It's around 20 or 30 miles east of the town of Stettler. From what I understand, the property is right in the heart of Paint Earth

County. It sounds to me like it could be just perfect for the first Circle Square Ranch. Incidentally, the quarter section is being offered to us free of charge, with no strings attached. Phil and Jane Doan own it."

Glen went on to explain that Phil was the famous rodeo star who was the 1967 World Steer Wrestling Champion and also the 1974 All-Around Cowboy Champion. Phil had read the article in the Crossroads magazine about the vision to raise up Circle Square Ranches across Canada. God had moved upon his heart to donate the entire quarter section.

"Praise God, Glen. That is tremendous! When can we meet Phil and view the property?"

"I'm flying in tomorrow to take a look at it. Phil asked me to meet him at his parent's farm, which is located a half-mile from the property."

"Hey, man, that's great!"

"Would you be able me to pick me up at the airport? We could head down straight from there—that is, if you are free."

"You better believe I'm free. This is exciting news."

"Sounds great, Pal. I'll be landing at 12:30 p.m. on Air Canada flight 107."

"Is it okay if Sandy comes along?"

"Of course. We want you both to have a good look at it. This could very well be your new home in the future."

"This is getting really exciting, Glen. Oh, by the way, you need to dress real warm. It's been colder than an Eskimo's deep freeze around here lately. Two pairs of long underwear and a heavy parka wouldn't be out of order. See you tomorrow."

Both Sandy and I had difficulty sleeping that night. This was finally it! We were about to begin the family ministry that God, over the past five years, had been preparing us for.

Glen's plane arrived right on schedule. I left Sandy in the car to keep it running. The latest weather report was that the wind chill factor had dipped to -35 degrees Fahrenheit. Fifteen minutes later, I tossed Glen's bags into the trunk and we were on the road to the ranch property. I had never heard of Halkirk, and I couldn't find it on the map in my car, but if it was near Stettler, I figured the shortest route would be through Camrose on Highway 13. With the help of gas station attendants in the little town of Heisler and then in Halkirk, we eventually pulled up to the Doan's farm just after 3:00 p.m.

We were greeted at the door of the old farmhouse by the friendliest people with the biggest smiles I had ever seen. Phil introduced us to his wife, Jane, his dad and mom (Muff and Bernice), and his brother, Merle, and Merle's wife, Donna. They sure made us all feel warm and accepted, in spite of the weather outside. Grandma Bernice served us hot coffee and cookies. I couldn't help noticing Grandpa Muff's perpetual grin. Every time I looked at him, he was smiling from ear to ear. His eyes seemed to be constantly smiling as well.

"Well, shall we go take a look at the property?" Phil interjected, just as we were finishing our coffee. "The snow is pretty deep, and there is no road into the back quarter, so we'll have to ride in on the stone boat. Merle will drive the old Massey tractor. I hope you've all got your woolies on. We have an extra pair if anyone needs them."

"Thanks, but we've come prepared," Glen laughed. At least he thought we had. The 10-minute ride across the neighbour's field was kind of fun, as we laughed and talked and tried to stay warm. Twice we were forced to stop and open the old-fashioned barbwire gates.

As the tractor pulled up to the second gate, Merle turned and shouted through the tiny hole where his eyes and nose peered out of his furry hood. "This is it. It doesn't look like much from here, but hold on for a few minutes. A third of the land is what we around here call a coulee."

"It's like a deep valley," Phil added, holding his hand over his face, which had already turned rosy pink. "Dad uses this back quarter for grazing the cows. That's really about all it's been good for, up until now."

"How much land do you own, Phil?" Sandy inquired, shouting over the roar of the old Massey.

"This is it," he answered. "Dad had nine quarters, and he gave this one to me, and the Lord told me that some day he would use it for children. A while back, God gave me an open vision, and I actually saw kids running all over this quarter section."

"That's fantastic, Phil," I yelled through my scarf. "God bless you, Brother, for your sacrificial offering to the Lord. I know He will reward you guys someday, whether we receive the land for our first Circle Square Ranch or not."

"Well, it all belongs to Him anyway, doesn't it?" he hollered back. "I just want to be obedient to His will."

Just then the tractor rounded a clump of thick bushes, and the most beautiful steep cliffs stood before us. The Paint Earth Coulees ran through the southern one-third of the property. The sheer cliff walls dropped almost 100 feet into the valley below. They reminded me of the Drumheller Badlands that I had visited years earlier. The many different frosty layers of brown and black and grey sandstone shimmered in the bright afternoon sun.

"Oh Lord, what a fabulous place for a youth ranch," Glen blurted out. "This is so much more than we had hoped for. What do you think, Garry? Does this land have potential or what?"

"When can we get started?" I responded.

"As soon as you'd like, fellas," Phil said. "I'll sign it over this afternoon, or whenever you like, if you're sure you want it. I just want to see this place bring glory to God and help a lot of young kids. If you like, we can head back to the farm and talk about it. I don't want anyone to suffer frostbite."

"I bet Mom has a fresh pot of coffee on by now," brother Merle offered.

As we made our way back to the tractor, which was still chugging away, I suddenly realized that Sandy was not with the rest of us. When I turned around, she was standing on the edge of the Coulee bank and staring out across the valley. She seemed to be oblivious to the fact that everyone was leaving. I walked up behind her and gently placed my hands on her shoulders.

"Isn't this a most incredible plot of land for the ranch? It's absolutely perfect, isn't it?"

She didn't respond.

"Is there something wrong, Dear?" I inquired. Other than the noise of the tractor in the background and the muffled voices of the others, the air was absolutely still. It seemed to be frozen along with everything else in sight. There wasn't even the sound of a bird. Sandy slowly turned, and I noticed a small tear that had crystallized in the corner of her eye.

"Garry, you've got to be kidding. You don't expect the children and me to move here, do you? Where would we live? This place doesn't even have a road to get to it. I'm not sure if I can handle this. I don't know what I was expecting, but this is too much to ask of me. I'm a city girl, not some wilderness wife."

"Honey, you're seeing it at its worst. Just wait until spring comes. This land will be fabulous!"

"But Garry, there's nothing here—not even a bird, or rabbit, or anything. Are you absolutely sure you heard the Lord right? I was expecting a building or two, or at least some sign of life. Garry, this land is gorgeous, but it's a hundred miles from nowhere."

Edmonton Eskimo Team Picture – 1975 Grey Cup Champions

CHAMPION DE LA COUPE GREY 1970 • *GREY CUP CHAMPIONS 1970*

Eskimo Punter

Team mates Mike Lambros, Stu Lang,
Ron Estay, and Me at 1975 Grey Cup

My New Team

Garry & Sandy at Grey Cup 1970

Garry & Sandy at Schupsky's

Brad
1989

Julie
1991

Jesse
2001

Our Family in Kelowna

Lefebvre Family Picture

Pat & Ken

Blaine & June

Bob

rray & Cathie

Mark & Alison

The Present and Past Ranch Directors

The Paint Earth Coulee

Lefebvre Family in 1985

...eaving Circle Square Ranch

Bee at Rodeo Days

Clowns - J.B. Tulips & Pic

Opening Ceremonies

Brad & Julie - Half Time Show

Mr. Chips & Brad on Phoenix

Mac and Colonel

Bully for You

ook Out Below!

Oops! Wrong Way

se & Cart

Pic at Campfire

Cowboy Dean
- Muddering to Himself

Home on the Ranch

Phil Doan - Cowboy Visionary

Bernie & Bee - Carrying the Vision

Shannon Cherry - Faithful Servant

Reynold Rutledge - First National Ranch Director

Mac Hyland - Home at the Chutes

Banquet Speaker

Garry, Doug Kooy & Willard Thiessen
on It's a New Day

Garry & David Mainse on 100 Huntley Street

Chéri
Special Olympic Skier

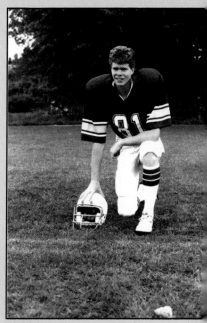

Brad - Sr. Bantam Football

Julie - St. Albert Ladies
Soccer Champions

Jesse - St. Albert Midget Hockey

Brad and Ted DiBiase

Gordon Ferguson
and Meadowlark Lemon

Jules and Jesse with Dean McAmmond

Ryan   Jarome   Shane
Smyth   Iginla   Doan

Paul & Ryan Collins
with Dean McAmmond

Garry, Sandy & Madeline Mims with
Mayor Bill Smith & Wife Marlene

Larry Kerychuk, Herbie Kuhn
& Ted "Million Dollar Man"
DiBiase

Brad & Bev
with Swamp Dog Estay

AWARDS BANQUET & CONVENTION

Jim Sandusky
CFL Man of the Year

Susan
Humphreys - St. Martins
Female Athlete of the Year

Leighann Doan
College Athlete of the Year

Garry Unger & Wes Reinheller
- Successful Bidder

Madeline & Brian Warren
Hall of Faith Induction

Paul Rutledge
Stunt Man of the Year

The Lefebvre Family Today

Sandy & Garry
35 Wonderful Years

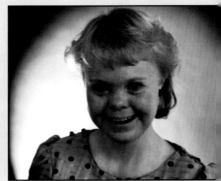

Chéri
Our Precious Angel

Jesse & Jules
A Special Relationship

Brad
Gospel Recording Artist

"I've never been more sure of anything, Hon. This is definitely it," I tried to reassure her. "Looks like we'll get to find out what it was like to be a pioneer."

"You know I have never been great at camping outdoors and all of that stuff," Sandy reminded me. "We don't own a trailer or even a tent."

"Well, we'll just have to cross that bridge when we come to it," I answered. "I believe God will supply everything we need. He hasn't failed us yet. I'm sure He has it all worked out. We just need to trust Him, that's all."

"You know I'm willing to do anything the Lord wants us to. I'm just afraid we might be a little off in our interpretation of His will . . . but if you are absolutely sure this is it, I'll try and flow with it the best I can. Where you go, you know I will go."

"That's the girl I married. I'm sure things will look much better in the spring. Someday we will look back on this and laugh. This is going to be the greatest adventure of our lives."

"I hope you're right," Sandy sighed.

We walked back to where the others were waiting. In my mind, I heard the familiar, quiet voice of the Holy Spirit say ever so gently, "*You are in the right place. My grace is sufficient for all you will need.*"

Muff &
Bernice Doan

Chapter 12

A NEW BEGINNING

Phil and Jane signed over their quarter section to Crossroads in March of 1977, and the Lefebvre family pitched our first tent on the property on May 17. That first spring and summer at the ranch were undoubtedly the busiest and most demanding four months of our lives. We often worked from sunup until sundown, stopping only for meals and bathroom breaks. Sixteen-hour working days were the norm for those early years.

In early July, some helpers from Ontario, Bill St. Pierre and his family, along with Paul Rutledge, son of National Director Reynold Rutledge, joined us. Bill had just been hired to build and direct the first Circle Square Ranch in Eastern Canada, near Severn Bridge, Ontario, where another property had been made available. Bill was the most industrious person I had ever met. He never seemed to run out of energy and lived in high gear most of the time—at least when he was awake. He never ceased to amaze me with his knowledge of building. There didn't seem to be anything he couldn't figure out or fix. He always seemed to be coming up with a new or better way of doing something. The man was a real genius. Bill, his wife, Gloria, and their children, David and Paula, were a tremendous help to us that first summer. I don't know what we would have done without them.

Before the St. Pierres arrived at Circle Square, we had been drilling for water without success. After four dry holes in a row, we finally drilled a 400-foot well and hit a natural gas pocket along with salt water. The water wasn't fit for human consumption, although the horses sure loved it. That was the last time we drilled. We eventually settled for a dugout filtration system, which has been doing the job to this day. Through this trial of faith, I realized how we city folks can take for granted a simple thing like having an ample supply of good drinking water.

Just prior to Bill and his family joining us at the Halkirk ranch, we had moved a small, 420-square-foot building onto the property. It came all the way from Lloydminster on the Saskatchewan border, about 200 miles away. Jack Allen, a wonderful Christian brother whom I came to know and love, had donated it to us. That little building served us well. In addition to housing the Lefebvre family that first summer and other volunteers later on, it eventually became the Trading Post (tuck shop) next to the rodeo arena, where it still stands today.

That first summer Sandy actually fed as many as 16 people for a sitdown dinner in that tiny building. And amazingly, she managed all this cooking on a tiny propane camping stove and without running water. Believe it or not, we actually had 12 people sleep over in wall-to-wall sleeping bags one night.

The Trading Post,
our first ranch home

When Bill realized that we had natural gas in our water supply, he decided to make use of it, so he rigged up the most incredible outdoor hot shower I have ever seen. The first thing he did was to run an 800-foot length of one-inch hose on top of the ground from the well down in the coulee to where we had placed the small building. Next, he drew the gas off the moving water with the use of a valve system and then heated a 45-gallon drum with the hose coiled inside. Finally, he ran the hose up into a third barrel, which was fastened on the front edge of the roof of our small home. He then attached a showerhead to the barrel and built an eight-foot–high plywood shower stall under it. We were in business. Oh, how much appreciated was that shower, by one and all!

We were all very grateful for Bill's ingenuity, and we enjoyed many a hot shower that summer. That was, until the valve stuck one afternoon. Thank God, no one was showering at the time, as the pressure built to the point where the barrel exploded. Everyone thought that a bomb had detonated nearby. Needless to say, that was the end of hot outdoor showers for the remainder of the summer. From then on, we all borrowed Merle and Donna Doan's bathtub, which was about a mile and a half west towards town.

There wasn't anything Bill St. Pierre was unwilling to do. The world could use a lot more workers like him. He drew up the plans for the Circle Square Hotel and would help to lay the foundation as well before returning to work on the ranch at Severn Bridge. The foundation footings for the Circle Square Hotel were poured in July of 1977. Now it was time to lay the bricks of our cement-block basement. But before we could do this, someone would have to drive to Red Deer to pick up the load of blocks. Bill volunteered to make the trip, in a truck borrowed from a neighbour.

The First Miracle

It had become our habit since the shower explosion to pray for God's protection over everything we did, trying not to take anything for granted. Before Bill left for Red Deer that morning, we all gathered around him and prayed, asking God to grant him a blessed journey and to send an angel or two with him to make sure he returned safely.

The neighbour's truck was a one-ton with dual wheels and a large flat-deck trailer. We were informed that it was licensed to carry 25,000 pounds, which was pretty close to Bill's estimation of the weight of the blocks we would need. However, our neighbour was somehow mistaken. The truck was only licensed to haul 12,500 pounds. If we had known that, Bill never would have attempted to haul such a heavy load. Besides being very dangerous, it was illegal.

He left late in the morning and arrived in Red Deer without any difficulty. The 12-by-8-inch concrete blocks were loaded onto the flat deck on pallets, with only plastic packing-wrap securing each individual pallet. They were not tied down either, as their own weight was sufficient to hold them on the deck. Besides, we didn't own any tie-downs. Bill could tell he had quite a load on, so he drove carefully as he returned home down Highway 12 back to the ranch. The old truck was working very hard, especially up the hills, and would climb to 55 miles an hour on the straightaway.

When Bill was about 30 miles from home, nearing Stettler, he heard a loud bang. The vehicle lurched as one of the dual tires from the passenger side soared over a fence and out into the field. The lug nuts had snapped under the pressure and both wheels had come off. The second wheel caught under the truck and jack-knifed the trailer, throwing the old truck across the highway and into the ditch.

Instinctively, Bill shouted, "Help me, Jesus!" and let go of the steering wheel, sprawling across the front seat. He felt the truck pitch a couple of times and then dive down into the steep ditch.

Seconds later, the truck climbed back up the embankment onto the road and came to an abrupt stop. Bill sat up just as a young man ran up to his door and swung it open.

"Are you all right, Mister?" he shouted.

"Yes, I'm okay—praise the Lord," Bill answered.

"I don't believe what I just saw with my own eyes," the young man went on. "When your trailer jack-knifed, it threw you into the ditch, and then the truck climbed back onto the road. What blows my mind is that you're untouched, and you didn't even lose one single block. Your whole load is still intact. I still can't believe it!"

"Thank God, my angels were on the job," Bill sighed. "The Lord sure was looking after me."

"Your what?"

"My angels. The ranch staff and I prayed before I left this morning for God to send His angels with me to protect me and, thank God, He answered our prayers."

"Do you really believe in that stuff?"

"You bet your life I do. Don't you? I guess I'm living proof that prayer works. By the way, my name is Bill St. Pierre. What's yours?"

"Jim is my name. Uh, can I give you a lift somewhere? I'm hauling this load to Saskatoon. Boy! It's a good thing I didn't try to pass you a few seconds earlier. We would have had a real wreck. Maybe someone really is looking after us."

"There's no doubt in my mind," Bill responded as they climbed into Jim's semi. They drove the 30 miles into Stettler, leaving the truck on the side of the highway. Bill wasn't able to secure the only towing service in town that evening, so Jim offered to drive him the 25 miles back to the ranch, which was almost directly en route to Saskatoon.

As they drove along, Jim opened up and began to tell Bill of how he had been raised by his grandmother, who was a Christian, and how he had run away when he was only 14. He knew his granny had been praying for him for years. A few minutes later Bill was given the honour and privilege of leading Jim to a saving knowledge of Jesus Christ, as he opened his heart and asked the Lord to come in.

Before they arrived at the ranch, Jim promised to call his grandmother when he got to his destination and tell her that her prayers had finally been answered. Grandma must have been thrilled.

The next morning Bill returned to Stettler and was able to get in touch with the towing company. When the owner realized that the blocks were for the new ranch at Halkirk being built to help young people, he didn't charge us a penny for his services. Since that day, this same man, who also owned a rental company, has blessed the ranch ministry over and over again and has never charged a red cent for the rental of his equipment.

The total cost of all the repairs came to a grand total of $65, which was miraculous in itself, but the greatest miracle of all was young 19-year-old Jim's salvation. It wasn't a *coincidence* that he was just about to pass Bill's truck when the accident occurred. I believe it was a *God-incidence*.

"And we know that in all things God works for the good of those who love him, who have been called according to his purpose.". (Romans 8:28).

A Horse of a Different Colour

Our first summer at the ranch was spent building roads and putting in power, gas, and sewer lines, as well as starting the basement of the hotel complex. But for a welcome diversion one Sunday afternoon, five of us decided to take a ride into unexplored territory on the south side of the creek that ran east to west through the bottom of our coulee. Up to that point, we had not found a place where we were able to cross. My brother Blaine took the lead on our palomino, Blondie. Her month-old colt came along for the exercise. She was a beauty—the spitting image of her mother.

Blondie was a spunky horse and loved to run. Stopping her was the difficult part. Sandy had already had two accidents riding her that spring. Both times she had fallen head-first to the ground when Blondie made a sharp turn and stopped on a dime with her front feet. Thankfully, Sandy wasn't seriously hurt either time. There was no way she would get up on Blondie again though, that was for sure. But Blaine was an excellent rider and loved to mount Blondie whenever he had the chance. She would prance and dance, and he knew he had gone for a ride when he climbed off her.

None of us was prepared for what was about to happen. After all, we were just going for a slow trail ride. Sandy was riding her horse, Rusty, and made us promise that we would go slow this time. She felt she had suffered enough bruises for one summer. Sandy's younger sister, June, reluctantly came with us this time. In her teen years, she had been on a runaway horse once before and wasn't keen on riding trails.

We walked the horses in single file down to the bottom of the hill, then slowly trotted them about 100 yards across the coulee bottom towards the creek. Blaine had told us earlier that he had discovered a way to cross the creek. He had found a place where it was almost completely dried up and would be, to all appearances, an easy crossing. Now we would be able to see what kind of riding trails were on the south side of the ranch property. We were always looking for new, unexplored territory.

Blondie was her usual energetic self that day and pranced her way to the edge of the old creek-bed 50 yards ahead of the rest of the group. Her young palomino colt trotted along beside her. When they reached the edge, which dropped down some three to four feet into the creek, Blondie stopped abruptly and refused to step down the short embankment, despite Blaine's kicking and even an occasional smack with the reins on her shoulders. Blondie had always been a very responsive horse. You never had to tell her twice to move. When she wouldn't move forward, Blaine should have realized there was danger looming ahead. Horses are often smarter than people when it comes to knowing where to walk.

Just as the rest of us caught up to them, Blondie gave in to Blaine's persistence and lunged into what appeared to be a dry creek-bed. She sank immediately into thick black mud, virtually to the top of her legs. The horse panicked and lunged forward, desperately trying to scramble up the far bank. As she drove her front feet into the soft bank, her hindquarters sank right up to her rear end, deep in the mire. She lost her balance and toppled over backwards, pinning Blaine face down under her 1000-pound body. Blondie began to thrash about wildly, trying to turn over onto her feet. Every few seconds she rolled enough to one side for Blaine to raise his head from the mud and gasp for air, and then she would fall back on top of him.

Everything had happened so fast that the rest of us were stunned. There wasn't a thing any of us could do. We were all powerless to help Blaine with Blondie's hooves slashing about. All anyone could do was cry out to God in desperation.

"Lord Jesus, help!" I shouted.

The others echoed my prayer.

"Jesus! Jesus! Help him."

After a few long seconds, Blondie quit struggling and just lay there motionless and exhausted. She had given up, trapped in a sea of muck. Blaine had disappeared from our sight, somewhere under Blondie. Just then, Blondie's colt, which had stepped into the bog hole after her mother, scrambled up the near bank and let out a shrill whinny as she bolted for the barnyard. Blondie swung her head in the direction of the sound to see her baby galloping away.

A new surge of energy burst into the horse's body, and with incredible strength she flipped herself over onto her side. Blaine was lying face down, his head below the surface of the quagmire. Suddenly his head flew up and his lungs gasped for precious air. The whole ordeal must have taken about two minutes or so. He had been just moments away from suffocating in the murky slime. We all rejoiced as horse and rider made it to the safety of the shore, both worn out from the ordeal.

In a time of crisis, the Lord should be the first one we call upon, not the last resort. If our heart is fixed on God, we will spontaneously cry out to Him in times of trouble. The Word says, "Out of the abundance of the heart, the mouth speaks." Sometimes all you have time to pray is, "Help, Lord!"

What a lesson we learned that day! None of us would ever likely argue with "horse sense" again. Everyone was in agreement that the ride was over for the day, so we all dismounted and walked the half-mile back up to the barn.

When we reached to the top of the coulee, I took one look at Blondie, her colt, and Blaine as they stood together, and I broke out laughing. The three of them were covered with mud on one side and almost totally clean on the other.

I couldn't resist flogging the old cliché: "Now that's a horse of a different colour," I laughed.

The New Ranch Director

Chapter 13

GOD'S PROVISIONS

From the time I was very young, I loved being around horses. My love for these majestic animals even extended to the smell of fresh horse manure. During my elementary years, I spent many of my summer holidays on my Uncle Harvey and Aunt Gladys's farm near Gibbons, Alberta. Cousins Clayton, Ross, Grant, and Kevin provided me with all kinds of great fun and adventure. Goofing around in Uncle Harvey's granaries when they were almost full was one of our favourite pastimes. As we grew into our teens, hunting and trapping gophers became a much more exciting past time.

The summers at the McWhirter farm were especially wonderful whenever they happened to have a horse around, which wasn't often enough to suit me. The only thing I hated about the farm was cleaning out the pig barn before breakfast, which was a chore that seemed to be designated to Ross and me more often than not. The up-side was that it sure created a big appetite for Aunt Gladys's delicious breakfasts.

As far back as I can remember, I have loved the old West and often wished I had been born a hundred years earlier. Whenever an old Western duster or a wilderness adventure came on television, you would find me perched in front of the set. If a John Wayne movie came to town, more than likely I would find a way to see it. More than anything else, I loved to watch the horses. There was just something about those splendid animals that drew my attention. So in the summer of 1976, when I knew that I was soon to be the first director of Circle Square Ranch, I bought my first horse. I had dreamed of that moment for many years.

Actually, what I bought was more like half a horse. Ron Mix, a friend of many of the Christian Athletes on the Eskimo team, owned a ranch on the outskirts of east Edmonton, where he raised a handful of horses. Quarterback Bruce Lemmerman and I had come to be great friends with the Mix family through our involvement with Athletes In Action. One day, Ron offered to sell Bruce a young two-year-old Appaloosa stallion. He was a beautiful steed but was untrained. Bruce offered me half-ownership if I would become involved in the training process, since he just couldn't spare the time during football season. Being a quarterback required him to spend a significant amount of time at the team office most days, watching and breaking down game films. I jumped at the chance to finally own my own horse, and we bought him together for $400. I thought I might as well start my ranching career by breaking my first horse.

Bruce wanted to name him Phoenix, and I didn't object. I was just excited to own my own horse, and Phoenix seemed to be as good a name as any. After we had him gelded, he turned out to be a great saddle horse, and the experience I gained in training him was invaluable. Either Bruce or I worked with him almost every day, right up until our move to Circle Square Ranch the following May, when Bruce generously donated his half of Phoenix to me. Phoenix was such an intelligent and gentle horse. Although he was fast and very responsive when an adult was on him, a small child couldn't make him run at more than a slow canter, no matter how hard they tried.

In the fall of 1976, I decided to buy another horse for Sandy and purchased a Welsh Morgan Cross named Rusty from the Mix family. He turned out to be the most reliable horse we ever owned at Circle Square Ranch, and he served the camp well until he finally had to be put down in 1991 at the age of 28. Three of our four children, who were raised on the ranch, learned to ride on faithful old Rusty.

In the spring of 1977, brother Blaine and I loaded up Phoenix and Rusty in Ron Mix's cattle truck and then drove to six different small Alberta farms to pick up 11 other horses that had been donated to the ranch. We pulled onto the ranch property at 1:00 a.m. the next morning. After we unloaded them all and turned them loose, they took off running to explore their new home. We were both ready for some long overdue sleep. The sleeping bags on the ground never felt more comfortable.

It wasn't long before we realized that we desperately needed a barn and some corrals. With the horses having the freedom to roam the whole 160 acres, it was very difficult to catch some of them. When one would start to run, the whole herd would often stampede. We had many a hair-raising chase, and only by the grace of God were none of us seriously hurt. During those early days, we would often go out on a trail ride in the evening, after a hard day's work. That is, whenever we could catch the horses.

Once in awhile, a few of us would play a game of night-tag on horseback, which proved to be a very dangerous way to let off a little energy. One evening after dark, I convinced Sandy to join the game. Against her better judgement, she finally consented to come along on Rusty. The game was going along well as usual and everyone was having a great time, when suddenly Rusty spooked when I darted in front of him. He ran headlong into a clump of thick bushes. Thank God he slowed to a walk, for a low hanging branch caught Sandy across the neck. "Whoa! Whoa!" she screamed, but Rusty wasn't listening. He kept trying to move forward, while Sandy was pinned backwards to the saddle, her feet caught in the stirrups. By this time I had jumped off Phoenix and grabbed the reins. Thankfully, I was able to back Rusty up before Sandy was seriously hurt. It scared her spitless, and needless to say, that was the last time we played that silly game. At that point, poor Sandy had had quite enough, and she vowed from that day forward not to go riding with me again.

The First Ranch Christmas

The most memorable of all our rides took place that first winter, the week before Christmas. One thing I had always wanted to do was to go out on horseback and cut down a Christmas tree in the woods and haul it home. Some of my fondest memories as a child were getting the traditional tree, but I had never done it with horses. I knew Sandy and the kids were sure to look back on our first Christmas together on the ranch with great joy. I wanted them all to remember this first one as a very special occasion.

Brad, Cheri and Julie

Unfortunately, on the day that I chose for this great adventure, the temperature dipped to -30º F. I had really talked it up with the kids and, amazingly enough, Sandy agreed to go along with the four of us, so I saddled up three of our horses, despite the bitter cold.

It will only take an hour or so, I thought, and we were tough pioneers. It was just a matter of dressing warmly enough for the occasion. Brad, who was six, rode our little Shetland pony, Dawn. Sandy rode double with eight-year-old Chéri on my horse, Phoenix, and I took Blondie, the palomino, with Julie our 4-year-old holding on behind me. I also carried a small hatchet and a lariat to haul the tree back with us.

Although the weather was bitterly cold, we all enjoyed the three-quarter–mile trek down into the coulee where the large, majestic evergreens grew in abundance. I figured we should look for one around ten feet high. The bottom or top could always be trimmed to make it fit in our newly acquired doublewide mobile home. We found the tree we wanted within fifteen minutes, and I chopped it down, while the rest of the family danced around trying to keep warm. Ten minutes later, we were back on the horses and towing the eight-foot tree towards home.

The moment we came up out of the small ravine, we ran into the rest of the horse herd that had curiously followed us down the coulee. None of us was prepared for what happened next.

The sight of the tree dragging behind Blondie spooked the herd, and they all tore off down the coulee bottom. Well, when the herd bolted, our horses were not about to stay put. Dawn, who was in the lead, took off. Phoenix followed right on her heels, dropping Chéri off his backside right in front of Blondie. She reared high in the air as I frantically pulled on the reins with all my strength. Chéri lay screaming right under my horse's front feet, while Blondie pawed the air.

At the same time, I felt Julie sliding off the rear end as she lost her grip on me. Quickly, I grabbed her by one arm and flung her as far as I could into a nearby snow bank. Blondie came down on all fours and somehow missed Chéri's head, only by inches.

Just then, I looked up to see Brad flying off Dawn's back as she disappeared over a steep embankment. To make matters worse, both of his boots stuck in the stirrups and vanished with his horse. Praise God, he landed in deep snow, unhurt. Phoenix was hot on their heels and just narrowly missed Brad as he too galloped for the embankment.

Amidst the wailing of the children, I could hear Sandy shrieking at the top of her lungs, "Whoa! Whoa! Whoa!" but Phoenix wasn't listening. Just as he hit the steep slope, Sandy let go of the reins and dove to safety, landing in a four-foot snow bank.

I finally brought Blondie under control and began to gather the children. Thank God, they were only frightened; nobody was physically hurt. They were all crying, including Sandy, and poor Brad was in his stocking feet. Fortunately, Sandy was wearing a pair of down-filled slippers inside her boots that she was able to give him or he might have frozen his feet off. We walked the half mile back up the coulee to the mobile home, leading the three children on Blondie, still dragging the tree behind.

By the time we reached the top, the bitter cold wind and the tears had formed large icicles on all their cheeks. As we pulled up to the house, I turned to my family and asked a simple question, "Now, wasn't that fun?"

I could not believe the four icy-cold stares I received. One thing was for sure, though. It was a Christmas none of us would ever forget.

Too Close for Comfort

Our first summer at the ranch was the most exciting and challenging time of my life, and our faith was constantly being tested. God often blessed and provided abundantly, even beyond what we asked of Him. On many occasions, He sent us wonderful, dedicated volunteers while providing building materials and finances according to our needs.

From the onset, I didn't have faith to believe that the money could be raised to build a much-needed barn for the animals. Instead, I felt that we somehow could find one somewhere in the area and move it onto the property. When my friend, Ron Mix, heard we were looking for a barn, he offered to move it free of charge through his company "Mix The Mover" if we found a suitable one in the vicinity.

In May of 1977, soon after our first tent was pitched on the property, Blaine, Sandy, and I began to pray together concerning our need of the barn. The first time we talked to God about it, a picture of an old, red, hip-roofed barn came to mind. That vision continued to grow stronger each time we talked or prayed about it.

One afternoon, as we were once again singing and praising the Lord for providing our every need, a thought came upon me very strongly that we should be more specific in our prayers about the barn. I shared my thoughts with the others and, as we committed it to God in prayer, I found myself asking God to supply a building within a 30-mile radius of the ranch property. I believe that the Holy Spirit dropped that number into my heart.

For those first few months of ranch life, our family spent most of our time driving back and forth from Edmonton, a two-and-a-half-hour trip one way. The early development stages were hard physical labour, but the excitement and joy we experienced made it seem like play. Even the children pitched in, and we often worked from daylight to dusk, stopping only for meals.

During those early months, I frequently thought of how blessed I was to be living out my childhood fantasy on a ranch, of all places. Again, I had done nothing to deserve it, but by the grace of God, a few more of my dreams were being fulfilled.

Before our family settled down to the busy ranch-ministry life, we decided it was time for the Lefebvres to have a long-overdue holiday. Being in professional football for the past 11 years, I had not been able to enjoy a summer vacation with my family since Sandy and I were first married.

Together the family planned for a two-week drive down the west coast of Oregon and California, with Disneyland as our destination. The children were so excited they could hardly sleep the last two nights before we were scheduled to leave. Chéri was eight years old, Brad six, and Julie had just turned four.

The morning before we were to leave, I received an unexpected phone call from Muff Doan, our nearest neighbour at the ranch.

"Garry," he began, "there's a barn that has just come up for sale over near Stettler, and I think it's probably just what you've been looking for. It belongs to a farmer named Campbell."

"Is it within 30 miles of the ranch property?" I inquired.

"I don't know for sure, but it could be pretty close to that. Why?"

"Well, we've been praying specifically for a barn that is within 30 miles of the ranch."

"Maybe you'd better come down and take a look at it, before someone else beats you to it."

"I can't, Muff, we're leaving for Disneyland tomorrow morning, and there's no way I can come down today. We'll be gone for two weeks. I guess it will just have to wait until then."

"I don't think it will stay there that long. Someone will probably snap it up while you're away."

"Well, I promised the children that we would leave tomorrow morning, so we will just have to trust God. If it's the barn that the Lord has for us, it will be there when we return."

I truly believed what I was saying, because the Lord had recently been increasing our level of faith, specifically through our children.

The Faith of a Child

A couple of months earlier, while we were still living in St. Albert, we had experienced a faith-building answer to prayer through our young son, Brad. Actually, it had started through an act of disobedience on his part. Sandy and I had just purchased a new skateboard for him, and we cautioned him that he could play with it near our house only and that he was not to take it off the block under any circumstances.

One evening he returned home with a sombre look on his face. When I asked him what was wrong, he burst into tears.

"Daddy, I'm sorry," he cried. "I disobeyed you and my skateboard was stolen by some big mean boys. I took it off the block like you told me not to. Please forgive me."

I was angry, but I found it difficult to scold my repentant little five-year-old. Instead, I just poured more guilt on him.

"Well, Son, you don't have a skateboard anymore, and Mommy and I are not going to buy you a new one. That's what happens when you disobey us."

His response totally caught me off guard. With great confidence he looked me straight in the eye and said, "It's okay, Daddy. I talked to Jesus and told Him I was sorry, and He said He would bring it back for me in the morning."

"Well, maybe He won't," I replied quickly, trying to lay more guilt on him and at the same time hoping to protect him from a real blow to his tender, young faith. Neither Sandy nor I thought for a moment that the skateboard would find its way back to our house, so we tried to change the subject as quickly as we could. He wouldn't give up that easily.

"Jesus will bring it back, Dad. He promised!" Brad insisted.

No matter how hard we tried, we could not convince him otherwise, so we dropped the matter, again hoping that he would soon forget about it.

The next morning, we rose early to once again make the long two-and-a-half hour trek to the ranch. When Sandy walked into Brad's room to awake him, she found him already up and rummaging through his toy box.

"What are you doing, Brad?"

"I'm looking for my skateboard."

"Son, you lost it yesterday, remember?"

"I know, Mom, but Jesus promised to bring it back. It's got to be here someplace."

By this time, he was on his knees looking under his bed. Just then, I walked into the room. When I realized what he was doing, I felt that as his parents, we had better bring this boy back to earth. I spent the next few minutes trying to let him down easy, but Brad's faith refused to waver, and no matter what I said, I couldn't shake his confidence. He kept repeating those same words, "I know Jesus is going to bring it back this morning."

Our family left for the ranch at 11:00 a.m., leaving our teenage houseguest, Karen, to look after things for us. She had given her life to Jesus through a Nicky Cruz Crusade and had come off the streets to live with us only two months earlier.

As the car rolled down the road, Brad kept looking back until our house was no longer in sight, and still he was confident that his skateboard would somehow come back. We returned home two days later and were greeted by Karen, smiling from ear to ear and holding a large familiar object in her hand.

"Some boy showed up at the door with this in his hand about ten minutes after you guys left."

We were all stunned, except for little Brad.

"I knew He would bring it back!" he shouted. "Thank you, Jesus."

It is written: *"A little child shall lead them."*

That spring morning, our family left for our long overdue holiday, confident that the barn we had been praying for would still be there when we returned, if it was indeed the one for us. After all, God could do anything. That's what our children believed, and what Sandy and I were learning slowly. By this time, we were wise enough to have the kids do the praying when a real need arose.

Our trip to Disneyland was a wonderfully relaxing journey for the whole family and also the most exciting thing the children had ever experienced. They talked about it for years afterwards. We returned to Edmonton in two weeks as planned, and I immediately called Muff Doan to see if the barn was still available. As far as he knew, it had not been sold. Brother Blaine and I jumped into my car the next day and headed for Stettler.

As we drove into the Campbell farm, my heart leapt. There it was, as big as life, the red hip-roofed barn that I had been envisioning in my spirit for three months.

"That's the one!" I shouted, "Thank you, Lord!"

Blaine and I rejoiced and praised God while we drove up the long driveway and pulled to a stop in front of the huge structure.

Just as we stepped out of the car, Mr. Campbell came around the corner of the house across the yard. He approached us curiously.

"Praise God, this is it!" Blaine blurted out.

"I hope you're not interested in this barn," responded Mr. Campbell.

"Why?" I asked.

"'Cause I just sold it last week to my neighbour down the road."

"You couldn't have," I responded without thinking. "By the way, my name is Garry Lefebvre and this is my brother Blaine. We are with Circle Square Ranch over near Halkirk."

"Campbell's the name."

"We have been praying for a barn exactly like this one, and I'm sure this is it. We're building a camp for children, and we really need this barn."

"I'm very sorry, gentlemen. I wish I could help you, but you're one week too late."

As the conversation continued, Blaine began to walk back and forth in front of the barn, with his hands raised towards it, boldly proclaiming, "Praise You, Lord. Thank You, Jesus. Thank You for the barn, Lord. Yes, sir, you belong to us—we've claimed you in Jesus' name."

Mr. Campbell's mouth dropped, and he stood speechless for a few moments as he stared at Blaine walking around and talking to the barn, and at me "amening" and thanking Jesus too. He must have thought he'd caught hold of a couple of real "wet-brains." A second or two later he regained his composure and began to speak again.

"Look, gentlemen. It sure sounds like you need this barn, and I'm sure you're disappointed, but my hands are tied. The barn has been sold."

"Have you received any money yet?" I questioned.

"No, not yet, but we've shaken hands on the deal, and I can't go back on my word."

There wasn't the slightest doubt in either Blaine's or my mind that this barn was the one we had been praying for, so I quickly responded, "I wouldn't expect you to, Mr. Campbell, but when your neighbour backs out of the deal, would you please call me first?"

I quickly scrawled my phone number on a piece of paper and handed it to him.

He stuffed it into his jacket pocket as he looked towards Blaine, who continued to walk around thanking Jesus. I noticed a smirk on old Mr. Campbell's face as he said, "He ain't going to back out. I'm sure of that."

"Just promise me you'll call when he does," I said, looking him straight in the eye.

"Yes, of course, but I'm sure it won't happen."

Blaine and I climbed into the car and drove back to the ranch, praising God all the way.

Mr. Campbell called me two days later to tell me that his neighbour had changed his mind and reneged on their deal. We were sure we knew why. God had earmarked that barn for Circle Square Ranch. He offered the barn to us for $1,600, and I gladly accepted.

Ron Mix rode down with me the following week to take a look at the answer to our prayer, to determine what it would take for his crew to move it. It didn't take him more than a couple of minutes to size up the situation.

"It will move all right," he said. "We just need to reinforce it a little, and she'll load on the back of our lowboy, and down the road she'll go. I suggest that we trace out a route down the back roads to the ranch. It just isn't possible to move it on the highway."

We drove down what he thought would be the best route, checking the power lines to make sure there wouldn't be any surprises on moving day. The only doubtful spot was about six miles west of the ranch, where a large three-phase power line crossed our path. Because of its size and the fact that it was the main line into Halkirk, it would be impossible to take down. Ron was a little concerned that it might be too low. I assured him that if God provided the barn, he would make it fit under the wire. As we neared the ranch property, I suddenly realized that I hadn't checked to see if the barn was within the thirty-mile range we had been praying for. I mentioned it to Ron and he agreed that we should check it out. We backed up to the ranch Texas-gate and took note of the odometer reading of his car and then proceeded down the back roads all the way to the Campbell farm.

When we pulled up to the barn, we had driven exactly 29.8 miles. Our faith had been tested and had been proven to be real.

One week later, Sandy, Blaine, and I watched with our hearts full of praise and a few tears of joy as the miracle barn rolled onto Circle Square property and was set down on its foundation. The move came off without a hitch, even though it took the better part of a day. It couldn't have come any closer to not making it under that three-phase line, either. In fact, we actually shaved a few shingles off the roof cap as we drove under it.he miracle barn still sits at the ranch today, no longer its original bright red, but wearing the brown and tan colours of Circle Square, a testimony to the glory of God.

The old red barn

Chapter 14

A LITTLE MIXED UP

The St. Pierres left for Ontario the last week of July, but the rest of our crew stayed until the end of August. Bill and Gloria had donated most of their summer, and we felt blessed to have had them with us that long. Now it was time for them to start working on the Severn Bridge Ranch, which they had been called to build and direct.

We were glad that young Paul Rutledge was able to stay on for another month and a half. Paul, at 21, the son of National Circle Square Ranch Director Reynold Rutledge and a recent graduate of Rawhide College in Arizona, was instrumental in setting up our horse programs and also a great help in many other areas of early ranch development.

Before he and his family left for Ontario, Bill St. Pierre had laid out the hotel complex and put in the footings and the first couple rows of concrete blocks. It was now up to the rest of us to finish the course. The Lord had graciously sent us many wonderful and eager volunteers, although not one of them had any prior experience in construction. Sandy and I were very appreciative of their willingness to help, but we knew that we had to rely on God even more. I had built a corner shelf once in Junior High School Shop, and now I was the rookie foreman of this inexperienced crew. God really does have a sense of humour.

One such young volunteer was Darcy Mabbot, a 13-year-old nephew of Phil Doan. Darcy, along with my 13-year-old nephew, Todd Rutkowski, laid 13 courses of blocks on an 80-foot long wall all by themselves. Miraculously, the wall is still standing perfectly straight, with less than a quarter-inch discrepancy from corner to corner. An engineer who visited the ranch five years later in 1982 told me that, in his opinion, there was no earthly reason why that wall had not collapsed the moment it was back-filled. Instead of staggering the blocks, which is sound construction practice, the boys laid many of the blocks almost right on top of each other. We didn't notice the mistake until it was too late. Consequently, we were unable to place any re-bar in from the top and could not pour any concrete in, which strengthens the wall. We decided instead to pray and trust God. Here we are, 24 years since the original construction, and the wall still stands strong and true to the glory of God.

Todd and Darcy both served as volunteer wranglers and counsellors during those beginning years. From the spring of 1985 until the winter of 1997, Darcy served at the ranch as full-time Horsemanship Director. Todd went on to become North American Director of King's Kids, a division of YWAM, and is presently the Associate Pastor at North Langley Vineyard in British Columbia. Both young men got their start in ministry by slinging heavy mortar and lifting 40-pound concrete blocks.

That first week in August was a scorcher. The temperature ranged from 90º to 95º Fahrenheit. It was backbreaking work, slinging those heavy blocks, but the person who suffered the most was Paul Rutledge. His main job was to mix the mortar by hand and keep four to six workers supplied at all times. He worked harder than all of us, and yet he never complained. By the end of that first week, I realized that he couldn't possibly keep up the pace. We needed an electric cement-mixer, no two ways about it.

I called my brother Murray in Camrose to see if he could find one we could borrow. Buying one was out of the question, as funds just weren't available. Murray was working for a paving outfit at the time and had worked in different construction jobs for years, so I was confident he would know someone who could help us.

Two days later, he called to tell me that he had come up dry in his efforts to secure a mixer for us. After spending another whole day trying to track down another friend in the construction business, I had exhausted all my resources. Paul, already a trim physical specimen, was dropping weight daily, and I knew I had to come up with a solution quickly. There was no way he could keep it up much longer. Something had to be done, and fast.

I walked into our mobile home that afternoon, feeling totally defeated. Sandy was standing at the kitchen sink busily preparing dinner. I dropped down on a kitchen chair and bowed my head on the table.

"Lord," I whispered, "what am I going to do? Where can I find a cement mixer? I don't know anyone else to call. Lord, please help me."

It is amazing how most of us usually wait until we have come to the end of our own efforts before we ask God to get involved. God delights in coming to our aid because He loves us. The Bible says that He resists the proud but gives grace to the humble. A true sign of humility is simple, total dependence on God, and I needed to learn this lesson. The quiet peaceful voice that I was learning to recognize spoke from within:

Interesting

"*It's about time you asked. Why don't you call Revelstoke Building Supplies in Castor?*"

"Sandy, I think the Lord is telling me to try Revelstoke in Castor. I'm going to call them and see if they have a small mixer we can rent. We have got to have one soon."

I called information and secured the number. The male voice on the other end of the line greeted me in a friendly manner.

"Revelstoke. Can I help you?"

"Hi, my name is Garry Lefebvre, and I'm the Director of Circle Square Ranch near Halkirk. We are a Christian youth camp and are presently in construction, and we're really in need of a small cement mixer. Would you happen to have one that we could rent for a couple of months?"

"I'm sorry we don't rent them out," he replied, "but we do have one that we will sell you if you like. What do you need it for?"

After I explained what we were doing, he replied, "Yes, I think the one we have here would be perfect for what you need."

"How much is it?" I inquired.

I don't know why I bothered to ask. We didn't have any funds to pay for it, no matter what the price was.

"It's only $150, a real bargain. We will need cash or a cheque, since you are just new in the area. Of course we will be glad to set up an account for you at a later date. We have an application you can fill out if you like."

"Could you hold on for a second?" I said, and covered the mouthpiece. "Sandy, they have what we need, but they want $150 up front. We don't have $150. What should I do?"

"I don't know, Dear. You'd better ask the Lord about this one."

So again I asked: "Father, what should I do?"

Immediately the thought came to my mind. "*Is this a real need?*"

"Yes, this is definitely a real need," I responded

"*Have I not promised to supply all your needs?*"

The verse from Philippians 4:19 came to mind: *And my God will meet all your needs according to his glorious riches in Christ Jesus.*" "Yes, Lord, you have."

Then tell them to send it out, for I have already supplied all that you will need.

My spirit leaped within me. "We'll take it," I said to the man who had been patiently awaiting my reply.

"Great," he said, "I'll deliver it myself tomorrow noon? I'd like to see what you're doing out there. Where exactly is your property?"

"We're six and a half miles north and east of Halkirk. Just follow the signs."

"Thanks. I'll be there somewhere between 12:00 and 12:30 p.m."

As I hung up the receiver, I turned to Sandy and said, "Well, I wonder how God is going to work this one out? I'm sure glad we serve the God of the Impossible."

"He has never failed us yet," Sandy said, adding, "I don't know how, but I believe the Lord will come through for us again."

The next morning, Sandy drove the ranch van into Halkirk around 10:30 to pick up our mail at the local post office. I was sitting at the kitchen table doing some paperwork when I heard her pull up. Seconds later, the trailer door burst open and Sandy ran in waving a white envelope above her head. She looked more exited than a young kid on Christmas morning.

"Praise the Lord! Praise the Lord! God has answered our prayers." She was shouting, her eyes glistening with tears of joy.

"What's happened?"

I knew that something dramatic must have taken place for Sandy to be reacting like this. She was normally quite controlled.

"Look at this," she said as she handed me the torn envelope. I took it from her and removed a slip of paper and two cheques. One cheque was for the amount of $67. It was dated a month earlier. The second one was dated only three days earlier and was for $86. They totalled $153, just three dollars more than we needed. Then note said, "Sorry for not getting this to you sooner. Hope it helps."

The letter was from Clarence and Linda Milke, our dear friends from Edmonton and, unknown to them, the cheques had arrived less than two hours before we needed them. I grabbed Sandy and started to jump and shout and dance all around the living room, praising God with abandon. We had us a glory fit.

"Alleluia! Praise God forevermore! Lord, You are so faithful. Thank You, Jesus. Praise Your holy name!"

We carried on for several minutes.

As I was bouncing down the hall, suddenly I stopped and looked up in the air and said, "What is the extra three dollars for, Lord? We needed only $150, and you sent us $153. If I was ever to write a book some day, Father, it sure would have brought You more glory if the amount had been exact."

Then I caught myself and repented aloud, "I'm sorry, Lord, for even thinking that. I know Your word says that You are able to do exceeding abundantly above all that we ask or even think. Forgive me, Lord. The three dollars are obviously for something else that we don't know about yet. Thank You for the $153. Lord, You are so good to us. Thank You, thank You, Lord."

At exactly 12:00 p.m., the Revelstoke Building Supply delivery truck pulled into the yard. By the time I reached the truck, the bright yellow cement mixer was already unloaded.

"Here it is," the driver said, as I strolled up to him. "I'm sure this will meet your needs just fine."

"It looks perfect," I said. "Thanks for bringing it out so quickly. It's going to save us a lot of work."

"Here's the bill," he said, as he handed me a green piece of paper. "Like I said yesterday, a cheque or cash will be just fine."

I looked down at the bill in my hand and my mouth dropped open when my eyes fastened on the amount owing: *$153*.

"Wow!" I exclaimed.

"Is there something wrong?" he asked.

"Oh! No! Not in the least, but I thought you told me that the mixer would be only $150."

"Well, yes, I did, but I had forgotten about the small rubber drive belt that goes with it, and that costs $3."

"Oh, that's okay," I said, "I just wanted to be absolutely sure. You see, in answer to prayer, I just received this exact amount of $153 in the mail, less than an hour ago."

"That's quite a coincidence," he said.

"I'd call it more of a God-incidence," I returned. "'Coincidence' left my vocabulary many years ago."

The man may have forgotten about the drive belt, but God surely hadn't. The Lord knew all along what we were going to need, and He used two of His faithful servants, 130 miles away, to release His blessing to us at just the right time. All we did was make the reception by faith.

"Trust in the Lord with all your heart and do not lean on your own understanding. In all your ways acknowledge Him, and He will make your paths straight" (Proverbs 3:5,6).

Chapter 15

DEDICATION DAY

In July of 1978, we began our first Circle Square Ranch summer camp season. Earlier that spring, the ranch staff had begun a crazy tradition, which carried on for many years thereafter—two months before the children began arriving for summer camp, we started on a new building project! This time it was the construction of the girls' wing of the main complex. We really had no choice because we needed to finish the bunkhouses to a point where they would be usable for summer camp.

For many years after that first spring, there always seemed to be one project or another that the staff had to rush madly to complete in time for camping season. The reason that this cycle went on for years is that the fiscal year began in September, and by the time finances needed for new projects became available, the ranch was into spring again. Consequently, we would often end up working 14 to 16 hours a day, right up until the ten weeks of summer camp began, and that's when the days became even longer, filled with even more activity.

By the time the last camp was over each summer, the staff personnel were ready for a long-overdue rest. Although these summers could be gruelling, no one really complained, for they knew they were there to serve the Lord and to help young people.

That first season found us frantically working on a number of projects, not only for camp but in preparation for our official dedication, which was planned for June 16. It had been advertised on 100 Huntley Street for a few weeks, and David Mainse, along with our National Ranch Director, Reynold Rutledge, were scheduled to fly out from Toronto to officiate. Our new Program Director, Gary "Coulee" Clifford, and a volunteer carpenter friend, Fred Lozinik, and I stayed up an entire night putting the arborite top and other finishing touches on the front lobby counter. That night, Fred laid my camp nickname on me. I was standing in the lobby wearing a pair of old carpenter coveralls when Fred looked over at me and said, "Hey! You look just like that old carpenter on TV, Mr. Chips."

Gary picked up on it right away, adding, "That suits you perfectly. Would you pass the saw, Mr. Chips?" That name stuck for nearly three years until I finally convinced them all that "Colonel" suited me much better. It took the permanent staff that long to realize that Colonel Sanders and I had to be very close friends, since it was hard for me to pass one of his Kentucky Fried Chicken franchises without stopping in for a short visit.

Our entire staff from that very first season set a precedent for the years that have followed, and I'm sure they will be eternally rewarded for their dedication. Their spirit of self-sacrifice still prevails at Circle Square Ranch. Thank God for the hundreds of volunteers from Alberta, Saskatchewan, British Columbia and beyond who gave of themselves those first few years to see the ministry launched. And thank God for those who continue to give of themselves to see that hundreds and even thousands of young people are given the opportunity to experience the love of Jesus at Circle Square Ranches across Canada every year.

The morning of the dedication, we were all still busy with last minute clean-up. Bernie Doan, our Operations and Construction Supervisor, had done a fine job in organizing the full-time and volunteer staff, and we had accomplished about all we could in the time allotted.

Bernie and his wife Bernice had come on staff with us earlier that spring. They came from Eston, Saskatchewan, where Bernie was the foreman of a construction company. He was Phil's younger brother, and their return to Halkirk was like a homecoming for all the Doans. Bernie's mom and dad were our nearest neighbours, and brother Merle and his wife, Donna, lived just down the road a way. Phil and Jane were on permanent staff already, as Phil headed up our Horsemanship Program. Bernice's family all lived over near Veteran, so the whole Doan and Ellerby clan were thrilled to have Bernie and Bernice back home—and so were we.

These two precious saints were the most dedicated and hardworking couple I had ever met. They will never know just how much they were needed, and how God was able to use them to launch the ministry and bring the ranch to the point that it is at today. It is one of the most blessed Christian camping facilities in all of Canada. I say that not just because of the beautiful facilities and wonderful programs that are offered, but also because of the spirit of love, of self-sacrifice, and of giving that prevails there. It is the Spirit of Jesus, shining through the staff, who reach out to all who cross that Texas gate onto the property.

Dedication Day had arrived and we were excited. We had no idea how many people would come, but we figured there would be quite a few, since David had been talking about it a fair bit on 100 Huntley Street lately. The ceremony was planned to commence at 2:00 p.m.

The phone started ringing around 10:30 a.m. The first caller was from Edmonton. A lady was calling to inquire if the dedication was still going to take place, because it was pouring rain up there. Our receptionist, Shannon, assured her that all systems were go, and that it wasn't raining down here at the ranch. Then there was a similar call from Calgary, and moments later from Red Deer, which was only 90 miles away. I was just putting the finishing touches on the counter when my secretary, my sister Pat, brought all of this to my attention.

"People are calling from all over the province. It's pouring rain north, south, east, and west. And they are concerned that they might come all this way for nothing."

Just then Sandy spoke up.

"Look! Rain clouds are headed this way."

I ran to the front door and looked out. As far as the eye could see, there were ominous black clouds, from the southeast to the southwest, rapidly moving our way.

"We need to pray," I said, trying not to sound too alarmed. "Call all the staff together. We need to do some serious praying—and I mean right now."

If it rained even a little bit, our Dedication Day would be totally ruined. Our homemade roads were fresh and new and still needed to be gravelled. We knew from experience that it was useless to try to negotiate the gumbo on the roads after the slightest rainfall. In the past, a number of vehicles had ended up over the edge of the coulee bank, close to disaster. If it rained, the cars would have to park beyond our Texas gate and the people would have to walk the half-mile in to the hotel—that is, if they would. Unless they were wearing gum-boots, they probably wouldn't even attempt it. And if they did, our beautiful hotel complex would be a disaster by the time it was over. To make matters worse, we had just installed our new rust-coloured carpet.

God wouldn't let this happen, or would he?

As the staff gathered in the hotel lobby, my thoughts wandered to the gospel of Mark, where Jesus took authority over the elements and calmed the storm. Then the Lord reminded me that He has given us authority in the name of Jesus Christ to carry out His will and to enforce His plan through prayer.

Lord, I thought to myself, *what am I to do?*

A voice from within answered, *"I do not rain on my own parade. You take authority and command it not to rain, in Jesus' name."*

Faith began to rise in my heart, and I turned with great confidence to the staff, who were milling about.

"Let's all go outside. We need to pray against this rain and put a stop to it."

The staff responded and soon we had all moved outside and were standing in front of the hotel doors. Instinctively we joined our hands together. We faced the storm clouds which by now were only a mile or two away. I felt an incredible boldness rise within me as I began to speak.

"In the name of Jesus Christ, I command you clouds to depart. Go rain on the farmers who need it, but you are not going to rain on Circle Square Ranch today. This place is being dedicated to God, and you are not going to ruin it."

I was actually talking to the weather.

Some gasped, a few jumped and shouted, and others praised the Lord, for within seconds of the prayer, the clouds began to part in the centre as if by some invisible hand. We all watched in amazement while they passed over to the left and to the right and then joined back together again on the other side of the property. Within the hour, the sky was pitch black as far as you could see in every direction—except for a great circle above the ranch property, where it was a beautiful blue. It stayed that way all day. People continued to call to ask if we were still going to go ahead with the dedication, as it continued to pour buckets over the whole province that day—except for Circle Square Ranch, that is.

At noon, we had all gathered for lunch in the dining hall, when suddenly a dirty green truck pulled up out in front. Bobby Hronek, our neighbour, walked in through the main doors. For a moment, Bob just stood there in his rubber boots with a dumbfounded look on his face. I got up from the table to greet him.

"What is going on around here?" he said. "It's pouring rain over at my place, so I figured you guys were in real trouble for your dedication ceremony. I came over to see what was happening to your roads. I can't believe it, but it's raining right up to your Texas gate, and it isn't raining on your property."

Bobby and Gloria were our closest neighbours, next to the Doan farm. He had been very negative toward the ranch from the beginning and had let us know, in no uncertain terms, that they didn't like us being there.

During that first year, a number of false rumours had been circulating in the Halkirk area concerning who we were and why we were there, and I guess the Hroneks must have believed some of them. Lately, however, they had seemed a lot warmer toward us and had made frequent visits. We all prayed often for Bobby and Gloria, and in the last couple of months, we had begun to notice a real softening of their hearts.

"Praise the Lord, praise the Lord," my sister, Pat, echoed from behind me.

"God has answered our prayers," I said. "We prayed for the clouds to rain on the farmers who needed it, but not on Circle Square Ranch. The Lord is at work."

"This is the strangest thing I have ever seen," Bobby replied. "I wouldn't have believed it if I hadn't seen it with my own eyes. There sure are some odd things going on around here."

"Well, Bobby, all things are possible with God," I said with a smile. "You haven't seen anything yet."

Bobby just shook his head and walked toward the front door.

"What time is this meeting supposed to start?"

"Two o'clock," I replied.

He didn't look back. Bobby had witnessed a first-hand miracle, and we all could see that he was deeply moved. God was revealing Himself to him, in answer to our prayers for his soul and for his family's, and his heart was slowly opening to the truth of the Gospel. The ranch staff had been sharing with the Hroneks, for over a year now, that Jesus really loved and cared for them, and they were gradually running out of objections. Later that summer, Bobby and Gloria both accepted Jesus Christ as their Lord and Saviour.

Our dedication day turned out to be wonderfully and gloriously blessed in more ways than one. We recorded 535 different people who attended the service and signed our register. During the service, Reynold ministered in song and David preached an anointed message from the Word of God. We were also blessed with an offering of over $15,000 that day, which was just what we needed to pull us through that first summer season. Once again, God had demonstrated His faithfulness and divine provision, reminding us that, as His children, we are called to be the recipients of His matchless grace.

Chapter **16**

THE POWER OF HIS PRESENCE

From the first summer camping season in 1978, many of the ranch staff were anticipating that God was going to do something very special in our midst. Different prophetic words had given strong indication that the Holy Spirit was about to move. The Lord had spoke to me during the initial stages of ranch development from Psalm 133, *"How good and how pleasant it is when brothers live together in unity.... For there the Lord bestows his blessing, even life forevermore."*

I had this expectant sense that God wanted to reveal Himself to us in a powerful way. All He was waiting for was for us to come into the unity of the Spirit.

I didn't have first-hand knowledge about the workings of God, except for the accounts I had read about various outpourings of the Holy Spirit in the church in times past. I hadn't been privileged yet to experience a real move of God myself. The opportunity of attending a Bible school hadn't been afforded me, either. However, I sure wanted to be in a place where God was pouring out blessings. So I did my best to minister the principle of spiritual agreement to our staff and tried to impress upon everyone that we must constantly strive for team unity, regardless of the cost to our personal feelings and opinions. One thing I had learned from many years in the football wars was that winning teams always were close-knit, manifesting a spirit of unity. It took us until the second camping season to gain what I believe was a measure of the true spirit of unity.

During the first three weeks of camp in the summer of 1978, we held a few emergency meetings to work out some differences between staff. Each time, God demonstrated His faithfulness to us. As the staff came into line with the principles of unity taught in the Word of God, The Holy Spirit was poured out in the most wonderful and unexpected ways.

The first outpouring we experienced came subsequent to a "cleansing and forgiveness" meeting in which the Lord dealt very specifically with bitterness and resentment between many of our staff members. The first heart that He graciously cleansed was my own. When my relationship with this one particular staff member was restored, it set off a chain reaction that brought deliverance to many of the other staff. The scriptures demonstrate that God always deals with the shepherds first, and then He moves upon the sheep. I believe that true unity moves from the head down through the body.

The next evening we took the entire camp to an overnight camp-out down in the Paint Earth Coulee. The twenty staff members along with about 60 ranchers set up camp a couple of miles from the ranch on a piece of beautiful valley property owned by our neighbour, Paul Nielsen. On special occasions, we took extended trail rides over onto Paul's place. The valley, or coulee, as the locals called it, was absolutely gorgeous. The hills were covered with bright reddish shale, which many of the farmers around the area used to spread on their driveways. The spot I'd chosen reminded me of many old western movies I had seen. It was picture-perfect. During one of our earlier trail rides, I had realized that this place was ideal for an overnight sleep-out. Paul had graciously given us permission to use the place, providing we left it as we found it. We would have had it no other way.

The group set up camp Thursday evening immediately upon arrival, and then we brought all the ranchers and staff together for a campfire. These late night times of singing and testimonies were always very special, and God often moved upon the hearts of campers and staff alike. The evening campfire meeting was always an exciting time, but none of us was prepared for what God had in store for us this particular night. He was about to command His blessing upon us and supernaturally change many of our lives forever.

As was customary, Sandy and my youngest brother, Mark, strummed their guitars and led the song service after dinner. The amazing thing is that we didn't do anything different from what we had done on previous camp-outs. The songs chosen were the same ones we had been singing since the first day of camp. As usual, the whole group was singing with great enthusiasm. About halfway through one of the songs, the atmosphere dramatically changed, as many of the staff and campers sensed God's presence beginning to envelope us. I became so caught up in what I was sensing that I stopped singing. It sounded like everyone's voice had simultaneously changed. The music and voices blended together in the most harmonious sound I had ever heard.

We had entered into a different realm of experience. Suddenly, the music and singing stopped. An indescribable peace filled the air, to the point of saturation. Everyone present knew that something unusual was taking place, although no one was sure just what that was.

After we had been standing for a few moments in silence, a 15-year-old camper named Stephen slowly walked over to me.

"Mr. Chips," he said very softly, "I have a serious problem. There is a tumour the size of an egg, right here in the right side of my chest. My doctor says that I have to have it removed when I get home from camp next week, and I'm scared. Do you think that Jesus would heal it for me?"

Without hesitation, I replied, "I sure do, Stephen. Would you like me to pray for you right now?"

"Yes, Sir, I would like that."

As I often did when praying for someone, I reached out to place my hand upon him. Just as I was about to touch the right side of his chest, he flew backwards like he had been shot out of a cannon. Stephen slammed backward onto the ground and smashed his head on a massive log. The sound of the impact of the back of his head against the hard wood stunned me. I was sure that he must have cracked his skull wide open, yet he didn't appear to be in pain.

Two of our young staff members, who were standing next to me, immediately rushed to his aid. To the amazement of everyone, Stephen was unhurt, and he just lay on the ground with a radiant, peaceful smile on his face. He seemed unaware of the rest of us and oblivious to the fact that he had just whacked his head hard enough to crack his skull. Young Stephen had been slain in the spirit, just as it happened in the Bible:

"When He (Jesus) said to them, 'I am He,' they drew back and fell to the ground" (John 18:6).

I had witnessed this manifestation before in Full Gospel Business Men's meetings around the country, but I had never been in the middle of it.

About ten minutes later, Stephen slowly got back up to his feet. At first, he didn't believe us when we told him that he had hit the log with his head. He said he had not felt a thing. In fact, Stephen thought he had landed on a pile of soft pillows.

In the meantime, other ranchers began to swoon under the power of God's presence. In a few minutes there were young bodies lying all around the campground. That night many of them were delivered of anger, bitterness, and resentment, while some were set free from demonic oppression. Others just basked in the sweet, holy presence of Jesus. No one even thought of going to sleep until after 5:00 a.m.

By noon that following day, Stephen's tumour had already shrunk to half its size. The next evening God sovereignly moved upon Stephen's older sister, Susan, and healed her as well. As we often did when the weather didn't cooperate, we held our evening campfire meeting inside the dining hall that night. I was led to speak on the subject of fear and how Satan uses it to hold God's children in bondage. When fear is ruling in our hearts, faith cannot operate through us because our receivers are out of tune. What Jesus has purchased for us on the Cross with His life's blood cannot be appropriated when our receivers are malfunctioning. At the conclusion of the message, I prayed a general prayer, binding the spirit of fear and asking God to release the spirit of faith. Moments after I dismissed the ranchers from the room, Susan came running back in shouting, "It's gone! It's gone!"

"What's gone?" I asked.

"The cyst under my eyelid. It just disappeared. I can hardly believe it. I was supposed to go in for an operation next week, just like Stephen. The growth has been there for a long time, and I was really worried about it too, but when you were speaking, something happened inside of me and all the fear left. Can you believe it, Mr. Chips? Jesus has healed me!"

"I don't have to believe it, Dear," I responded, "I already know it. The evidence is right in front of me."

"Thank you, Jesus, I am healed," she declared.

She could barely contain her joy and ran off to the girl's wing to share her good news with her other bunkmates. Susan was blessed that night with a wonderful revelation of God's unconditional love and forgiveness. Stephen wrote us later from Vancouver to tell us that his tumour had totally disappeared by the time he got home on Sunday evening.

Even the Demons Flee

Over the eight years that our family lived and ministered at Circle Square Ranch, we were privileged to see God perform many incredible miracles. From reaching hard-hearted teenagers to many miraculously healings, God's blessings were showered upon us. Of all of them, there was none more dramatic than when God's Spirit touched young Rhonda and her cousin Dayna.

These two 17-year-old girls had come to camp under definite protest. Their aunt had sent them, and from the moment they arrived, it was obvious that they didn't want to be there. We found out later that the girls had actually made a pact to do all they could to disturb the camp and to prevent other campers from coming to the Lord. The two of them had been dabbling in witchcraft and Satanism and were intent on exercising their dark spiritual powers to disrupt the camp. Little did they know that darkness can never overpower the light.

Rhonda and Dayna were assigned to the same cabin, and on Sunday evening their counsellor knew she was in for a real spiritual battle. It had become obvious that these girls were more than your average rebellious teenagers. During our regular staff devotions on Monday morning, we all prayed for them, and we continued to do so throughout the week. Somehow we knew that we were up against more than met the eye.

On Wednesday night during our outdoor campfire meeting, the Holy Spirit broke through to Rhonda. Once again, I was speaking that evening. This time I felt led to talk about true commitment and what it really means to follow Jesus as His disciples. I closed the meeting with a prayer, as was customary, and dismissed the campers and staff to return to their cabins to discuss the message before lights out. As I was in the habit of doing, I asked those who wished to stay behind to talk or have prayer to stay seated while the others left.

Immediately, Dayna made a quick exit and scurried for her cabin, and Rhonda started to go after her. She took two or three steps and then suddenly froze in her tracks, unable to move a muscle. A couple of seconds later, she let out a spine-tingling shriek that startled everyone present. She had tried to run from the conviction that she was feeling, but God mercifully arrested her, for He knew that in her heart Rhonda really wanted to know the truth.

I called for two of our counsellors, John and Rena Groot, and asked them to take her outside the tepee and pray for her, so as not to frighten the campers who had stayed behind for prayer. Fifteen minutes later, the three of them strolled back in, smiling from ear to ear.

I have never in my life seen such a dramatic change in someone so fast. Rhonda looked like a different person. Her countenance radiated the love of God. The darkness that had shrouded her only minutes earlier was completely gone.

Therefore, if anyone is in Christ, he is a new creation; the old has gone, the new has come! (2 Corinthians 5:17)

When Dayna found out that night what had happened to her cousin, she was fuming mad. They had made a pact together with the devil to disrupt the camp, and now that Rhonda had become a Christian, Dayna felt betrayed. She didn't even try to hide her feelings, and the chip on her shoulder grew larger. The other ranchers made sure they stayed out of her way. It wasn't hard to see that this girl was looking for trouble.

That Friday night, we did something we had not done before. A young music group from Kindersley, Saskatchewan, came out in the evening to do a contemporary concert for us. The band was made up of four of our alumni counsellors. That evening we experienced the most incredible time of high praise to God of which I had ever been privileged to be a part. The band began to play at 9:00 p.m., and immediately the staff members began to dance and praise the Lord. Soon the whole camp joined in, with the exception of Dayna, who just sat there glaring at everyone.

The music and dancing continued for nearly four straight hours. Just before midnight, Dayna slipped out and headed for her bunkhouse. Margaret, one of the volunteer staff, saw her leave and quietly went to cut her off before she reached the bunkhouse. When Dayna saw her coming, she turned around and scampered back into the rear of the dining hall. A few minutes later, she tried to make her getaway again and discreetly edged her way out. Margaret was watching her closely and headed her off once more. This time I noticed what was happening and walked out into the foyer after Dayna. She was already on her way back in. As she came around the corner, the power of God hit her so hard that she pitched forward and slammed face first to the floor, right in front of me.

She let out a piercing scream and began to sob uncontrollably.

"Jesus, forgive me. Jesus, help me," she wailed.

Margaret dropped to her knees and grabbed Dayna into her arms and held her tightly as she poured out the pain and bitterness that had been bottled up inside her for years. She could run from God no longer. His love had overtaken her. God had arrested the two cousins dramatically, and demonstrated His unfailing love to them both. They were both changed in a moment of time, but their lives from then on took altogether different courses.

From that time on, Rhonda has continued to grow stronger in her walk with the Lord. Later that summer, she was involved in teaching Vacation Bible School in Edmonton. She attended Bible school for a few years, and completed a degree in Christian education. She has a strong, growing desire to know the Lord and to serve Him wherever she has been placed. This young lady has a true servant's heart and radiates the love of God. She has often returned to Circle Square Ranch to lend a hand and volunteer her services in whatever capacity she is needed. For a number of years, she served full time in the secretarial position. Anyone who knows the "new Rhonda" would find it virtually impossible to reconcile the description of what that "other girl" was like—before her commitment to Christ—with the woman of God that she has now become.

On the other hand, Dayna's journey became a series of struggles. Unlike Rhonda, she didn't submit herself to the Word of God, prayer, and fellowship with God's people. Shortly after she returned home from camp, she began to hang out with some of her old friends whose influence was far from God's ways. It wasn't long until Dayna fell back into her pre-Christian behaviour, and she and Rhonda slowly drifted apart. It broke Rhonda's heart to see her cousin fall so far after the incredible encounter she had with Jesus that summer, but Rhonda continued to pray for her often.

Thank God, a few years later Dayna came to the end of herself and once again surrendered her life to the Lordship of Jesus Christ. To this day she continues to love and serve the Lord and is happily married with beautiful children of her own.

David, Ron (Itchy) and Norma-Jean Mainse

Chapter 17

I TOLD YOU SO

From the beginning of creation men and women have looked at life diversely, and Sandy and I are no different. It is said that opposites attract and that is certainly true of us. A man of God once prophesied over us that Sandy is like a plodding horse and I am like a prancing one. I am impulsive by nature and tend to want to run with an idea before I think it totally through. Thankfully Sandy weighs everything through and checks out all the available facts before she makes a decision. Together we make a great team. I help move her into action and she slows me down.

In the fall of 1978 it had become very evident that the ranch was in need of a tractor. During our first year at Halkirk, we were blessed by a heavy-equipment company from Edmonton, who loaned us a brand new 977L Track Loader for three months. My brothers Blaine and Murray, both experienced heavy-equipment operators, used the powerful machine to excavate and to build our roads. Now that the loader was gone and the ranch was growing, we needed some type of tractor to maintain the roads in winter and to perform numerous other tasks.

When we began to make this a serious matter of prayer, Sandy and I actually wrote our prayer request out in the form of a covenant. By this time we were learning to be very specific in our petitions to God. A John Deer 4020 was the tractor we asked for, complete with a front-end loader, which we were sure would meet our needs perfectly. We began praying in late August and tried to stand in faith and not waver for the next two months. When the first snowfall came in early November and the tractor hadn't arrived yet, I decided to take matters into my own hands. With the sale of our St. Albert home, Sandy and I were able to deposit $50,000 of the equity into a savings account at the Alberta Treasury Branch in Castor. It was the first time in our married lives that we actually had more than a few dollars in savings.

One morning shortly after the first snowfall I was sitting in our mobile home at the breakfast table, when these thoughts invaded my mind: *"Maybe God hasn't answered your prayers for the tractor like you expected because you are supposed to buy the tractor for the ranch. You do have $50,000 sitting in the bank. You could easily purchase it yourself. If* *you are a man of faith, what do you need money in the bank for anyway? Maybe it's just in case God dies and you have to begin providing for yourself again. Are you asking God to bless you with something that He has already provided? Why don't you take some money from your savings and buy the ranch whatever tractor you need?"* I turned to Sandy, who was standing at the kitchen stove and spoke my thoughts.

"Honey, I was just thinking about the John Deer tractor that we have been asking God for. I believe the Lord is telling me that He has supplied the need already and that we should take some of our savings and purchase a tractor."

"That doesn't sound right to me," she responded. "We made a prayer covenant with the Lord, and I believe He will provide what we asked for."

"I think you are being a little covetous, don't you?" I continued. "Are you afraid to spend some of our savings for fear that we might need it later? What do we need money in the bank for anyway, just in case God dies?"

"Of course not! I just think you are giving up on the Lord answering our prayer and trying to make it happen yourself, that's all. If you feel that strongly about it, go right ahead, but I don't have a good witness about it."

"Well, the buck stops here, if you know what I mean. I feel assured that I should pursue this course. I am going to call Ron Mabbot right away and see if he can find what we need." Ron and his wife, Melba, lived in Coronation, where they ran a farm implement dealership.

"Okay," Sandy complied, "if you really think you should, but I still don't feel a peace about it. You are the head of this family, so I defer to you."

When I called Ron later that afternoon, I was delighted to find that he was in possession of a tractor with front-end loader that he was trying to sell. It was an International, not a John Deer 4020 like we had been praying for, but they were an old and reputable farm-implement company. Ron mentioned that there was no warranty on it, but that it was in good shape; besides, he said, those old International tractors seemed to run forever. He was willing to sell it to me for only $5,000.00, so I asked him to hold it for me. The next morning I drove to Coronation and purchased the long-awaited and much-needed tractor.

It was delivered to us the following afternoon, and we put the new machine into immediate action, building a mound of earth for "Boot Hill," our imitation graveyard near the boys' bunkhouse wing. The old International was doing a great job, and we used it daily—until the transmission blew out of it the second week. After we brought it back from the shop, it lasted for another week and then the front left wheel broke off. The front right wheel broke the following month. In the first three months, the old International spent as much time in the shop as she did in the field.

To make matters worse, five days after I purchased the tractor, Pastor Lorne Fisher from the Killam Pentecostal Church showed up at the ranch to give us a hand with some carpentry. As we were working together on the girls' bunkhouse wing, Pastor Lorne turned to me and said something I will never forget. "We heard at the church that you guys are in need of a tractor. Have you got one yet?"

"Yes," I replied. "We just purchased one this past week. Why do you ask?"

"Oh, that's too bad," he responded. "My church board asked me to check, and if you didn't have one yet, they felt they were to buy you whatever you needed." I gulped and swallowed hard but was too embarrassed to say anything. I knew I had made a grave mistake, an expensive $5,000 one.

When I told Sandy, she was very gracious and only said "I told you so" once. She kindly let me know that I had presumptuously missed the will of God. Like Abraham of old, I had impatiently attempted to help God out by the arm of my flesh and had unwittingly created my own Ishmael. When I finally understood my error, I repented before God and asked His forgiveness, then confessed my sin to Sandy and the entire ranch staff. The old International then became know as Ishmael. Six months later, by the grace of God, I was able to return the tractor to Coronation, and Ron Mabbot agreed to put it on consignment at his dealership. Within two weeks, Ishmael was sold and I received the entire $5,000 back. It was a lesson learned or at least so I thought.

Losing Face

The following spring after Ishmael was sent down the road, Sandy and I came to loggerheads once more on the matter of a purchase. In rural Alberta, spring is the time when most calves are born, and many of them end up on the auction block. Phil Doan and I were discussing this fact one morning when he mentioned that he was going into Stettler to the auction the next day to buy himself a calf. I decide right there and then that it was time I bought some livestock of my own. Since we were living on the ranch with all the space and pasture land our quarter section afforded us, it seemed like a natural thing to do. However, when I talked with Sandy later, she was not the least bit enthused about my idea.

"Look," I said. "You may have been right about the tractor, but what harm could there be in spending a hundred and forty or fifty dollars on a little calf. All we do is pick him up at the auction, bring him out here and turn him loose in the pasture. Sometime this fall, when he has grown to 600 or maybe 700 pounds, we can sell him back at the auction or butcher him and fill the freezer. That is very inexpensive beef. What could possibly go wrong? We can even use him for the calf scramble races during camp rodeos. The ranchers will love it. Phil is going into Stettler tomorrow to buy one for himself and has offered to purchase one for us at the same time."

"I know it all sounds so simple," Sandy responded, "but I don't feel right about it, and it has nothing to do with the money. I do not feel that it is the right thing to do. I am not going to stand in your way if you are set on it, but I am not in agreement with buying this calf."

For the second time, I went ahead with my decision without her agreement and in spite of her caution. After all, I was only going to buy a little calf.

Phil drove into Stettler the next morning and returned that afternoon with a gorgeous little white-faced Hereford calf. He got a great deal and purchased him for only $135.00. The calf was quite a bit smaller than other calves his age, which were selling for $150.00 to $160.00. That just made him all the cuter. The kids and I named him Face. At the time of Face's arrival, our one and only ranch cow had just calved herself, so we had two babies about the same size to tend to. After a month had passed, the ranch calf had noticeably grown a couple of inches more than little Face. I wrote it off to him having a slow start in life and didn't think much more about it, until mid summer, by which time he still hadn't grown at all. By the time fall had rolled around, I finally realized that I owned a midget calf. In six months Face hadn't grown an inch. Once more Sandy let me know in no uncertain terms, "I told you so."

When November arrived, it seemed logical that we should keep Face through the winter and give him one more year to grow up and become a steer. At that time, my kid brother Mark was on full-time staff as our Horsemanship Director and was responsible for tending all the livestock.

By then the ranch boasted a herd of 35 horses, which required constant care. For Mark, daily chores included feeding and watering the horses and the cow and the pigs we were raising for food.

In December the temperature dropped below –30° F and the dugout that the animals drank from froze over solid. One of Mark's responsibilities was to chop a drinking hole every morning and evening. He continued this ritual through Christmas and on into the New Year. On the afternoon of January 8, 1980, Mark visited our director's mobile home to announce that he had just found Face frozen to death under the dugout ice, his hind foot sticking up where the drinking hole had been cut. He had obviously fallen in the hole while attempting to get a drink. Sandy and the kids were broken up over it, and I felt sick. Not only had our little calf come to a tragic end, but my $135 investment, although perhaps it doesn't seem like much, ended up at the bottom of the ranch dugout.

Through these two specific experiences, we came to understand that there is great power and strength in *spiritual agreement* between a husband and wife. By that I mean that both husband and wife need to feel at peace concerning decisions that affect the family. If I had waited and prayed for even a day more with Sandy, the outcome would have been very different in both of these incidents. The decisions I made were obviously premature, and my timing was definitely off.

Cousin Shannon, Brad, Julie and the calf.

Chapter 18

THE TRUTH WILL SET US FREE

Since the fall of 1971 when I had sustained my serious spine injury, my neck had not bothered me, with the exception of that one incident in our apartment in Montreal. My seventh vertebra never slipped out again, and I really hadn't thought about it for many years.

By 1979, the ranch was growing and prospering wonderfully, and we were into our second summer camping season. Our expectations were for an increase from 300 ranchers to over 600, an average of 60 per week. Most of our staff were quite athletic and loved to participate in the different outdoor games with the ranchers. One such game, to which an Edmonton church youth group introduced us to, was called Capture The Flag. We later refined it and renamed it, "Christians and Communists."

Virtually the whole camp would divide into two groups. The object of the game was for the Christians to smuggle their pretend Bibles across enemy lines to a prescribed area. Of course the Communist team would do all they could to prevent them from succeeding. The teams would wear armbands made from pieces of garbage bags of two different colours. The enemy would be taken out of commission by simply tearing off their armbands. Young people and staff alike sometimes got carried away. In the heat of the moment and in their exuberance, there were some minor physical bumps and bruises. I was one such casualty.

I was trying to avoid being put out of commission by a couple of campers, when, out of nowhere, one of the exuberant staff, Bernie, physically tackled me around the ankles, and I mean *physically*. Bernie, an ex-pro hockey player, was as strong as an ox. He knocked me flying, and I landed hard on my left side, jamming my shoulder into the hard clay. In the few moments after the dust settled, I realized that I was all right, though somewhat shaken. The game ended shortly after that, and everyone headed to the tuck shop for a sweet treat before evening campfire. During the fireside meeting that night, I noticed a few twinges of pain in my left arm but didn't think much of it. It wasn't until I awoke the next morning with throbbing pain down the arm in that old familiar place that I realized my seventh vertebra must have slipped out again.

For the next month, a number of us prayed on different occasions for the Lord to heal me of the nagging injury, but it persisted and gradually grew worse. God had been teaching us about relying on His promises and standing on His word, no matter what life's circumstances dished out. So I patiently waited and stood the test of faith, continually praising God for His promise of healing, even though the manifestation wasn't there. The pain grew more intense, but I just kept confessing with my mouth that *by His stripes I was healed,* trying to believe in my heart, according to 1 Peter 2:24.

I was sure I knew what was causing the pain, so I didn't bother to have a doctor check it out. Besides, we were in the middle of camp, and I didn't want to take the time to drive all the way into Stettler. I didn't have a problem with seeing a doctor; I just didn't think it was necessary at the time. I think that we too often run to the doctor for minor aliments, instead of going to our Great Physician, Jesus, and giving Him a chance first. If I had thought it was really serious, I am sure I would have had it checked out.

The second week in August, Sandy and I were made aware of a Full Gospel Business Men's Convention that was being held in Edmonton. We decided to run up one evening and take in a meeting, which was strange because we had never before left the ranch during the camping season, for any reason. The Full Gospel Business Men's Ministry had blessed us both before, and I had shared my personal testimony at a number of different chapters in British Columbia, Alberta, and Saskatchewan. I wasn't thinking in terms of my physical problem when I decided to go that night. Sandy and I were in need of a spiritual refreshing, and we really went on that basis alone. Bernie and Bernice were directing the camp program, and we knew they were very capable of handling everything while we were away.

After a two-and-a-half-hour drive, we arrived in Edmonton early for the meeting and were able to secure a seat near the front of the ballroom in the Edmonton Inn. Sandy and I were greatly refreshed and ministered to by the Lord during the time of praise and worship. A number of businessmen shared their personal testimonies that evening, and that, too, was a tremendous blessing to us.

The main speaker, Earl Moore from Texas, spoke for about 40 minutes concerning his life and how God had turned him right side up after he gave his life to Jesus. He then made an altar call, which has been the custom of the Full Gospel Business Men's Fellowships all over the world.

A number of people went forward for prayer, some to surrender their lives to Jesus for the first time and others to pray for different spiritual, emotional, and physical needs.

As I stood by my seat, praising God for what He was doing in the lives of those who were being prayed for, the Holy Spirit spoke to my heart and said, *"Go up there and ask for prayer, and receive your healing."*

I turned to Sandy and asked her to go up with me. When we reached the front, the Canadian President of Full Gospel, Jim Jarvis, met us.

"Hello, Garry. Hello, Sandy." He greeted us with his usual warm, friendly smile. "What are you guys doing here? I thought you'd be down at the ranch. It's sure good to see you two. What can I pray for you tonight?"

"Well, Jim," I replied, "I've been battling a severe pain in my left arm for over a month, and it seems to be getting worse. I slipped a vertebra in my neck back in 1971, and the symptoms were exactly the same. I'm sure it's the same problem."

"Come over here and sit in this chair," he said. "I want to check your feet to see if your spine is out at all."

I had seen this method of ministry done before at a few other Full Gospel meetings, and frankly, I wasn't really sure if it was truly the way God operated. I had witnessed people's backs apparently being healed when their feet would grow out after prayer offered on their behalf. However, there was still that element of doubt. Would God really heal someone that way?

As you can see, I was more than a little doubtful when I sat down in the chair. Jim asked me to sit back all the way in the hard chair, and he lifted my feet together, holding them in his hands.

"Look, Sandy. Watch what Jesus is about to do," he said confidently. "These legs are out by five eighths of an inch. Your spine must really be out of whack so . . ."

Sandy stood directly behind Jim, staring over his shoulder and watched intently as he knelt in front of me.

"We're going to ask Jesus to heal this problem right now—if that's okay with you?"

"Go for it," I said.

Jim offered a simple prayer to our Heavenly Father in the name of Jesus. Before I even felt anything happening, Sandy let out a little gasp.

"His leg just shot out. They're both the same length. That's incredible!" she exclaimed.

The pain instantly left.

"I'm healed, praise God, I'm healed," I blurted out. "My arm never felt better."

We all were excited, and we praised the Lord for His wonderful healing power.

As Sandy and I were about to leave, Jim grabbed me by the arm and said, "Garry, would you consider coming to our men's breakfast tomorrow and testifying about your healing tonight? I know it would be a great blessing to everyone if you would."

"I would love to, Jim, but we are expected back at the ranch tonight. Tell you what—I'll call home and see if I can arrange it. I'll make the call from the pay phone in the lobby."

After I talked with Bernie, he thought it would be great if we stayed on, and so I felt comfortable with it.

The next morning, I rose early for the breakfast and felt just terrific. I had slept like a baby. It had been so long since I had been free of that constant pain. Jim agreed to get me on first thing so we could get back to the ranch as soon as possible. When the dishes had been cleared, he stood up to the microphone and began to introduce me. In the middle of the introduction, the pain came back into my arm, worse than it had ever been before. My arm throbbed and throbbed with a sharp, pulsating pain.

Oh, no! What am I going to do?

Then this voice inside my head began to speak: *"Are you going to stand up there and lie to these people? You're not healed. Your vertebra has slipped out worse than it ever has before. Are you going to lie?"*

Just then a quiet, peaceful voice cut into the conversation in my head. *"Son, you were not healed last night. I healed you nearly 2,000 years ago. Does not my Word declare that by my stripes you were healed? You just received it last night. Tell the people that and nothing more. If you speak what my Word says, you can't possibly tell a lie. My Word is Truth."*

The faith that rose up within my heart was powerful. I stood to the podium with absolute confidence and began to speak. I shared about how I had been injured and how I had re-injured my neck that summer. Then I said, "Last night Jim prayed for me, and I received my healing. You see, Jesus purchased it for me almost 2,000 years ago, and I just received it last night."

The pain left instantly, and, at the time of this writing, I have been free from it for over 22 years. Thirty minutes later, Sandy and I hopped into the van and headed back to Halkirk. We couldn't wait to share the great news with our staff.

Jesus said, "Then you will know the truth, and the truth will set you free" (John 8:32).

Chapter 19

THE TRIP OF A LIFETIME

The summer camping season of 1981 had come to a close, and Circle Square Ranch was once again into off-season retreats. This segment of our yearly calendar moved at a much slower pace and was a welcomed and much-needed rest for all the permanent staff. One of the tremendous blessings of the ranch camp also being a retreat centre was that we were privileged to have many different churches and denominational groups visit our facilities. From my early years as a child of God, my heart was touched with a concern for the unity of the Body of Christ. Being involved in ministry with Crossroads and David Mainse was a wonderful blessing to me. David's love for all of God's people, regardless of their denominational affiliation, was central in the Crossroads' ministry. His burden for unity of the church was very obvious to all who knew him.

At Circle Square Ranch we were blessed to meet and fellowship with numerous other church bodies, both charismatic and non-charismatic. Through our many associations, we learned to appreciate how each had its own unique revelation of the many-faceted Christ, who is too wonderful and great for one denomination alone to contain. Although we humans do sometimes put God in our denominational boxes, He is far too large to remain there. A wonderful woman of God once said, "One thing that I have discovered is that the more I have come to know God, the less I know Him. He keeps getting bigger, and I keep getting smaller."

Although the summer camping season was a physical drain, with 16-hour days for 10 consecutive weeks, Sandy and I decided that we would wait until the end of the year before we took our holidays. We chose December 28 to January 12, so that we could attend some conferences in the southwest USA. The first was a Full Gospel Business Men's Regional Convention in Phoenix. The second was the World Deeper Life Conference in Los Angeles, and the last was a conference on faith in Anaheim. Along with the three conferences, we were looking forward to spending some time with our dear friend and spiritual father, Larry Kerychuk.

When Sandy and I arrived in Phoenix, we were pleasantly surprised to find Bob and Sandy Nelson, who had just flown in the day before. Larry had purposely kept their visit a secret from us and knew we would be excited to see them. We hadn't seen or heard from the Nelsons for a couple of years.

At the time of our arrival, Larry was heavily involved in putting together an evangelistic outreach at the Fiesta Bowl in Tempe on New Year's Day. He had been working with a few of the players from Penn State, so he asked Bob and me if we would like to meet with a couple of them for breakfast the day before the game.

Larry arranged the meeting at a small Spanish restaurant the next morning at 9:00 a.m. The five of us sat down in a U-shaped booth, and Bob and I were introduced to Keith Brown, the Penn State centre, and Leo Wizaluski, one of their defensive ends. I soon realized that Keith and Leo were on fire for God and full of His Spirit. There was a boldness and yet a sweet tenderness about them both.

Larry, as the one who knew all of us, carried most of the conversation.

"Garry," he began, "could you share with the guys your testimony of when you were voted the outstanding Canadian Player in the 1973 Grey Cup? I think it will be a real encouragement to Keith and Leo."

I began my story at the point where Sandy was impressed with the thought that if I should win that award, I would be handed a golden opportunity to share Jesus' love with millions of people at one time. I went on to tell them how God had given it to me by enabling me to play the finest game of my life, and then I shared what I had said during the postgame interview.

Just then, Larry interrupted.

"Bob, why don't you tell us what was happening on your side of the camera when you saw this football player talking about Jesus."

"I was absolutely disgusted," Bob began. "What right has some jock to talk about God? He wasn't no priest. That religious stuff, I thought, belongs in a church—not at a Grey Cup game." Bob proceeded to take us back to his earlier life and began to recount how he had become a slave to alcohol.

Just then, a man with a glass of beer in his hand came sliding over to the end of our booth on a chair equipped with casters.

"Are you guys talking about God?" he blurted out.

"Yes, as a matter of fact, we are," Larry replied without hesitation.

"Do you mind if I join you? I would like to hear what you guys have to say."

Larry handled our introductions, and the man introduced himself as Halley Yekel.

Then Larry looked across the table at Bob and said, "Why don't you continue on with your testimony?"

As Bob talked of his enslavement to alcohol, Halley seemed to hang on every word. Of course everything Bob said spoke volumes to Halley. A man doesn't sit and drink a beer by himself at nine o'clock in the morning unless he has a real drinking problem.

After Bob talked of his conversion experience and deliverance, Larry turned to Halley and began to ask him questions about his own personal relationship with God. He opened up and began to share with us of his horrendous experiences in Vietnam. I could hardly believe the horrid stories he relayed of young children being slaughtered. Halley poured out his heart to us, and finally Larry asked, "Halley, would you like to receive Jesus Christ as your personal Saviour and Lord?"

"Uh, yes, I would, but how do I do that?"

"We'll all just bow our heads and Garry will lead you in a prayer," Larry explained, "and if you are serious, the Lord Jesus will come into your heart."

"Can you pray . . . in a restaurant?" Halley asked, his eyes surveying the room.

Just then Bob Nelson piped in, pointing to the beer, which Halley hadn't touched since arriving at our table.

"Mister, if you can drink Satan's puke in a restaurant, you can pray for sure."

"Yah, I guess you're right!" he agreed. "Let's pray."

He grabbed my left hand and squeezed it so hard, I thought my wedding ring would cut through the skin. Halley followed me as I led him in a long prayer.

A few moments later he raised his head and opened his eyes. His very countenance had literally changed and was reflecting the inner joy and peace he was feeling. Halley was a new man. It says in 2 Corinthians 5:17, "Therefore if anyone is in Christ, he is a new creation; the old has gone, the new has come!"

There is nothing on this earth that can compare with the joy experienced when one lost soul is found. The Scripture also says, "Even the angels in heaven rejoice over one sinner who repents."

God's timing is always perfect. By His wonderful grace, He had brought all of us together that morning to share His love and forgiveness with Halley. Of all the restaurants in Phoenix, we had been led to that particular one for a divine appointment. We all left the restaurant that morning ready to soar like eagles, supercharged with the Spirit of God.

Bob and I returned with Larry to his home, and Keith and Leo headed back to their hotel to join their team-mates in preparation for next day's game against the powerful University of Southern California Trojans.

The Trojans were highly favoured as, in many an expert's opinion, they boasted the top running back in the country—the great Marcus Allen. I didn't have the opportunity to watch the guys play that next afternoon, as Sandy and I attended the Full Gospel Business Men's Convention over at the Hyatt Regency. After the evening meeting was over, I called Larry at home to see how the game had gone.

"What an incredible game! Penn State won. Leo played the game of his life and spent most of the first 30 minutes in USC's backfield. It was unbelievable! He personally held Marcus Allen to 15 yards rushing in the first half. Leo was voted the Outstanding Defensive Player of the game, and he gave a bold, clear witness for Jesus on national TV to millions of people. Alleluia! Praise the Lord!"

From there Leo went on to win the same award again in the Hula Bowl and later in the Japan Bowl as well. Each time, he gave a bold witness of his faith in Christ to many millions of people.

Once again, I was awed at the amazing timing of the Lord. In His sovereign will, He had brought the six of us together for Halley's salvation, and to bring a witness for Jesus to millions of lost souls watching the three successive bowls in two different countries. Psalm 34 says, "The eyes of the Lord are on the righteous and his ears are attentive to their cry."

Of course, Christians are righteous in God's eyes only because of the righteousness of Jesus, not on any of our own merits. By our faith in Jesus alone and by His blood atoning for our sin, we are declared righteous by God.

It's Time to Clean House

Sandy and I flew out the next day for Los Angeles to take in the World Deeper Life Conference, which was being held at the fabulous

Bonaventure Hotel. I was especially excited because one of the main speakers advertised was Dr. Edwin Louis Cole. A set of Dr Cole's teaching tapes, which were given to me a year earlier, had blessed my socks off. Dr. Cole was truly a man's man, and he was anointed with a tremendous ministry to men. As a gifted communicator, he travelled extensively, teaching his famous seminar on Maximum Manhood. The sole reason I had suggested to Sandy that we take in this conference was that I wanted to hear Dr. Cole in person.

He was scheduled to speak in the last morning session on the second day, and I excitedly anticipated the ministry I was about to receive. Somehow I was sure that my life would be revolutionized. Dr. Cole was due up at 11:00, so the other morning sessions couldn't move fast enough for me. As expected, the moderator rose to the platform to introduce the speaker, but instead he called up another young man from Nigeria, who spent the next fifteen minutes giving his personal testimony. What he had to share was great, but by the time he finished there was only forty minutes left for Dr. Cole. As I looked at my watch, the moderator once again deviated from the schedule and called another brother from Zambia to testify as well. He spoke for almost thirty minutes, so by the time Dr. Cole climbed the stage to the podium, there was only ten minutes left until the conference lunch break. Dr. Cole handled himself graciously and suggested that he share a short story during the time remaining, as there obviously wasn't sufficient time to deliver the message he had intended.

Maybe Dr. Cole was able to handle the last-minute change, but I certainly wasn't. I sat in my seat and silently boiled. *What's wrong with you people?* I thought to myself. *I've flown thousands of miles to hear this anointed man of God speak, and you give him ten minutes to tell a short anecdote!* The anger inside me continued to grow, so much so that Dr. Cole's words barely registered.

Suddenly the meeting was over and it was lunchtime. Earlier, Sandy and I had found a nice little restaurant on the fifth floor of the ten-floor shopping plaza, dwarfed by the four towers of the hotel rooms, which were an additional twenty-five floors each.

"Would you like to have lunch at the same place again, Garry?" Sandy's voice interrupted my thoughts.

"No!" I barked back at her. "I'm not hungry."

"Are you feeling sick?"

"You bet I am. I can't believe these people took up all of Dr. Cole's teaching time. How could anyone be so insensitive? I came all this way just to hear him, and he doesn't even get to speak. I thought we were coming to a spiritually uplifting conference. That moderator is out to lunch. I used to have some respect for the guy, but he just lost what little I had for him."

"Maybe we'd better go back to the room," said Sandy. "I've never seen you like this before—you're fit to be tied."

"You'd better believe I am. Let's go up to the room. Nothing would taste good right now anyway."

We headed for the elevator. As we entered our hotel room, I began to pace back and forth. I was so agitated that I couldn't possibly sit still.

Sandy, sensing my turmoil, offered to help the only way she could.

"Honey, would you like me to pray for you?"

"Go right ahead," I responded. "It sure won't hurt."

She carefully placed her small hand on my left shoulder and prayed softly.

"Please, Lord, help Garry through this."

Then she began to pray in the Spirit in her prayer language.

After a minute or so, I wheeled around and said, "Thanks a lot, but that didn't do a thing for me."

Praise God, she didn't give up that easily, and continued to pray.

"Oh Lord, Garry's in real trouble. Please take this heart of stone and change it to a heart of flesh. Thank you, Jesus."

Seconds later I threw myself on my face on the bed. A dam burst from somewhere deep in my soul and gushed forth uncontrollably. I wept bitterly for close to an hour, until there were no more tears left. God graciously revealed the bitterness of my heart that had been pent up for years. The incident with Dr. Cole had just brought it to the surface. During that precious hour, God showed me many different people that I had judged in my heart. Each time He revealed another one, I poured out my heart in true repentance.

At last, when the cleansing process was completed, the Lord began to fill me with His incredible unconditional love, first for me, then for many others, and finally for Sandy. Suddenly, I saw her as God saw her and for what she really was, and she was absolutely perfect. The revelation of the way God looks at His children, through the finished work of the Cross, and hidden in Christ, completely overwhelmed my soul. When I finally rose from the bed and looked into Sandy's face, she was radiant.

"Darling," I said, "you are absolutely gorgeous. There isn't anything that I would change, even if I could. God made you perfect."

"I've been trying to tell you that all along," she laughed.

"I know, Honey. God has just given me a new set of eyes. They're His. I can now see you and everyone else as He does. As far as I'm concerned, God made you for me, and He did a perfect job."

For the next three days, Sandy and I walked on a cushion of air. We basked in God's wonderful love and the world seemed to drop into slow motion. During those three incredible days, we often went until two or three in the afternoon before realizing that we hadn't eaten anything yet. Food just didn't seem to be important, except for the purpose of keeping up our strength.

The desire to tell others about this wonderful loving God grew with intensity. It just seemed natural to introduce Jesus to them, as anyone would their best friend.

There were three days between the Los Angeles Conference and the Anaheim Conference, so Sandy and I booked the extra nights at the Bonaventure Hotel with the thought of taking in some of the sights. We had enjoyed a wonderful day at Knott's Berry Farm a few years earlier with Bruce and Brigitte Lemmerman and were looking forward to visiting there again. Having obtained directions from the hotel clerk, we hopped on a city bus in front of the hotel and headed for a relaxing day at Knott's Berry.

We took a seat near the centre of the bus and sat back to enjoy the 30-minute ride. As we were being seated, I noticed a young couple sitting just behind us who were engrossed in a serious conversation. They were talking quite loudly and seemed to be unaware that everyone on the bus could hear them. My ears perked up as I picked up the conversation.

"I've just purchased a $25,000 insurance policy, and I've named you as the beneficiary," she said. "In case I die, I want the money to go to you, Tom. You're my only brother and my only kin. It also has a double indemnity clause in it, so if I am killed accidentally, you will get $50,000."

As I listened to the lady's words, I was impressed in my spirit to share the Gospel with them. It just seemed like the natural thing to do.

What should I say to them? I asked the Lord quietly in my heart.

"Ask her if she has her death insurance," I heard the Holy Spirit say.

"Thank you, Lord," I whispered and slowly turned to face them.

"Excuse me, I can't help but hear your conversation, and I would like to ask you a question. Do you have your death insurance?"

"Yes, I do," she replied. "That's what we were discussing—my Mutual of New York policy."

"I'm sorry, you misunderstand me," I continued. "That's your life insurance. I'm talking about your death insurance."

"What company are you with, Sir?" she asked.

"I'm with the Blessed Assurance Company, Jesus Christ," I replied.

The look on her face reflected her shock, but I was more shocked than she. Those words were completely spontaneous. I had never thought of Jesus in those terms before.

"Are you covered?" I continued.

"What do you mean, am I covered?"

"Are you covered by the Blood? Have you received the sacrifice of Jesus Christ's blood for your sins? Are you sure that you will go to heaven when you die? That's what I mean by 'are you covered?'"

"Well . . . uh . . . uh . . . I don't know about that," she stammered. "Oh! Here's our stop. We have to get off here—bye."

As quickly as the conversation had begun, they were off the bus.

Lord, I thought to myself, *I didn't get to finish. They left too fast.*

"You shared what I wanted you to. That's all I ask."

Suddenly I realized that everyone on the bus was looking at me, and they had been listening to the whole conversation. I had been talking to more than just a couple of young people.

"Where did that come from?" Sandy interjected.

"It must have been the Holy Spirit," I answered. "That was all new to me."

"We need to pray that they will never forget what you said, and that every time they think of insurance, they will remember this moment, until they are saved." Sandy was always the one who was quick to pray.

That day we enjoyed ourselves immensely at Knott's Berry Farm, on occasion pausing to breathe a short prayer for the young couple.

"Miss Direction"

The entire trip to date had been nothing short of incredible, but God wasn't through blessing us yet. We still had another conference to take in. The Conference on Faith was a spiritual eye-opener for both of us, and it lifted us to new heights. The Anaheim Convention Centre was filled to capacity with over 8,000 enthusiastic Christians, all seeking to know God in a deeper way. The times of worship were exhilarating, and God's presence permeated the building.

Part way through the Thursday evening meeting, I sensed the Lord prompting me to leave the meeting. It didn't make sense. I was thoroughly enjoying myself and receiving the ministry. However, I was learning to obey that still, small voice within, so I immediately turned to Sandy and said, "Honey, I feel the Lord is telling us to leave right now."

"Where do you think we are supposed to go?"

"That restaurant down the street where we had lunch today," I quickly answered.

"Well, we'd better get going then," Sandy agreed.

Minutes later, as we stood inside the restaurant entrance waiting for the waitress to seat us, I was still puzzled as to why we had been prompted to leave such a great meeting.

"Smoking or non-smoking?" the young hostess asked.

"Non-smoking, please," Sandy replied. "Smoke gives me an awful headache."

"Follow me, please."

What happened next had to have been totally orchestrated by the Lord. A handful of people were seated in the large area to our left, and none of them appeared to be smoking. To our right was a long, narrow area with booths along the windows and a long counter running parallel to them. Seated three-quarters of the way down were two men with their backs to us, and they were both smoking. The hostess seemed to be oblivious to this fact: she sat us directly across from them and walked back to the front counter.

"Uh, Miss ! Miss!" I called as she turned and walked away. She didn't respond and kept right on going, as if she were deaf.

"Well, Dear," I said apologetically, "maybe their smoke won't blow over this way."

As we sat down, Sandy picked up the strong smell of the smoke and wanted to move to another booth as far away as possible, but before we could get up again, her bionic ear picked up the two men's conversation.

"Just a minute," she said. "One of those men is witnessing to the other. Maybe we should stay here and pray."

"Okay," I agreed.

Within a few seconds, we both could hear the conversation much more clearly.

"My Lord!" I whispered. "He isn't witnessing for Jesus; he's witnessing for the devil."

"You're right," Sandy replied. "We need to intercede right now."

We clasped hands across the table and began to pray softly under our breath. It is times like this when you are thankful that you are able to pray in tongues. It was certain that we did not know how to pray in English for this situation, other than to bind the powers of darkness. The two of us hadn't been praying for more than 30 seconds when the young man on the right, who was on the listening end of the conversation, jumped to his feet and said, "You're crazy, man. I'm getting out of here."

He immediately took off to the men's washroom, as if his life depended on it.

Suddenly the other man wheeled around on the bar stool and looked in our direction. I tried to catch his attention, but he seemed to be staring directly above our heads. He looked severely agitated. Without a word, he stood up and quickly headed for the exit, disappearing out the door.

Moments later the first young man returned from the washroom. As he approached our booth, I smiled up at him and said, "Young man, would you like to hear about the real Jesus?"

"Yes, I would," he replied. "Man, that guy was weird. Would you believe he was making the train in that picture on the wall move? He gave me the creeps."

"Come, sit down and have a coffee with us," I said. "We're Garry and Sandy Lefebvre. What's your name?"

"Victor's my name. Nice to meet you," he replied as he sat down next to Sandy. Five minutes later, after we shared the simple Gospel message, young Victor bowed his head, prayed a prayer of repentance and received Jesus into his heart.

As he lifted his head, a middle-aged lady appeared next to our booth, looked at Victor and said, "Did you just receive Jesus into your life, young man?"

"Yes, I did," he answered a little timidly.

"Well, God has given me a ministry in leading Christians in the Baptism of the Holy Spirit. You need to be filled with the power of God, Son. Would you like to come over to our table?"

"Yeah, okay—if it's all right with these folks."

"Sure, that's great," I said. "This lady will lead you in the next important step. Welcome to the family of God, Victor."

He shook our hands and thanked us, then left with the lady and her other companions. We never did see him again, but we are confident we will see him in heaven some day.

That evening, as we lay in bed, I reflected on the goodness and the perfect timing of the Lord. My mind went back to the winter of 1975, when I had first witnessed God move in this way. That was when I first realized that, as I committed my way unto the Lord on a daily basis, my every step was under His control. That year, over 50 football players and their wives, along with twenty-five or so Christian businessmen, met in Calgary for the Third Annual Athletes In Action Conference. The meetings were held in southwest Calgary at the Holiday Inn on McLeod Trail. It was a tremendous time of learning and encouragement, while the athletes, their wives, and business people were being challenged to become more deeply committed to the cause of Christ. The speakers the Lord had sent to minister were outstanding and all of them delivered great motivational messages.

The conference began on Thursday evening and concluded Sunday after lunch. There were players and wives in attendance from all nine CFL teams, and business people from all over Canada. These off-season conferences, which started back in 1973 under the direction of Larry Kerychuk, were a wonderful source of inspiration for all of us, and many players and family members made first-time commitments to Christ during these great times together. Throughout the course of the weekend, many of our hearts were knitted together in the love of God. When the 1975 conference drew to a close, many a tear was shed as the goodbyes were said and loving hugs exchanged. The family of God is closer than any earthly family could possibly be. When God blends hearts together, there is nothing, in terms of human relationships, that can compare.

Sandy and I had driven to Calgary with Ron and Debbie Estay, after picking them up at the Edmonton International Airport that Thursday. They had flown in from Louisiana that afternoon. We planned to drive them back to the airport on the way back home. At the conclusion of the conference, the four of us headed north to Edmonton. When we had been on the road for about twenty minutes, I noticed that we were very close to the home of some dear Christian friends, the Shermans, who lived in northeast Calgary.

"Why don't we drop in and say hi?" I suggested. "I'd like you guys to meet the Shermans. They're the parents of Jerry, the Campus Crusade for Christ Director at the University of Alberta."

Since we were all in agreement, we exited on McKnight Boulevard and pulled up at their home minutes later. When you are part of the family of God, you can drop in at unexpected times and be assured of your welcome, just as you would be at your natural sister or brother's house. None of us had any inkling that our last-minute decision to drop in was part of God's wonderful plan.

We all were invited in for tea. Of course Ron would never turn down food, so the rest of us thought it best to not let him eat alone. The Shermans were gracious hosts, and we fellowshipped with them for over two hours. Realizing the long drive that was still before us, I finally suggested that we hit the road.

As we were gradually heading for the door, Ron, right out of the blue, turned to Debbie and said, "Deb, do you have my car keys?"

She responded with a humorous, matter-of-fact reply: "What would I be doing with your keys, Crocket?" That was her pet name for this robust Cajun who answered to "Swamp Dog" for all his team-mates.

"Deb, they've got to be in your purse, or I left them in my room at the Holiday Inn."

"You'd better have them, or we're in trouble, 'cause I don't know what I've done with my set," Debbie responded, as she rummaged through her saddlebag purse. "I haven't been able to find them since last week."

Sandy and I stood at the top of the stairs with the Shermans, laughing as the Estays bantered back and forth. After two or three minutes of checking and rechecking his pockets, Ron hollered up at me just as he went out the door to search his luggage in the car.

"Garry, would you call the hotel and see if they found the keys in my room?"

I picked up the yellow pages from the telephone table in the hall and located the number. As I dialled the number, I thought to myself, *What am I doing calling the hotel? I don't even know what the keys look like!* Just as the hotel clerk answered, Ron came back in from the car.

"Hello, Ma'am. We were just at your hotel for the AIA Conference. Did you by any chance find a set of keys that might have been left in one of the rooms?"

"Yes, sir," she replied. "There was a set of keys turned in just a few minutes ago. What do your keys look like?"

"Just a moment, please, they actually belong to a friend."

I felt a little foolish asking for a set of keys that I couldn't even describe. I held my hand over the mouthpiece and hollered down to Ron at the bottom of the stairs.

"Ron, they've found some keys. What do yours look like?"

As I tried to hear what Ron was saying and talk to the clerk at the same time, what Ron described and what she said seemed to jive.

"Thank you, Ma'am," I said. "We'll be right down to pick them up. Praise the Lord!" I shouted down to Ron. "Your keys are at the desk. Someone found them and turned them in."

We said goodbye to the Shermans, jumped into my car, and headed south to the Holiday Inn. Thirty minutes later as I pulled the car up to the lobby doors, Ron jumped out and hustled inside to fetch the elusive keys. Debbie made a wisecrack—something about Ron holding onto his keys.

As I watched him disappear through the lobby doors, I received a strong impression to follow him inside. It didn't make any sense to me, as all the players had probably left for home some three hours ago. Although the thought didn't make natural sense, I obeyed it anyway.

As I opened the car door, Sandy said, "Where are you going? Ron will be right back."

"I know, Honey, I just feel I should go inside for some reason."

Ron was standing over at the registration desk talking to the clerk as I entered the lobby. Instead of walking over to him, I felt compelled to go over to the other side towards the entrance to the hotel restaurant. As I strolled under the archway, I sensed that I was going to meet someone. All of a sudden, I heard a familiar voice.

"Oh, my Lord, there he is! I can't believe it!" I glanced in the direction of the voice and my eyes fastened upon the huge saucer-like eyes of Eskimo running back, Keith Barnett. His mouth was hanging open and his face was beaming. There was another man sitting with him, whom I didn't recognize, and he was staring at me too.

"This is unbelievable," Keith exclaimed as I approached the table.

"What's going on?" I questioned.

Keith wiped a tear from his eye as he began to explain.

"My friend Bill and I have been sitting here for the last couple of hours, and I have been sharing the Lord with him. Would you believe that Bill just asked me a question that I don't have an answer for, and I said, 'Oh Lord! If only Garry Lefebvre were here, he could answer your question.' Not seconds later, I looked up and you were standing in the doorway. This is incredible, Garry. What are you doing back here? Didn't you leave for Edmonton hours ago?"

"Well, I did, but obviously the Lord wouldn't let me out of the city. He knew I was needed back here. What was that question, by the way?"

Five minutes later, Bill bowed his head right there in the restaurant and invited Jesus Christ to be the Lord of his life. Keith was still shaking his head as I said goodbye and walked back out to the car to share the good news of Bill's conversion with the others.

I was overwhelmed with God's grace and absolutely perfect timing. He had brought me all the way back there at the precise moment that I needed to arrive, for Keith's sake and especially for Bill's. I was even more amazed when Ron announced that the keys we had returned for were not his. A few minutes later, Debbie pulled the lost keys out of her huge purse. We all broke out in praise to God and hilarious laughter.

"God is truly awesome!" I shouted.

"Amen to that!" chimed Ron.

Chapter 20

BIRTHED IN PRAYER

Sandy and I were blessed with three beautiful children and they had been fortunate enough to be raised in the wonderful atmosphere of Circle Square Ranch. We were both positive that three children was the ideal family for us, although during our engagement I had suggested that we should have four. We had long since forgotten about that and were quite content with our little family. Chéri, Brad, and Julie were now eleven, nine, and seven, respectively, each of them unique in their own special ways.

One cold October day in 1980 while I sat at the kitchen table finishing some paperwork, Sandy stood across from me preparing dinner at the sink. Suddenly I saw a young toddler, who would have been around eighteen months old, run across the floor right between us. The vision lasted for only a second or two and quickly vanished.

What was that? I thought to myself. Then I heard that familiar, still, small voice inside me say, *"That's your new son. I want you and Sandy to have one more child."*

I swallowed hard and spoke to Sandy, who was still standing with her back to me.

"Honey, you will never guess what I believe the Lord just showed me. I just saw a vision of a little boy . . . and then I sensed God telling me that he was our son. I believe He wants us to have one more child."

Sandy spun around faster than I had ever seen her move and with a look of amazement on her face blurted out, "Over my dead body!"

"Hey, watch your confession," I gently rebuked her. "This isn't my idea."

"But Garry, you know what difficulties I've had with my pregnancies. If the Lord wants us to have another child, maybe we can adopt one. I am not going to go through another pregnancy. Besides, you know what the doctor said about my inverted womb. He doesn't think I could ever conceive again."

"Well, I guess it will have to be a miracle then," I said confidently.

"No way," she said stubbornly. "I'm not about to go through another pregnancy. Adopt, yes. Pregnant, no way!"

"It's okay," I assured her. "I told you this isn't my idea. You just pray about it, and the Lord will show you what He wants."

Three months later, after continual prodding from the ranch staff, our children and me, she finally consented not to take any more precautions to prevent conception and to just trust the Lord. The next day I left for a speaking engagement in Regina. That morning, as Sandy was reading the scriptures, God spoke to her out of Isaiah, chapter 11. Her attention fell upon verse 10 and the words "the root of Jesse" (King David's father). Immediately she fell in love with that name and knew that this was God's chosen name for the son who was yet to be conceived.

That same day, when I was standing in the Edmonton International Airport near a newsstand, I sensed the Lord speaking to me. A word jumped out at me, not from a page of the Bible, but from the cover of an issue of *Sports Illustrated*. It was an article about the great Jesse Owens. The word *Jesse* loomed larger than life before me and seemed to block out everything else for a few moments. I instantly knew that this was the name of our son-to-be. Later, after I arrived home and we compared notes, Sandy and I were confident that God had spoken. The name Jesse came to us twice more within the week. Obviously, by now we were absolutely sure what we were to name him, and Sandy felt confident that this new child was definitely the Lord's plan. Our three children were so excited about this new brother-to-be that, for the next two years, they prayed over and over for God to send him. It seemed that Julie wanted this baby brother more than any of us, and she prayed fervently and faithfully that God would answer her heart's desire and bring Jesse to us.

Christmas Eve of 1982 turned out to be a very special time for us. Our family tradition was for each child to open one gift that evening after dinner. As we all sat around the warm crackling fireplace, the children excitedly awaited their gift to be handed to them. Sandy walked over to the tree and picked up three small packages, handing one to each of them. We then instructed them to open the gifts one at a time, starting with the eldest and ending with Julie.

Chéri opened hers right away as the other two peered anxiously over her shoulders. They all looked quite puzzled when the package contained only a small piece of paper with writing on it. The message read, "He is faithful Who has promised. Now open the next one."

Brad opened his package and again there was only a message.

"All things are possible with God. Now open the last one."

"What is this?" Brad exclaimed. "Where are the presents?"

"Julie, you open yours now and you'll see," Sandy and I replied. Quickly she tore open the small box on her lap and stared at the tiny boy doll in her hand.

"Read the note on his neck," I said.

Julie read aloud, "Hi! My name is Jesse. I am seven weeks old and I live in your Mommy's tummy, and I will be here in July."

Julie burst into tears and ran and flung her arms around Sandy's neck and gushed, "I don't care if I ever get another Christmas present. This is the best gift I could ever have!"

Brad was very quiet and looked a little dumbfounded.

"Does this mean you're pregnant?" he said nonchalantly. We all laughed and rejoiced together over God's goodness.

"By the way," Sandy interrupted, "Dad and I were looking at a book of names the other day, and you'll never guess what the name Jesse means."

"What?" Julie responded.

"Would you believe it means 'gift from God'?" I said.

"Oh Mommy, Daddy! This is the greatest gift you could ever give me," she shouted.

"Yes, he truly is a precious gift from Jesus to us all, and I think we should stop right here and thank God for this wonderful blessing," Sandy interjected.

For the next few minutes each of us gave thanks to the Lord for His faithfulness. From that day until the day he arrived, we oftentimes laid hands on Sandy's abdomen and spoke blessings upon baby Jesse. We called him "Precious One." We even sang love songs to him and continually blessed him with the power of our words, telling him how wonderful he was and how blessed we were to have him.

The morning of February 19, 1983, I was awakened at 6:00 a.m. to the sound of Sandy moaning softly.

"What's wrong?" I said sleepily. "Are you all right?"

"Garry, I'm in a lot of pain," she whimpered, "I think I'm having contractions."

"Oh no—you can't be! You're only three months pregnant!"

"The pains are strong and only ten minutes apart." She winced as another strong contraction overcame her.

By this time, I had reached for the phone and was frantically dialing the Stettler Hospital.

"Get dressed!" I yelled, as the receptionist's voice came on the line. "My wife's in labour and she's only three months along!"

"Bring her right in," she replied. "We'll do what we can, although there are no doctors here until later this morning."

I hung up the phone and quickly dressed. Sandy was struggling to put on her shoes when Julie walked up the stairs from her bedroom and stepped into the upstairs hallway.

"What's going on?" she said rubbing her eyes. "Where are you going?"

"Quick! Wake up Chéri and Brad. Mom is in real trouble. I've got to get her to the hospital right away. Pray for Mommy and Jesse. This is really serious," I blurted out.

I'll never forget her little face as she looked up at me and smiled.

"Don't worry, Daddy. God promised."

Little Julie's words, spoken in childlike faith, calmed my fears as quickly as light dispels darkness. Faith rose up in my heart as I calmly replied, "You're absolutely right, Sweetheart. This baby is God's idea, not ours. I'm going to take Mommy to the hospital, but I'm sure that she and Jesse will be just fine."

I helped Sandy into the car and quickly ran back into the house to call my brother Murray and Cathie. I asked him to bring the other ranch staff together immediately to pray and intercede for Sandy and Jesse.

The ride to Stettler took 25 long minutes. We worshipped and sang praises to the Lord all the way there, confident that He would act on our behalf. By the time we arrived at the hospital, Sandy was in too much pain to walk. I carried her into the foyer, where two nurses helped me put her in a wheel chair. They immediately rushed her into a small room to the left of the corridor, while I gave the nurse at the desk all the particulars.

"She's aborting! She's aborting!" the older nurse exclaimed, as the two of them helped her onto a bed. The younger one immediately hooked up an intravenous and began monitoring her vital signs. Minutes later, I entered the room and walked over to take Sandy's hand. Just then, the receptionist stuck her head around the corner and said, "Mr. Lefebvre, there's a phone call for you at the desk."

"I'll be right back, Sweetheart," I assured Sandy and rushed out.

It must be the ranch. Nobody else knows we're here.

Murray's familiar voice greeted me on the other end of the line.

"We've just been praying, and the Lord spoke a word of knowledge through Mac Hyland. It seems that some type of a curse has been put on

Sandy and the baby. You need to take authority over it and break its power."

I thanked him and told him I would let him know as soon as there was any change.

As I headed back to the room, I wondered how I was going to do this with the nurses there. I didn't want to come across as some kind of nut. Strangely enough, as I entered the room, both nurses, as if led by an unseen force, quietly left the room, and Sandy and I were alone. I explained the nature of the call to Sandy, just as she began to have another intense contraction. I immediately placed my hands on her abdomen and began to pray with intensity and authority.

"Devil, in the name of Jesus Christ, get your hands off this child—he belongs to God."

Within seconds the contraction ceased and a calm peace and assurance swept over us. We both began to praise and magnify God.

The head nurse returned moments later and was completely surprised to see Sandy sitting up, out of the woods. However, due to what they called her unstable condition, Sandy was admitted and placed under close observation.

Dr. Karia, Sandy's obstetrician, arrived an hour later and gave her a thorough examination. He then informed us that in her present condition it would be impossible for her to carry the baby to term. It was imperative that her uterus move to its proper, upright position in order for the fetus to have room enough to grow.

During the days that followed, we all waited for this to occur naturally, but to no avail. After five days, she was taken by ambulance to the Red Deer General Hospital to be seen by a specialist in obstetrics. After an extensive examination, he determined that our only option left was surgery. At this point, his main concern was that an operation might be very dangerous for Sandy and possibly fatal for Jesse, but he felt we really didn't have any other choice. The surgery took place that evening. It was successful, thanks to the prayers of many friends and loved ones and, of course, thanks to the doctors as well.

A special rubber device called a pessary was inserted to hold the uterus upright until it was strong enough to stay in its proper position on its own. Sandy experienced a great deal of discomfort for the next nine days, and remarked that it felt like sitting on a broomstick. Then the doctor attempted to remove it under a local anaesthetic, but the procedure was just too painful. We were all concerned about her going under a general anaesthetic again, but we felt we had no other options. We thanked and praised God when Sandy came through the second operation and the womb stayed in place with no apparent harm to Jesse. The rest of the pregnancy went without further difficulty. Jesse was due right in the middle of camping season, so we had to trust the Lord for good timing.

The week Jesse was to arrive, we were blessed to have a guest speaker at camp, which was a rarity. Bob Holland was an anointed schoolteacher from Montana. The 1983 camping season was as physically taxing as ever, and the staff really looked forward to Saturday evenings after the rodeo, when they all had the night off. Most of the staff headed for Stettler, and Sandy, Bob, and I decided to go there for dinner as well. Just as we were finishing our dessert, Sandy informed us that she had been experiencing labour pains for the past hour.

"It's not for awhile," she informed us. "The pains are quite irregular and about 20 or 25 minutes apart. It will be some time yet before this precious one arrives."

"Why don't we go for a walk over towards the hospital?" Bob suggested.

"Perhaps the walk will speed things up," I added. We were all in agreement, so we went for a stroll down Main Street. We met some staff and informed them that Sandy was getting close.

As we strolled slowly down the street, carloads of teenage staff would holler at us as they passed by, "Is it time yet?" By the time we arrived at the hospital, the word was out, and about fifteen staff members were there to meet us. The contractions were not any stronger yet, but we decided to go into the emergency anyway.

The nurse on duty examined Sandy, and she suggested that we all go home and come back later when the pains were about five minutes apart. Then almost as an afterthought, she added, "If you would feel more comfortable, you could stay here if you like. We do have an empty bed, and we can call your husband when you're more fully dilated."

"What should I do, Garry?" Sandy asked.

"I don't know," I replied, "but I think we should pray and see what the Lord says." We joined hands and prayed, and I heard a distinct word in my spirit, *"Stand still and see the salvation of the Lord."*

"I feel God is telling us that you should stay here," I said, "but I'll go back out to the waiting room and see if Bob confirms it."

Bob felt very strongly that Sandy should stay right where she was. I went back to her room and assured her that I would be back in plenty of time to be in the delivery room with her. I wouldn't miss Jesse's arrival for anything.

I kissed her, and Bob and I left for Circle Square Ranch, thirty miles away. We figured it would be at least five or six hours before I would need to be back. We stopped for a coffee for about a half-hour and then headed for home.

As we drove up to the Texas gate, we were met by some of the staff driving out to find us.

"Get back to the hospital!" they yelled out the window, "Sandy is having the baby!"

I turned the car around and headed back to the hospital as fast as I dared. Twenty minutes later I arrived to find Sandy in heavy labour, with her contractions five minutes apart. She told me that right after we had left, Dr. Karia had come in to see another patient. When he realized she was there, he examined Sandy only to discover that her membranes were bulging and her water was on the verge of bursting. He wanted to break the membrane right away, because this would help bring on hard labour. She asked him if he would wait until she could phone me at the ranch, as I definitely wanted to be there for the delivery. He reluctantly agreed to wait. When Sandy returned to her room after making the call, Dr. Karia decided to give her another internal examination. As he examined her, he found that the umbilical cord was wrapped twice around Jesse's neck. Thank God he was able to slip it off before hard labour began.

Sandy continued in intense labour for the next four hours, and Jesse arrived right on schedule at 3:15 a.m., July 31, 1983. Our miracle boy entered this world without any complications; however, he did come down the birth canal so fast at the end that Sandy was bruised right down to her knees. I'm almost sure I detected a bit of a smile in the corners of his little mouth. From his entrance into our lives, Jesse has been an incredible blessing to the entire family. In turn, he has been the recipient of loads of love, a response to the joy he has brought all of us from day one. The only real difficulty we had with him in his early years was when Brad or Julie would argue over whose turn it was to have Jesse sleep in their bed. To this day, Jesse has continued to be a loving and obedient son who has been blessed with a kind and gentle nature. He has indeed been a precious gift from God.

Jesse at 6 months

Jesse at 4 years

Shot Between the Eyes

Our experience with Jesse wasn't the first time that God miraculously intervened during those years.

During our eight-year stay at the ranch, it was often my joy to take in young people who needed help getting their lives on track. In exchange for room and board, we required them to help out around the place. There was always a need for more help. Relatives, friends, and other concerned Christians often sent these youth to us. Most of them were quite helpful; some were a real handful. On occasion, one or two campers stayed on for a time after summer camping season ended.

A 16-year-old lad was one of these holdovers. We will call him Jim in order to protect his family. Jim's mother had volunteered her time in the kitchen that summer of 1980, so when she asked us to keep him on for awhile, I was happy to oblige. His help would be welcome—there were a lot of preparations needed to get ready for the fall and winter retreat season. For the most part, Jim was a pretty decent, well-mannered young man while he was with us. It was when he hung around his peers back in Edmonton that he seemed to get into trouble. After a few months, he earned my trust and I gave him free rein of the ranch property. I decided to keep him on through the winter and possibly right through until the next summer's camping season. Jim was very helpful to us and carried out his duties and responsibilities, in addition to faithfully attending morning staff devotions and Thursday evening Bible studies.

On the afternoon of May 5, 1981, I returned to my house from the barn after helping with the chores. As I stepped onto the back porch, I beheld an open vision right before my eyes. This experience was similar to the vision I had had of our yet-unconceived Jesse, six months earlier. But this one was of a very different nature. Before my very eyes, I saw my ten-year-old son Brad lying dead in a coffin. I immediately began to rebuke the devil and bind the satanic forces, declaring that Brad was a child of God and therefore under God's protection. I lingered there on the porch landing for a couple more minutes, praying in tongues, until I sensed a release in my spirit. Not wanting to worry Sandy unnecessarily, I kept the experience to myself and pondered it in my heart through the rest of the day. For several years now, Sandy and I had known that Brad had the call of God upon his life. If the Holy Spirit had been warning me of a satanic attempt on Brad's life, I was confident that God would intervene. I felt quite at peace about it.

A few years earlier, when Brad had just turned six, he told us an amazing story. We were sitting at the breakfast table when he informed us that he had dreamed the night before that he had gone to heaven and seen Jesus.

"Mom," he said, "did you know that heaven has golden floors?"

For the next 15 minutes, he described in amazing detail this incredible experience. He spoke of angels around the throne of God. Some had wings and some didn't, while others had wheels with hundreds of eyes around them. Brad told us that Jesus had taken him by the hand and led him to a beautiful city. Near the city was a river of crystal clear water, which had trees with luscious fruit growing along its banks. Finally, he said that Jesus had told him he had to go back, because he had a job for him to do on the earth. From that day on, Brad has never feared death in the slightest, and we knew that he was definitely called of God.

Two days after my vision of Brad in the coffin, Sandy and I took Julie to Calgary to see the dentist. We left Brad and Chéri with my mom at the ranch hotel. When we returned the following evening, we were immediately informed that Brad had been rushed to the hospital in Stettler earlier that afternoon. He had been shot between the eyes from six inches away with a 22-caliber blank. Young Jim had taken the ranch's 22 rifle that afternoon and gone gopher hunting. When he returned, he found some blank shells in the hotel and began shooting them off as he sat out on the front porch. When Brad heard the gunshots, he went out to investigate. Suddenly, Jim wheeled around, held the barrel just inches from Brad's face and said, "Say your prayers, Brad—you're going to heaven."

The gun went off and knocked little Brad to the ground. The impact from the blast hit him dead center between the eyes and flattened the bridge of his poor little nose. The ranch staff rushed him to the Stettler General Hospital, but they had no way to get in touch with Sandy and me as we were en route from Calgary. When Brad was examined, the doctor found fourteen tiny metal fragments deeply embedded in his left eye.

Mac and Irene Hyland drove Sandy and me to Stettler to find our son. He was handling the whole affair extremely well and was very happy to see us. He had already forgiven Jim for shooting him and was very much at peace. That evening, we were informed that Brad had to be sent immediately by ambulance to the Red Deer Hospital for an operation on his eye. At midnight, the ambulance came and took Brad to Red Deer. Mac and Irene and Sandy and I stayed up the entire night interceding for our son. Thankfully, the operation went well, and they were able to remove twelve of the fourteen particles from his eye. The remaining two were embedded so deeply that the doctor would have been unable to remove them without causing permanent damage to his sight. Today these particles are still there in his eye, yet he enjoys 20-20 vision—once again a testimony of the grace of God.

I have never known anyone who has undergone more accidents and health problems than our son. Beginning with the three operations immediately after birth, Brad has come through five car accidents, one motorcycle accident, seven major intestinal operations, a collar bone broken in two places, a fractured ankle, and numerous sprained ankles culminating in an Evans repair. And on top of all that, at the age of six he was kicked in the side of the head by a wild horse. In spite of the constant barrage of attacks on Brad's physical body, his faith has grown stronger. Through it all, God has given him an unwavering faith and a passion to reach young people through music. In 1997, Brad released his first CD entitled *Cry Out*. Eight of the ten songs on the album are his own compositions, birthed out of life's adversities. His heart's desire is to be known as a worshipper of his God.

CFLer's son makes a vocal debut

POP

BY STEVEN SANDOR

*Pre*VUE

Brad Lefebvre

Garry Lefebvre enjoyed an 11-year career in the Canadian Football League as a wide receiver and punter for both the Edmonton Eskimos and the Montréal Alouettes.

Now, 20 years after his dad retired from the game, son Brad Lefebvre is kicking off his musical career.

The junior Lefebvre is celebrating the release of his debut independently-released CD, *Cry Out*. With a mix of both up-tempo tunes and ballads, Lefebvre hopes his music has the right mix to attract youngsters to his inspirational message.

"I've been singing since I was six years old," says Lefebvre. "I've always had an ear for music and a love for singing. I tried to record an album before but it didn't work out at the time. But then this opportunity came up and my friends were saying I should go for it. So I decided 'yeah, let's go for it.'"

The recording session lasted from January of this year to the middle of May. Lefebvre has pressed 1,000 copies of his new disc and 300 cassettes.

Lefebvre doesn't feel that his music is voiceless. In fact, he counters that his lyrics carry a strong message.

"I have always had a strong connection with young people. I hope young people can start to see my inspirational message. My music carries a message of hope.

"My message is that there isn't anything in the world that you can't achieve." ●

Brad Lefebvre
CD Release Party
West Edmonton Christian Association
Sept. 12

VUE WEEKLY
ISSUE # 102
Sept 11 - A, 1997

Brad & Bev

Chapter 21

ANGELS WATCHING OVER US

As my 11-year professional football career came to a close, the Lord's favour was upon me. For many professional athletes, there are certain feelings of emptiness and a very real vacant spot when their careers are over. For me, it was quite the opposite. It was the closing of one thrilling chapter of my life and the opening of an even more exciting one. I left the football field to work in God's great harvest field, and the vision that the Lord had given me left no room for looking back to what used to be.

I had no idea of the magnitude of the calling that I was launched into, but the Lord did, and so did the devil. I praise God that nothing catches God off guard, for the Scriptures tell us that the Lord neither sleeps nor slumbers. The devil tried to kill me three times within a two-year period, but the angel of the Lord was there to protect me each time. The first attempt on my life was in September of 1976, just six months after God had spoken to me about leaving my football career for the youth ranch ministry.

The Car Angel

As a Canadian ball player, my salary was a lot lower than that of many of the American players, although I played for 11 years. We Canadians had to scratch for every dollar we got. Consequently, most of us had to work other jobs on the side to make ends meet. Since we didn't usually begin football practice until 4:00 in the afternoon, many of the players, like me, were able to hold down other employment. I performed a few different jobs during my 11-year career, mostly in sales. During my last two years in Edmonton, I sold office equipment for Olivetti of Canada.

One Friday afternoon, I was held up in an appointment in West Edmonton until 3:45 and was rushing to the stadium as fast as I dared drive. There was an automatic fine of $100 levied for arriving late for practice, and I was doing my best to see that didn't happen. My blue 1975 Mercury Cougar pulled up to a red light on 97 Street and 108 A Avenue. I was only half a mile from Clarke Stadium, but it was already 3:55. My eyes were fastened on the overhead lights to the left of the intersection.

"Come on, light—change," I said impatiently. "I've only got five minutes." Just then it turned amber, and my eyes swung to the right anticipating the go-ahead green.

The moment the light turned green, I pulled my right foot off of the brake and hit the accelerator to the floor as hard as I could. The car didn't move. An invisible force held my foot a fraction of an inch from the pedal.

"What!" I exclaimed, just as a car, undetected from my right, flew through the intersection in excess of eighty miles per hour. If I had moved at all, he would have splattered me all over the intersection. Thank God, there were no other cars there at the time; and thank God, I sat there for another moment and praised the Lord for saving me, for another car, which must have been chasing the first one, also raced through from my right, even faster than the first maniac. God's angel had spared me from a fatal accident. I praised and worshipped my Saviour all the way to the stadium. I knew that the devil had tried to wipe me out, and the incident caused me to realize more deeply the importance of constantly praying and trusting God for His divine protection.

I am sure there have been other times that God has spared me even when I haven't been aware of it. There is a great book written by Pat Boone called *A Miracle A Day Keeps The Devil Away*. It deals in great detail with this subject.

The Construction Angel

A year and a half later, I experienced my second near-miss. The main complex, the Circle Square Hotel, was under construction, and we were working on the upper balcony. I had left Bernie, our foreman, with two of our young teenage volunteers working on the railing, while I climbed down to ground level to get some nails. I bent over to fill my carpenter's pouch with spikes, and as I straightened up, a two-pound hammer slipped out of one of the boy's hands and bounced off the top of my head. The blow stunned me, but I was unhurt.

An hour earlier, during lunch, I had put on a construction hard-hat that someone had left on one of the picnic tables. I had never worn one before on the job. In fact, none of us owned one. Where it had come from, none of us knew, but again the angel of the Lord had preserved me.

The Pry-bar Angel

The third time that I was consciously aware of God's protection was during our second spring construction push at Circle Square. We had been putting some finishing touches on the main complex and had just finished pouring the basement floor. A large, forty-five–gallon drum full of sand was sitting at the bottom of the outside stairwell and needed to be removed. My younger brother, Mark, and I decided to lift it out with the front-end loader on the ranch tractor. Mark ran over to the barn to fetch the old Ishmael, while I proceeded to secure a couple of large chains around the barrel. It would be a simple job.

As I carefully worked with the cumbersome chains, I heard the tractor pull up to the top of the stairwell and the sound of the hydraulics as Mark raised the loader to its maximum height and tipped the bucket forward, directly above my head. Unknown to either of us, someone had left a five-foot-long, twenty-pound steel pry-bar in the bucket.

I heard the rattling sound of the bar as it rolled off the end of the metal bucket, but I didn't realize what was happening. In a split second, I felt an invisible force push my upper body about a foot to my right. The sharp point of the heavy bar nicked my left shoulder and slammed into the floor right next to my left foot. If the angel hadn't moved me, the bar would have gone through the centre of my skull. The only evidence of the incident was a tiny bruise the size of a fifty-cent piece on my upper left arm. For the next two weeks, I praised the Lord for His mercy and faithfulness every time I stepped into the shower and noticed the small bruise—a mark of His favour and divine protection..

The Van Angel

The winter of 1976-77 was another bitterly cold one, with temperatures dipping down to -40º F on occasion. That wasn't much fun, especially when you had to visit the outdoor facilities in the middle of the night. David and Norma Jean paid us a visit in late November of that year. They were travelling in the area and drove out to spend the evening at the ranch with us. They brought us a small wall plaque that they had picked up somewhere on the way. We still have it to this day. It was a picture of a goofy-looking mountain lion draped over the branch of a tree. The caption read simply, "Hang In There."

It was a real encouragement to Sandy and me, and we appreciated their kindness and thoughtfulness, but we weren't about to give up anyway, no matter how cold it got. We were there to stay forever, or until the Lord said otherwise. The Mainses spent that night with us and got to try out our fancy, ice-cold, non-flush outdoor facility. That evening, David informed us of a little bit of wisdom he had picked up while on the farm back in Ontario. Apparently a tush-sized piece of Styrofoam is able to pick up body heat instantly and will do wonders for the backside. We truly appreciated this tidbit of information. I only wished it had come to us a whole lot sooner. The Mainses were a real blessing to us in coming out to stay over that evening, but I think they were glad to get back to civilization the next day.

A couple of weeks later, Sandy and our three children experienced an incredible miracle, and again it was through the kids' faith. The temperature had dropped 20 degrees that day to -35º F. Brad and Julie had left for school that morning, not dressed warmly enough for such temperatures. We certainly did not want Brad and Julie to have to walk the half mile in from the Texas gate when they were dropped off by the school bus. Being the good mother that Sandy was, she warmed up our 1976 brown and tan Chevy van, drove the six and a half miles into Halkirk, and picked them up after school. Since I was busy with chores, she decided to take Chéri along for the ride.

On the way back, as they came around a bend in the road about two miles from home, the van went out of control on the icy road, skidded sharply to the left, and came to a stop at the bottom of a deep ditch. No matter what she tried, the van wouldn't move even an inch forward or backward. The underside of the van was hung up in the heavy snow up to the axles, so the wheels just spun. They were two miles from the ranch on a rarely travelled country road, hung up in a ditch, with no help in sight. The children were not dressed warmly enough to walk, and Sandy wasn't about to leave them alone and make the long trek by herself.

"Oh, Lord! What are we going to do?" she cried out in desperation. Just then, six-year-old Brad piped in, "Why don't we just ask the Lord to send an angel to push us out?"

"Yeah, God will send an angel to help us if we ask Him," Julie added quite confidently. Sandy admitted later that her faith wasn't up to asking for that much, so she suggested that the children do the praying.

Brad boldly led off, "Jesus, we need Your help. Would You please send us an angel to push us out of this ditch?"

"Thank You, Lord," they all chimed in unison. Sandy dropped the column shift into drive and slowly stepped on the accelerator. She could hardly believe what was happening. The van rolled out of the ditch with no problem. It felt like an invisible force was lifting the back end as they climbed up onto the road. The children cheered and praised God as they headed for home. Sandy was in shock. All she could say was, "Thank You, Lord! Thank You, Lord!"

I was engrossed in some paperwork when the ranch van pulled up to our mobile home. The door burst open and Brad came rushing in with the others close on his heals, "Dad! Dad! Mom drove into the ditch and an angel pushed us out!"

"Well, tell me what happened this time," I asked. Miracles didn't surprise me anymore. In fact, I was beginning to expect them quite regularly. Hardly a day had gone by since we came to Circle Square Ranch that something exciting hadn't happened.

The Tired Angel

The Bible says that the angels of God are sent to assist the children of God, and that they respond to the voice of God's Word. (See Hebrews 1:14; Psalm 103:20.) When we speak the word that God gives us (in faith), the angels respond, and that's when miracles happen. We are simply the recipients of the grace of God: that is, we are simply "receivers." Faith is a gift from God and is basically our spiritual connection, much like a receiver on a television or radio brings in the signal and manifests it in sound or a picture. Faith, when exercised, releases the angels to carry out the will of God on our behalf, in accordance with the plan and purposes of God.

In September of 1978, at the end of the summer camping season, our family was privileged to take a short vacation to Valemont, B.C. Tom and Donna, friends whom we met through the Full Gospel Business Men's Fellowship, had invited us to spend time with them. My brothers Murray and Mark came along with us, but that's another story, which I'll share later.

As we were packing the van that September afternoon, I noticed that we didn't have a spare tire. Aware that our trip would cover over 800 miles, I didn't want to take any chances, so I resolved in my mind to buy a new spare in Stettler on the way. Since the Lord had been teaching me to commit everything to Him, on the way to Stettler I asked Him what He wanted me to do. Within my heart I heard, *"Don't take a spare, just trust me."*

When I shared my revelation with Sandy and my brothers, they all bore witness to it right away. "If you feel that's what God wants, then let's go in faith," Sandy said.

Sandy and the children really enjoyed their stay in Valemont. They spent three days with Donna, while Tom, Murray, Mark, and I did our thing. But I'm getting ahead of myself again.

The evening before we were to leave for home was when the miracle began. I say "began" because this was the longest continuous display of God's power I have ever witnessed.

It was 9:00 p.m. and all of us had just returned to our friends' place, two miles north of town. When we climbed out of the van, I noticed a loud hissing sound, which was coming from the rear of the vehicle. The sound got louder as I drew closer. It seemed to be coming from the rear tire on the driver's side. When I bent down and touched the tire, I could feel the air gushing out of a large 1/4 inch hole in the outside of the tire wall. Something had obviously punctured it. I instinctively prayed out loud, "Lord, please keep this tire up until I can get it fixed or replaced. Please send an angel to help us."

Immediately I thought of the testimony that my brother Blaine had shared with me years before. God had kept his tire inflated for thirty miles while the air was blowing out of a hole in it. "Jesus," I prayed again, "You did it for Blaine. I know You can do it for us too."

I wasted no time as I jumped back into the van and raced to town, praising God all the way and praying in the spirit. When I arrived in town, I drove straight to the local Shell Station, only to find it closed. I checked the tire to find that it was still up. Amazingly enough, it didn't appear to have lost any air at all, but of course that was impossible, as the air was blowing out as hard as ever. I didn't try to figure it out, but just praised the Lord and drove over to the Esso Station, only to find it closed for the night as well. I took another look at my tire, to make sure it was still up, and drove back to the house. The tire was still full when I climbed out of the van. By this time the air had been blowing out of it for close to twenty minutes since I first discovered it. "Lord, please keep an angel watching over this tire," I said, and I walked into the house.

To be honest, I was surprised when I walked out into the yard the next morning to find the tire still fully inflated, air pouring out as fast as ever. We were all totally amazed. The tire had stayed up for over eight hours by this time. Sandy and I loaded the children into the van, said goodbye to our friends, and headed for town. We pulled into the Shell Station, and I asked the pump jockey if there was someone around who could help me with a tire. He said that he was the only one there and he didn't know anything about tires. I thanked him, glanced back at the tire, which was still as full as ever, and proceeded over to the Esso. When I pulled up to the garage door, I climbed down to greet the attendant coming out to meet us. "Do you have anyone here who could help me with a tire?"

"That one there?" he said, pointing to the rear of the van.

"Yes, the left rear," I responded as I turned around. The tire was absolutely deflated. The Lord had answered our prayer. He had somehow, miraculously, kept it inflated until we found someone to help. God had demonstrated His faithfulness to us once again.

With a thankful heart, I purchased a new tire for the trip home. The attendant told us that he couldn't fix the old one, as the hole in the sidewall was too large to repair. He actually held the tire up in front of us and stuck his baby finger through the large hole. As we drove onto the highway and headed back to the ranch, a funny thought struck me, and I turned to the others in the van and asked, "I wonder if angels get tired?"

"What makes you ask that?" Sandy responded.

"I just had this picture in my mind of an angel blowing air into the stem of our tire all night."

Years later, I read of how God had performed a similar miracle with a bicycle tire for Tony Campolo Jr. when he was a young lad. God can transcend His own natural laws any time He chooses to do so, and in that sense, *nothing* is impossible.

My Brothers Really Got My Goat

During our eight years at Circle Square, the ranch was blessed with numerous gifts from many generous donors. One of the most unusual donations was a beautiful bighorn sheep head, which I hung directly to the right of the huge 12-foot stone fireplace in the main dining hall. Mounted next to the fireplace, the majestic ram's head received many comments as well as inquiries as to how we acquired such an outstanding trophy. One afternoon, as I was pouring myself a coffee, I looked up at the sheep's head and the scriptures in Matthew chapter 25 ran through my mind. That is where Jesus speaks of a time in the future when He will return and separate the sheep to His right and the goats to His left. The sheep are the ones who did His will and the goats, the ones who didn't. Right there and then I decided that we needed a goat's head to hang on the left side of the fireplace, which would serve as a powerful message to all who entered the room.

When we had left for Valemont that September, the main purpose was to bring back a mountain goat's head. Tom was a registered hunting guide, and he set up the hunt for us. My brothers, Murray, an experienced hunter and Mark, a rookie, came with me to join in the goat hunt. Tom secured another local guide for us, his friend Joe, since there needed to be one guide for every two hunters for everything to be legal. The morning after we arrived in Valemont, we left Sandy and the kids with Tom's wife, Donna, at their log cabin, and the hunting party drove in two vehicles to about 20 miles southeast of the town. When we arrived at the base of the mountains, Murray suggested that we all join together in prayer before getting underway. Joe, the only non-believer in the group, recoiled at the suggestion and immediately responded with, "What do you mean 'pray,' and for what?"

"We want to ask God to protect us and bless us with a successful hunt. We didn't come all this way to get skunked," I answered.

oe folded his arms across his chest in a slightly defiant manner and backed up about ten yards, while I led in prayer. As soon as I said "Amen," Joe returned to the group and we began our assent. He didn't say anymore about the prayer, but I could tell by his manner that he thought we were a bunch of religious kooks.

After three hours of climbing straight up through the heavy woods, Joe and Tom led us to an open area directly above the tree line, where we immediately set up our base camp. When our tents were up and everything else was in order, to my surprise Joe bid us all farewell and headed back to town. "Oh, I hope we didn't scare Joe off." Murray responded.

"No, that's not the reason he left," Tom informed us. "He planned to leave all along and will be back in two days to meet us down at the van. It wasn't our prayer that chased him away, but it sure did throw him off some." After sundown, the four of us snuggled into our warm sleeping bags, for we wanted to get an early start in the morning.

We rose at 6:00 a.m., and Murray and I made breakfast while Mark and Tom packed lunches for the four of us. Tom suggested that we break into pairs and scout out the area, so after cleanup, with back packs and rifles Tom and I began to climb the mountain peak immediately to our west. Murray and Mark ascended the peak two mountains over towards the east. At 11:30 a.m., after a grueling four-hour climb, Tom and I reached the top of our mountain. I was exhausted, and my thighs were burning. Even though I had trained for a month by climbing up and down the coolie at home, I could not believe what poor shape I was in. Immediately Tom pulled out his spotting scope and began to scan the range. After 20 minutes of gazing at the awesome scenery, Tom spotted a single goat standing on a high, narrow ledge, four mountain peaks to the west. "Look here!" he shouted. "There's the one you want, Garry. He's just waiting for you to come and get him."

"Let's go," I responded. "He looks just perfect to me from here."

"Hold on a minute," Tom answered back. "We'll never get to him in time. He's too far away for us to reach him by nightfall, but if your brothers see him, they might be able to, since they were headed in that direction when we last saw them." Minutes later, Murray and Mark came into view, positioned about halfway between us and the goat. They were ascending the west side of the mountain face, so the mountain itself blocked their vision. They were within easy striking distance but couldn't see the goat, which was standing only two mountain peaks beyond them, about 2000 yards directly to the east.

"Oh, Lord!" I said. "Please show them the goat in time, and help them get to him." Suddenly, as quickly as he had appeared, the goat vanished from our sight. Shortly thereafter, the guys disappeared from our view as well. Tom and I spent another couple of hours looking for more signs of game, but with no success. Finally, after two full hours of scanning the horizon and coming up empty, we slowly made our way back down the mountain. Every so often, I breathed a prayer, trying to exercise faith by thanking the Lord for a successful hunt, trusting that He had heard and was answering our prayer from the day before.

Tom and I arrived at base camp around 3:30 p.m. to find that my brothers were not back from their trek, so we still didn't know whether they had seen the lone goat or not. By 5:00 p.m. they still hadn't returned, so we decided to put something together for supper. Tom started a fire while I drew some water from the nearby stream. Moments later, as I was placing the pot on the open fire, Mark's familiar voice came from behind me. I wheeled around to see the two of them only a few yards away. Mark face was downcast and he looked just awful.

"I am so pooped," he began. "I can't walk another step. I've never been so tired in my life. As far as I'm concerned, this hunt is over. If you guys want to continue on, it's totally up to you, but I am not going to climb another hill, let alone another mountain. If you three want to go out again tomorrow, then I'll stay here and look after base camp and cook the meals if you like. My legs are killing me. I am done."

"Mark, you can't give up so easily," I responded. "We've just started. Tom and I spotted a big goat up there, just beyond where you and Murray were this afternoon. We were hoping that you saw him too." I turned and pointed to the mountain peak where we had seen the goat, hoping to encourage Mark not to quit. When I turned back, Mark had taken off his backpack and pulled out a large chunk of raw meat.

"You guys hungry?" He laughed, throwing the slab of goat ribs onto the tarp next to me.

"Holy cow! You nailed him!" I shouted.

"We saw him all right," Murray added. "Boy, have we got a story for you."

"Why don't you tell us over dinner?" Tom suggested. "Let's cook this baby right now. I am starving and anxious to taste it."

"Me too," I said. "I've never had the pleasure of tasting goat meat myself. I wonder what it tastes like? It'll probably be real stringy and tough," I answered my own question.

"We're excited to taste these ribs for sure," Murray chimed in. "You'll never believe how we brought him down."

I roasted the meat until it was medium rare, just the way I like it, then the four of us sat down to feast on the ribs along with some boiled potatoes and warmed beans. I couldn't believe how great the goat tasted. The meat was so tender, you could cut it with a fork. I would compare it to the best filet mignon I've ever eaten.

"Well, you've got to tell us what happened," I began. "When Tom and I spotted Billy here, he was too far away for us to reach him, so we prayed that you guys would see him in time. Then we saw you climbing up that peak halfway between us and the goat, but you disappeared and that was the last we saw of you." As we sat around the fire and enjoyed the fabulous meal, Murray began to tell the story.

"First of all, I think the reason this meat tastes so good is that it is a *miracle goat*, and totally blessed by God. We must have seen him about the same time as you did, so Mark and I decided to climb to the top of the mountain to get a better look at him. That's probably when we came into your view. When we arrived on top, the goat was nowhere to be found, but when we had last seen him, he was headed in our direction. I knew he couldn't have just vanished, so we sat there and ate our lunch. Mark and I prayed and asked the Lord what to do. We both felt we were to just sit there for a while and if the goat didn't appear, then we would continue to move east in his direction. After about 30 minutes with no sign of him, we crawled down the slope and crossed the saddle and climbed up the next ridge.

"When we reached the top, he still wasn't visible. Just before one o'clock, he came back into view. I think he must have been sleeping in a cave on the south side of the mountain. He started towards us, so we crouched down and held our position. When the goat got to the saddle directly between his mountain and ours, he went right past it and headed slowly back east on the north, or opposite, side of the peek. This is where the miracle began to happen. Old Billy had walked about 30 feet when I realized I had to do something. He was out of range, even for Mark's 300 Magnum, so trying a shot from there was useless. Suddenly a surge of faith rose up within me and I spoke out loud to the goat. 'Oh, no, you don't, Billy,' I declared. 'You get back here right now, in the name of Jesus.'

He halted instantly and just stood there for at least two or three minutes. It was like an invisible force was preventing him from going forward. I believe it was an angel sent by God. All of a sudden, the goat went into reverse and began backing up. The path was too narrow to turn around on, so I guess he had no choice. When he reached the saddle, he turned and started walking towards us. When he was about 70 or 80 yards from us, I told Mark to take the first shot, since he's never had the chance to bag any big game before. I was afraid he might see us if he got any closer. Mark opened fire, but the shot missed. To our amazement, the goat ran to his right and looked over the edge, then he jogged back to the middle of the saddle and moved a few steps closer. This time, I fired, and I missed him too. Then he ran over to his left, looked over the edge, came back to the middle and moved closer again. Would you believe that between us we fired seven times, and after each shot that crazy goat came nearer to us! The angle was so steep that I guess our bullets were flying above his head. I finally nailed him at about 50 yards, when I aimed at his front feet and got him in the throat. For a while, I actually thought he might get so close that I'd have to knife him as he ran by me."

"Wow!" I exclaimed. "What an amazing story! I wish I could have been there. Is the Lord good or what? God sure answers prayer in the most incredible ways."

"Halleluiah!" Tom shouted. "God is good."

We stayed up until the wee hours of the morning, talking about the greatness of our God and praising His name.

Early the next morning, the four of us climbed to the saddle where Murray and Mark had left the remains of the goat. When we reached the spot, there he was, just as my brothers had described. Immediately, Murray pulled out his hunting knife and began to cut him up into four equal parts for us to carry back to camp. As Murray carried on the carving, Tom pulled out his map of the area and began to study it.

"What are you looking at?" I asked.

"I am just checking our location," he responded. Then: "Holy cow! You guys are not going to believe this!"

"What are you talking about?" I asked.

"The Mount Robson National Park boundary runs right through the middle of this saddle."

"Are you absolutely sure?"

"No doubt in my mind."

"What does that mean, Tom?"

"When you guys started shooting at Billy here, he was inside the park boundary. If you had hit him with one of your first six shots, it would have been an illegal kill. You dropped him ten feet outside the park boundary line."

"Praise God!" Mark hollered. "God protected us in our ignorance, and all the time I thought we were just bad shots."

"Amen, He surely did," I interjected. "God wouldn't have answered our prayer and blessed us with this goat and have us break the law at the same time, now would He?"

Jumping up from his crouched position, Murray raised his arms and shouted, "Praise you, Jesus! Glory to God Almighty! The Lord blesses us even in our ignorance. This was a greater miracle than I thought." After Murray finished quartering the goat, we headed back to camp, packed up the rest of our gear, and made the long trek down to where we had left the van. Joe was nowhere to be found.

When we arrived in Valemont, we immediately took the goat's head over to the ranger's station to register the kill. As we walked through the door, to our surprise, Joe was there visiting with the ranger. When they saw the goat, they were both taken aback.

"Where did you get him?" Joe exclaimed.

"Just above where we camped," Tom responded.

"That's impossible! After I left you guys, I came back down and Ranger Ted and I went up in the helicopter to see where the goats were gathering. They are all over on the north range about 50 miles from where you guys were. At this time of the year, goats herd together and they don't travel alone. How this one got over to you doesn't make any sense."

"Obviously the Lord answered our prayer," I pointed out. "He must have brought him to us."

Joe just shook his head in disbelief, and the ranger didn't say another word about it. However, he was able to determine the goat's age by the length of the horns. To this day, the miracle four-year-old Billy Goat hangs to the left of the ranch fireplace, a testimony to the glory of God.

Julie's Angel

The summer of 1984 was my last one as director of Circle Square Ranch. It was as wonderful and rewarding a season as all the other seven had been. That summer was truly memorable for the whole family, especially for 11-year-old Julie. She was privileged to have an encounter that few people on this earth have ever had.

That spring, our family came very close to a real disaster. But for the protection of God, we all could have perished. Sandy was awakened at 5:00 a.m. by the sound of baby Jesse crying. This in itself was unusual, as he had been sleeping until at least 7:00 a.m. for the past three or four months. As she stumbled into the kitchen to fix him a bottle, Sandy could smell smoke. She ran back to our room and shook me awake. "Garry! Get up!" she shouted. "Something's burning!"

I jumped out of bed like a shot and ran out into the hall. I smelled the smoke too. It was coming from downstairs where the other children slept. As I descended the stairs, I could see smoke coming out from under

Brad's door. I flung open the door without thinking. The room was filled with smoke and Brad was fast asleep in his bed, oblivious to what was happening. The night before he had taken the shade off his reading lamp to see better and had fallen asleep. He inadvertently knocked the lamp over during the night and the 100-watt bulb had burned a hole the size of a softball through his jean jacket. It then burned through the bedspread, the sheets, and three inches deep into the side of the mattress. The embers were aglow. I awoke Brad, pulled him out of bed, picked up the smouldering mattress, and ran it outside to douse it with water. In the meantime, Sandy had aroused the girls. In the midst of all the commotion, Jesse had fallen back to sleep. To this day, I wonder if he had ever been awake in the first place.

All of the children seemed unaffected by the incident, except for Julie, who was so frightened that she cried hysterically for nearly five minutes. The spirit of fear had gripped her heart. She kept repeating, "What if we hadn't woken up? We would have all died!"

"It's all right," I tried to reassure her. "The Lord is watching over us all the time."

"But Daddy," she cried, "it was so close. We could have burned up in our sleep."

"That couldn't have happened, Dear," I replied. "God has an angel standing right outside our front door, and he watches over us even when we are sleeping." She calmed down, but I could tell she had been badly shaken by the whole ordeal. It left a mark on her young mind and put real fear in her heart.

Later that week, God did something very special for Julie to remove that fear permanently. During the first week of August, there were 11- and 12-year-old campers at the ranch. Along with this young group was a 15-year-old Downs Syndrome boy named Kevin. Julie took a very special interest in him and personally helped him with all the different activities. She made sure that he didn't miss out on anything. Wherever you saw Kevin that week, there was little Julie right beside him, holding his hand.

On Thursday evening, we closed campfire around 11:00 p.m. and sent the counsellors to their cabins with their campers. Sandy had gone back to the house earlier to put Jesse to bed. Julie, Chéri, their cousin Shannon McIntyre, and I headed for home. Julie began to talk about Kevin.

"Daddy, isn't he the most precious boy you've ever seen? There is something so special about him." As she spoke about Kevin I could hardly believe my ears. In my whole life I had never heard anyone speak with such compassion. Tears welled up in my eyes as the presence of God overwhelmed me. It was as if pure liquid love was flowing through her words. As we approached the house, still about forty yards away, suddenly Julie, looking towards the house, let out a gasp.

"Dad! Look!" Her eyes almost popped out of her head.

"What? What is it?"

"There—there on the porch, Daddy."

"What are you talking about?"

"Can't you see him?"

"Who? What?" I shouted, as I crouched down and shifted my head to left and right in an attempt to see what she was staring at.

"Can't you see him?"

"Who?"

"The angel on the porch."

"The angel!" I exclaimed. God had opened her eyes to see into the spirit realm. *Blessed are the pure in heart, for they shall see God.* Aloud I said, "No, I don't see anyone."

Chéri and Shannon moved all around, but they couldn't see anything either.

"What does he look like?" I asked. I had never seen an angel in real life, and I wanted to know.

Julie began to describe him. "He's about two feet above the roof line."

That would make him around 8 or 9 feet tall, I calculated.

"He's wearing a white robe down to his ankles, and his feet are bare," she continued, "and his arms are folded across his chest, like a guard or something."

"He is—he's guarding our house," I declared. "God, you are so good."

"His hair is blond, and it comes down to his shoulders," she added excitedly. "Dad, how come his hair isn't moving?" A strong wind was blowing, about 20 miles an hour.

"Honey, if his hair was moving in the wind, it would mean he was in the natural realm, and we would all be able to see him. You are looking into the realm of the spirit, where the angels live. I guess it's not windy there."

Moments later, he disappeared from her view, and the four of us ran inside to tell Sandy about Julie's amazing experience. Since that memorable day, Julie has never again been afraid of a fire in our home.

Julie's baby picture

Julie, age 10

Chapter 22

LAUNCH OUT INTO THE DEEP

When the summer of 1984 camping season came to a close, so did an exciting chapter in the life of the Lefebvre family. We had left my football career and city life behind in the spring of 1977 and spent eight glorious years developing and directing the Halkirk Circle Square Ranch. But now it was time to move on to another episode in our lives. Our three eldest children, Chéri, Brad, and Julie had spent their formative years in what amounted, spiritually speaking, to a protective cocoon. Sandy and I were very thankful, as not only were they raised in the wonderful atmosphere of God's presence, they were not subjected to many of the temptations that young children often have to face. As a result, they had grown into three very well-adjusted, loving and obedient teenagers.

That summer, when the final rancher crossed our Texas gate and the last volunteer staff member shed a teary goodbye, I knew that our time at the ranch had expired. God had been speaking to me for quite some time, so it did not come as a shock to me. I knew in my heart that we had run the course and finished the race that God had asked us to run, although the finality of it all was disturbing to say the least.

I was absolutely positive that our ministry at Circle Square was done and that we were being asked by the Lord to lay it all down. I felt like a dark curtain had dropped over my eyes and the vision that had led me for the past eight years was suddenly gone. It was frightfully unnerving to know that our time there was completed, as God had not yet given me any specific direction as to where we were to go and what He had in store for us.

As I walked up onto the back porch of our gorgeous 3,200 square foot hillside bungalow, which overlooked the beautiful Paint Earth Coulee, I wondered how Sandy would react to the bombshell I was about to drop on her. This was her dream home. We had built it in faith only three years earlier at a miraculous cost of $40,000, mainly due to a few generous gifts and some amazing deals. Our operations manager, Bernie Doan, had done most of the work on the house, with some help from me and a number of other volunteers. As I opened the back door, I remembered the day we had moved in and what Sandy had said to me: "I wonder how long God is going to let us enjoy this wonderful home. You know something, Honey? It's amazing, but for some reason I don't feel attached to this house. It's gorgeous, and it's all that I have ever dreamed of living in, but somehow I feel like it is only for a time. It's God's house, and as long as He wants us to stay here, I will enjoy it to the fullest. I know it doesn't belong to us."

Will she feel the same now?

"Sandy," I hollered into the kitchen, "I have something important to share with you, but you had better sit down."

"I don't know if I like the sound of this," she replied as she walked into the spacious living room and sat herself down on the hearth of our 12-foot-wide by 11-foot-high rock fireplace.

"Well, Sweetie," I began, "the Lord has been speaking to me for the past month. To put it bluntly, our time here is up. Our ministry at Circle Square Ranch is over. I didn't want to say anything to you until I was absolutely certain that it was God speaking, but I can't deny it, Sandy. We're done here."

"I know."

"You know!"

"Uh huh. God has been speaking to me too. So, where do we go from here?"

"I don't know. The Lord hasn't told me yet. All I'm sure of is that our ministry here is about to come to an end."

"Well, you had better find out soon. Maybe you should go for a long walk in the coulee and ask God to make it clear to you. We can't just leave if we don't know where we are going and what we are going to do when we don't get there." Sandy had a way of cutting to the quick.

"That's exactly what I'm going to do. Where's my NIV New Testament?"

"In the bedroom on the dresser."

It was a warm, sunny evening as I strolled through the valley, praying in tongues and worshiping God. Every now and then, I would stop and sit down on the ground and read some scripture, waiting for Him to speak. God had spoken to me many times before, directly through His Word, and I expected He would do so again in this crucial time of our lives.

After an hour or so, I came up out of the coulee and wandered over to the rodeo arena and sat on the faded grey wooden bleachers. As I enjoyed the Lord's presence and the warm sunshine on my face, I felt absolutely at peace. I was confident that God would lead us in the path

He had chosen for us. My Heavenly Father's unfailing love had become very real to me in the past few years, and I was depending upon His faithfulness. He had never failed us yet, and I knew He would not fail us now. Then I heard that familiar, quiet voice of the Holy Spirit speaking to my heart, *"Read the fifth chapter of Luke."*

I opened my Bible and began to read Luke's account. Jesus' disciples had been fishing through the night and had caught nothing. When Jesus arrived at the shore early in the morning, He told them to put out into the deep water and let down their nets. Peter replied, "Master, we've worked hard all night and haven't caught anything. But because you say so, I will let down the nets."

The story goes on to declare that when they pulled up the nets, they were so full that they began to break. The disciples called another boat to come alongside and help, and there were enough fish to fill both boats, so full that they even began to sink.

As I read this passage, the words *"put out into deep water"* lifted off the page into my spirit, and I knew that God was calling us to thrust out into deep waters. I knew, too, that this move would have to be a complete act of faith. With the word came the calm assurance that God would be there with us in this new step in our exciting walk with Him.

I immediately returned to the house to share the news with Sandy. As I walked through the door, she was seated in the living room. The moment she saw me, she said, "Did the Lord give you an answer?"

"Well, yes and no. He spoke to me out of Luke, chapter five. The word I received was for us to launch out into the deep, which I interpreted to mean that God is asking us to step out in faith. I think what He is saying is that He wants us to make a decision in our hearts to resign from the ranch and turn the directorship over to someone else. Then I believe He will clearly show us where we are to go and what we are to do next."

"Praise God," Sandy responded. "The Lord has directed our path this far, so I am sure He won't lead us astray now. If you are confident that you heard His voice, then I am at peace too. If you want to call Crossroads and share the news with Uncle Reyn, I am with you all the way."

"I'll call him first thing tomorrow morning."

We went to bed very much at peace that night, knowing that God was in control of our destiny and that whatever He was leading us into would truly be another exciting adventure for the Lefebvre family. As we lay in bed, I thought about how God had lifted me out of my football career and led us to the ranch.

A thought crossed my mind: *When our Great Shepherd is about to lead us into another pasture, He surely knows how to make us dissatisfied with the grass in the present one.* The Lord had done that for us when it was time to make the last big move, and now He was doing it again. As great as the ranch ministry was, somehow it just didn't fulfill me anymore. My vision had vanished, and now someone else would be called to carry it through the next phase.

As I contemplated our future and the future of Circle Square Ranch, Bernie and Bernice Doan were impressed upon my mind. Bernie and Bea had been with us since 1978 and were as loyal and as dedicated to the ranch ministry as anyone we had ever had on staff. They had served the Lord faithfully for seven years in nearly every area of responsibility from horsemanship directors to program directors to operation managers. Bernie knew the ranch ministry inside and out, and Bea was a gifted administrator and excellent communicator.

As I reflected upon these things, I thought to myself, "Wouldn't that be just like you, Lord, to turn the directorship over to the Doans and have them move into this beautiful home that Bernie faithfully built for our comfort and enjoyment? On top of that, to have the brother of the one who donated the property end up directing it? Lord, You are so amazing." I drifted off to sleep, wondering how Reyn and David would receive the news about us leaving.

When I awoke early the next morning, the thoughts were stronger in my spirit, and I was now more confident that we were moving in God's plan. Since Head Office in Toronto was two hours ahead of us, I was able to call Reyn right away. When I broke the news to him, he was a little taken aback. We had been through much together, and our love for each other had grown strong over the years. The Rutledges and Mainses were as close to Sandy and me as were our own flesh and blood. As I shared my heart, it didn't take long before Reyn knew that I had heard from the Lord, and he added his blessing to our decision. Before the conversation was over, he prayed a wonderful prayer from his heart for God's guidance and protection over our family.

A week later, after discussing our departure at length, we mutually decided that we would stay on until the end of February, 1985. Upon my recommendation, the Doans were asked to take over the directorship when we left, and after a time of prayer and waiting upon the Lord, they gratefully consented. That week I was asked to join in ministry with an evangelist friend, Doug Kooy. He was the president of Crossfire

Communications, which was a traveling ministry primarily focused on youth. Doug had ministered at the ranch on a few occasions, and we really worked well together. Doug and Terry and their family lived in Brentwood Bay on Vancouver Island near Victoria, but they felt very strongly that they were to move their headquarters to Kelowna. Crossfire's executive administrator was a man I highly respected in the Lord, Barrie Silliker. His administrative experience included 30 years with Sears. The plan was for the three of us to travel and for Doug and I to preach and teach in tandem. The two of us were so much alike that it was almost scary. We agreed to all move to Kelowna on March 1, 1985, and set up the ministry offices.

It was much harder for our family to leave the ranch than any of us anticipated. It had not been difficult when the Lord called us from football, and I thought it would be somewhat the same this time. However, that was surely not the case. This time it was as if we were leaving our baby behind. Our family had literally been involved in the birth of the ranch, and much of what was now a prosperous ministry had come from our own blood, sweat, and tears—and much prayer. These eight years had been our "on-the-job" training in the school of the Spirit. God had blessed us with many deep-heart relationships.

Shannon Cherry, my secretary, had been with us from day one. The standing joke around the ranch was that Shannon was my second wife, who was there to boss me around and keep me in line during office hours. Of course it was just a joke, as she was anything but bossy, and I counted myself truly blessed to have such a loving servant of God and a dear friend to help me keep things running, administratively. My brother Murray and his wife, Cathie, and their family had served with us for six years. Bernie and Bea and their children had been there almost as long as we had. Our love for the staff had grown deeper and deeper over the years. We all had forged through many valleys together and had been blessed with numerous mountain-top experiences as well. The ranch staff was as close-knit a bunch as any earthly family.

At our farewell party, Sandy and I and the children all broke down emotionally. As a family, we attempted to sing the song "Friends Are Friends Forever" and barely got through the first chorus before the tears exploded and we all became basket cases. It was the most emotional time of our lives together, but at the same time all of us knew that this change for us was the will of God and we really had no other option.

The Kooys, the Lefebvres, and Barrie and Maureen Silliker all arrived in Kelowna in March, and within a week we were on the road. The Lord miraculously provided us all with beautiful homes in the Mission District, so our families settled right in and began to enjoy the fabulous Okanagan Valley. We moved into a gorgeous 2,500-square-foot hillside bungalow on Curlew Drive, and the Kooys and Sillikers found homes just down the mountain from us.

Ours was a quiet and peaceful neighborhood, and we soon made many new friends. The Roys across the street were the first couple we met. Jill was a believer and her husband, Jules, although unsaved, was a very open, kind, gentle-spirited and gracious neighbor. After a time, Sandy and I were privileged to lead him to the Lord.

Three houses down from us were the Schupskys, a Christian family who were soon to become our very dear friends. Ed was a building contractor who owned Spur Construction, and I was blessed to help him build a new home down the block. His wife, Linda, was a fabulous cook and was gifted with a gorgeous singing voice. Their children, Christie and Drake, were close to our kids' ages. Drake, Brad, and Julie shared many fun times together. To this day, whenever we visit Kelowna, we always make a point of spending some quality time at "Hotel Schupsky." It still feels just like home to us.

Crossfire Communications started out in Kelowna with a big bang, and not just in name only. We were invited by Kelowna Christian Centre to hold evangelistic meetings for five full days. Doug and I taught from Sunday through the following Friday, with Monday off. The meetings were extremely well attended with people coming from all over the Okanagan Valley. We taught every morning, held intercessory prayer meetings every noon, and preached in tandem every evening. God moved in a marvelous way, and many were saved, delivered and healed of different diseases.

The most dramatic incident was a man from Vernon who was miraculously healed instantaneously of multiple sclerosis. The local newspapers got ahold of what was happening, and we hit the front page. The Holy Spirit moved in a dramatic fashion and the revival meetings carried on for five consecutive weeks. It was the most exciting thing I had ever witnessed, and I was positive that this was the beginning of a powerful ministry team that God had anointed for the last days.

Doug and I began traveling around North America, conducting evangelistic meetings in many different churches and youth groups. The spiritual high that I was on lasted for a couple of months, but gradually dissipated until I finally came to the place where I couldn't go on any longer pretending that I was enjoying myself.

In my own heart I wanted desperately to be assured that God was indeed leading us and that we were fulfilling His will in the ministry. It seemed to me that we were trying to push ourselves around under our own steam and my kettle had quickly run dry. In the process of our travels, I witnessed some behavior from other professed "men of God" that was anything but godly. By September of 1985, I had become totally discouraged with the ministry and with myself for being a part of it. I knew I couldn't go on much longer, but I didn't know how I could just up and quit. Neither did I have any other direction to go at the time.

Crossfire was scheduled for seventeen days of meetings in a charismatic church in Denton, Texas, beginning the first week in October. Travelling had become difficult for me lately. Not only was my heart not in the ministry, but it had become increasingly hard for me to leave Sandy and the children at home. During the last series of meetings in Cranbrook, B.C., I had become terribly homesick. I could hardly wait for the meetings to end so I could get back home to my loved ones.

The first meeting in the church began with a bang. When I stepped up onto the platform, the congregation broke out in laughter. I looked down to see if my fly was open and thankfully it wasn't, then down at my white dress shoes and then my tie, but nothing seemed to be awry. Just then the pastor leaned over and said, "It's the shoes."

"What's wrong with my shoes?"

"Oh, nothing! This is Pat Boone's home town."

"Are you serious?" I responded. "Well, I guess I know how to pick the right shoes."

After that first night, the assemblies in Denton seemed to drag on for me, and they must have done the same for the church, as the pastor called us into his office and shut down the meetings after just five days, although we were scheduled to speak for two weeks. The afternoon before, I had spent some time in prayer and God had given me a tremendous release concerning my family, totally setting me free from my homesickness. Doug and Barrie decided to stay in Texas and try to put some more meetings together in the area, but I knew my time was up. Doug found it difficult to accept my resignation, but I knew that I was doing exactly what God had led me to do.

I left Doug and Barrie in Fort Worth and caught the first plane back to Kelowna the next morning, at peace in my heart for the first time in months. A little later I realized that God had been gracious to me in delivering me from homesickness, so I would never have to doubt my motive in walking away from Crossfire that day.

On the plane ride home, I made a promise to the Lord that I would never again take a meeting or any place of ministry just because I was in financial need. I promised that, if necessary, I would take a secular job or even go on welfare to keep my word. If God's Holy Spirit didn't open the doors for me, then I wouldn't teach or preach again. The Lord held me to my word, and the next two years proved to be a real test.

During that time I performed many different secular jobs in order to keep the wolf away from the door, the last as a car salesman for Kelowna Plymouth Chrysler. I found it increasingly difficult to make a decent living, and in the process, we were forced to give up our lovely home in the Mission District. God did bless the sale of the house: it went for $15,000 above our purchase price. But the equity we had built up slowly trickled away, and within the year we were broke and in debt.

Through this time of testing, our family learned to live on a lot less than we once figured we needed. The Lefebvre family learned to live lean, while learning to lean on Jesus all the more. In spite of the tight squeeze we were in, I held to my word and refused to make any calls to try to book any meetings for myself.

In April of 1987, I finally was invited to hold ten days of teaching meetings in a Full Gospel Church in Merritt, B.C. It had been a long time since I had been asked to speak anywhere by anyone, so I was very excited about the opportunity. I secretly hoped that it was a sign that the trial was over and the doors of ministry were beginning to open. The pastor of the Merritt church had asked me to teach seventeen times in the ten day period, beginning the last Sunday of April. I would have to speak on average nearly twice daily, so I knew it would be a real stretch for me. At the same time, I was confident that God would give me the messages that he wanted communicated to these saints.

The morning that I was to leave for Merritt, we found ourselves absolutely broke. The last pop bottle in the house had been cashed in and the money spent on milk. There was barely anything else left to eat. Not only was our cupboard bare, but there wasn't even enough gas in our little Ford Fiesta to make it to Merritt. I knew that the church would bless me with an offering at the end of the meetings, but what were we to do for now? I couldn't leave Sandy and the kids alone, without any food.

As we prayed together that morning, asking God to meet our need and thanking Him for His faithfulness to us in the past, I looked up at Sandy and said confidently. "I wonder how the Lord is going to work this one out? He has never failed us before and I don't believe He will fail us now."

"Well, it certainly will have to be a miracle," she replied. "We definitely are not in a position to help ourselves." Just then I remembered something I had read about a month earlier in the great book, *Reese Howells Intercessor*, and I blurted it out. "Man's extremity is God's opportunity."

"I think we are about as far out on the limb as we can get," Sandy agreed.

I was scheduled to be in Merritt at 2:00 p.m. that afternoon, so I would have to leave by 11:00 a.m. at the latest. At 10:00 a.m. I strolled down to the corner mailbox to meet the mailman, and he was right on time. He handed me a brown government envelope and my heart leaped within me. I hoped against hope that it was a cheque. I tore it open as I turned and walked briskly towards the house. When I saw the cheque I shouted, "Praise the Lord!" and ran to the top of the front steps, where Sandy was standing. "Look Sandy!" I exclaimed. "Your income tax refund cheque just arrived and would you believe—it's for $1,537.18."

"Thank you, Jesus!" she shouted as she burst into tears.

"What a miracle!" I said, grabbing her and hugging her tight. "Hon, do you realize we just sent in your return two weeks ago?" Sandy and I had actually laid our hands on the form and anointed the envelope with oil. We had then asked God to send an angel along with it and to return it to us as fast as possible. I think the Income Tax Office set a new record just for us. God has unlimited ways to provide for our needs. He is truly Jehovah Jireh, "the Lord our Provider."

Chapter 23

FORTY DAYS AND FORTY NIGHTS

Two months after the tax return miracle, I was put to the ultimate test: Did I really believe that God was able not only to supply our needs but to totally sustain me physically? Four years earlier, while we were still directing Circle Square, I felt very strongly that God had called me to a 21-day fast on water alone, beginning on New Year's Day. It had been a difficult decision for me, since we were in the process of building our new home and I needed my strength during the construction. However, the Lord supernaturally sustained me when I reluctantly obeyed, and I enjoyed amazing energy along with tremendous peace through the entire 21 days. The Sunday following the end of the fast, my pastor, Lorne Fisher of Killam Pentecostal Church, prophesied over me and said that sometime in the future God would call me to fast for forty days.

It was now June 22, 1988, and we were enjoying another gorgeous summer day in Kelowna. I was sitting out on the back porch reading the Scriptures when I recognized the Lord's voice speaking to me in my heart again. *"Have you noticed that you have no engagements booked in July and August? This is that time that Pastor Fisher spoke of four years ago."*

Immediately, I knew exactly what the Lord was referring to, and I was ready for it. I desperately needed some clear direction as to what the Lord wanted me to do and whether I was still called to full-time ministry. I felt strongly that by setting aside these forty days through the summer to seek the Lord in fasting and prayer, I would find the answer. When I had gone through the 21-day fast back at the ranch, the downside was that I always felt cold in my extremities. Fasting in the middle of the summer in the sunny Okanagan sounded a whole lot better to me.

Since the Merritt meetings, my ministry opportunities were few and far between, and I knew that something had to change—and quickly. At this time I was willing to do almost any type of work just to make ends meet, but somehow I knew in my heart that we were to keep on trusting God to supply our every need. The scriptures say "To obey is better than sacrifice," and I really wanted to be obedient, whatever the cost.

After a few more times of prayer, I sensed that I was to begin this long fast on July 22 and end it on August 31. I also felt I was being led to prepare my body for it, by slowly cutting down my food intake over a period of three weeks, until only liquids were being consumed over the final three days. I knew this would take real discipline and much prayer to accomplish. I set my heart to begin the process on July 1. At this time our family was in serious financial need to the tune of $13,000, a debt which had accumulated over the past two years.

Before the week was out, I received an unexpected long distance call from Long Island, New York, from Dr. Raymond Damadian, the inventor of the MRI. Our family had come to know the Damadians back during Circle Square Ranch days, when Dr. Raymond had flown his two boys Tim and Jevin all the way to Halkirk for camp. A while later, in thankfulness for how the boys' lives were turned around, the Damadians blessed the ranch financially and later sponsored my sister, Pat, and her three children, Todd, Dean and Tracey, through Bible school in Montana. It had been at least two years since our families had communicated in any form.

He said the reason for his call was that he felt God had impressed upon him to donate 1000 shares of his company, Fonar Corporation, to our family. He then asked me if Sandy and I would be willing to fly to New York the next week, at his expense, because he wanted to share a vision for a new ministry with us. I told him that I couldn't come right away because God was calling me to this fast. We were living by faith and out on the limb at the time, believing God to supply our daily needs. At the same time, I was expecting our Heavenly Father to open a door of ministry opportunity for us. It was not easy to delay Dr. Damadian with his generous offer. He kindly consented to wait until September 14, which would give me two weeks to come off the fast and gradually accustom my body to full meals again.

Dr. D couriered his generous 1000-share donation to our home within a few short days. Amazingly enough, the Fonar shares were worth $13 Canadian per share. With thankful hearts, we cashed them in and paid off our debts.

Throughout the entire forty days, we witnessed the miraculous hand of God, as time after time money dropped into our lap in the most unusual ways. People came right to our door with cash and cheques and food. We even found a one-hundred-dollar bill underneath a plate in our dining room. Amazing as it may seem, those forty days were the most financially lucrative we had ever experienced during our entire ministry lives, and I didn't go out to minister even once.

Jehovah Jireh, *the Lord our Provider,* showed Himself faithful once again. The hand of the Lord was so graciously upon me during this time that I was enabled, by His grace, to prepare and serve all of our family's meals from the twentieth day until the fortieth without being even slightly tempted by the food. I did, however, bake my favorite carrot cake and put it in the freezer until I could eat again. By the time the fast was over, I had dropped 49 pounds from 208 to 159. Thankfully, the Lord sustained me through the entire duration. It was during this time of setting myself apart unto God that I learned to lean upon Him even more.

Spotted Butterflies

I stayed close to home for the entire 40 days with the exception of the 31st to 33rd days. During that time I accepted an invitation from my dear friend Herb Sheath to spend a couple of days with him up in the mountains near Lumby, B.C. We pulled into a remote area that first evening and set up camp a few yards from a small stream, which we could drink from. As Herb and I sat around the campfire that night, he began to talk about the Lord and His 40-day fast in the wilderness. Herb was talking about the Lord being one with His creation and how even the animals must have been attracted to Him. It made me think of an amazing experience that God had given me back at Circle Square, about five years earlier.

"Herb," I began, "I want to tell you about an unbelievable experience the Lord blessed me with about five years ago. One afternoon I was sitting on the sun deck of our home at Circle Square Ranch. In my hand was a book entitled *The Ultimate Intention,* which I had been slowly working my way through. The moment before I opened it to begin reading, I closed my eyes and breathed a short prayer. *Father, please reveal to me who I really am in Christ.* When I opened my eyes, sitting on the middle of the book cover was the most beautiful white butterfly I have ever seen. I sat there spell-bound and motionless, holding my breath, afraid to scare it away. In my heart I heard these words. *'This is who you are. Like the caterpillar, you were once a worm crawling in the dirt and earth-bound. In Christ, I have made you a pure, white butterfly, and you are free to soar in the heavens.'* With that the butterfly lifted off the book, flew around my head, and soared off into the sky."

We talked some more, and then Herb and I thanked and praised God together until the fire went out. Then we bedded down in our sleeping bags for the night. When I awoke the next morning, Herb was sitting in his lawn chair next to the warm campfire, reading his Bible. I sat down in my lawn chair across from my friend and placed my Bible on my lap. I paused and breathed a short prayer, asking the Holy Spirit to teach me and lead me to the scriptures He wanted me to read. When I opened my eyes, I was shocked to see a white butterfly sitting on my Bible. "Herb, look," I whispered.

"That's incredible!" he exclaimed. "This is absolutely amazing! It's happening again." Seconds later the butterfly flew off into the trees.

"Herb, I think God is speaking to me again. I think I'll walk down to the water and spend some time there alone." I got up from the chair, leaving my Bible on it, and strolled slowly down the gradual slope to the clear, gently flowing stream. After bending down and lapping some of the cold, clear water, I noticed a long straight branch on the ground next to me. I picked it up, took out my hunting knife, and began to strip the loose bark away. When I was finished, I whittled a point on one end as I prayed in the Spirit and talked with my Lord. I thought the branch would make a great walking stick. About 40 minutes later, I gradually made my way back up the slope to where Herb was still sitting next to the fire. Before I sat down to read my Bible again, I jammed the sharpened end of the stick into the ground immediately to the right of my chair. After placing my Bible on my lap, I once again closed my eyes to pray.

"Father," I began, "is there something you want me to read?" In my inner man, I heard these words: *"Turn to the book of Galatians and start with chapter 6."* After opening to the page, I felt I needed to shut my eyes and pray again. "Holy Spirit, please teach me and show me what You want me to understand." When I opened my eyes, I was again startled, as a small black butterfly with dark orange spots was perched on my open Bible, right on top of the first verse. "Herb," I called out softly, "here's another one."

"What is going on?" he exclaimed.

"I don't know," I responded. "I think God is trying to get something through to me." At that moment, the butterfly lifted up and flew off into the distance at an amazing speed. My attention was immediately drawn to the verse it had been standing on. I read out loud. *"Brothers, if any man is trapped in some sin, you who are spiritual should restore him gently. But watch yourself; you also may be tempted."*

"I'm not sure what is happening, Herb. I think I need to pray some more."

I closed my eyes once again and began to talk in my heart with the Lord. When I opened my eyes, there was an identical, but much larger, black and orange butterfly stuck to the staff, just a foot above my head.

"Herb, look!"

"What is going on?" he said. "All the butterflies are being drawn to you. None of them have even come near me."

"I know," I replied. "God, what are you trying to get across to me?"

All at once, these words flooded into my mind. *"I sent the white butterfly first to confirm your last experience and to remind you of who you are in Christ. Then I sent the next two spotted ones, because many of my children are just like them. They have forgotten who they are and have become spotted by the world and are bound by sin. I am calling you to fulfill Galatians 6:1 and restore them by teaching them who they are in Me. The first spotted butterfly was drawn to my Word. The second one was drawn to you by the anointing of my Spirit, as represented by the wooden staff. I will show you when you are to begin. Be patient."*

After sharing these words with Herb, we talked for another hour as I contemplated what this all meant. We spent the rest of the day reading, praying, and sharing our thoughts, once in a while taking a stroll down to the creek for a cool drink. It became increasingly difficult for me to walk back up the little slope, as I was rapidly loosing my physical strength. I was grateful to have the wooden staff to help me. I slept very well that right. The still mountain air was very refreshing, and it most assuredly had been a full day.

Herb drove me back to Kelowna the next morning, and we talked all the way home concerning the strange events of the previous day. I knew that God had used His creation to bring a message across to me, yet what it was all about still escaped me. I would not fully come to understand the meaning of it all until more than a year later.

Green Light—Red Light, One, Two, Three

On September 14, Sandy and I flew to New York, excited about the possibility of working with Dr. Damadian, although we really knew nothing of his vision or how we fitted into his plan. "Dr. D," as I affectionately called him, and his wife, Donna, picked us up at John F. Kennedy Airport and drove us out to their house on Long Island. Although their home was equipped with a large swimming pool, it was really quite modest. We soon learned that they were very down-to-earth people who didn't believe in extravagance, even though they were wealthy. Dr. D actually drove a two-year-old Pontiac. Sandy and I spent the entire week with the Damadians. Our second day there, we were treated to a tour of Manhattan, an incredible dinner at a famous French restaurant, and a Broadway play. We were treated royally and felt quite spoiled. I was also honored to speak at their church that Sunday, and we were warmly received by the 2000-plus-member congregation. Unfortunately, their pastor was away, so we didn't have an opportunity to meet him at that time.

The vision that Dr. Damadian shared with us involved the home-mission board of their church. What he envisioned was holding evangelistic crusades across America, beginning on Long Island. The plan was to plant a new church with the new converts, set a pastor over the flock within six months, then move on to the next crusade and repeat the process. Dr. Damadian asked me if I would oversee the whole operation, beginning with the planning and the choosing of an evangelist. After the crusade I would assume the responsibility of teaching the young flock for the first six months or until such time as a pastor could be set in place.

After explaining this whole vision to us, he then blew our minds when he said, "You will be working together closely with the church board. I will deposit $500,000 in an account to begin with. When that runs out, the account will be replenished." While we were still reeling from that statement, he then added, "Of course you will need to pick out a house and a new car or van, whichever you feel would be more suitable. I am sure we can come to an agreement for a comfortable salary for you guys as well. We will move all your belongings here through my company, and I will have my lawyer begin immigration proceedings just as soon as you say the word."

We were both stunned and in shock to say the least. When we had left Kelowna, we were penniless, trusting God for our daily bread, and now we were being offered more money than we had ever dreamed of, to do the Lord's work in a new and fresh way. I had to stop and pinch myself. Through the long fast, I had been trusting God for new direction, believing that He would show me clearly what to do next; but this was unbelievable, a *chance of a lifetime*. When we left for home at the end of the week, our heads were still spinning. We told the Damadians that the offer felt good to both of us and that we would commit it to prayer and get back to them in a couple of days.

During the flight back, Sandy and I committed the matter to God. We both felt that we should accept the offer; after all, we didn't really have any other options. When we arrived home, I immediately called Dr. Damadian in Long Island and gave him our answer. We then called my brother Murray and sister in-law Cathie to tell them what Dr. D had offered us. Murray and Cathie had served the Lord faithfully with us at Circle Square for the last six of our eight years there. They had then followed our family and moved to Kelowna the year after we did. Murray and Cathie had always been very encouraging and supportive to us, even through the dark and tough times in Kelowna Their children Jacquie, Sara, Michael and Matthew were also very close to our kids' ages, and the eight of them enjoyed many great times together. I thought for sure that they would be excited for us. Although Murray agreed that this move could ultimately be a good thing for us, he didn't seem overly excited about it. My kind and gentle brother didn't let on at the time, as he didn't want to throw cold water on our fire, but he later said that both he and Cathie felt very uneasy about the whole idea.

Murray and Cathie were part of a mixed Bible study group of about 20 men and women that Sandy and I had been leading for a little over a year. Earlier that spring, prior to my extended fast, a few members of our group had asked me to consider starting a church. At the time, most of them were not in fellowship with any other church, although a few attended Kelowna Christian Centre with us. In essence, many of them were stray sheep and they were looking to me to be their shepherd. Despite their continual prompting, I refused to step into that role, as I knew it was a serious responsibility. I let them know that I wouldn't dare take it on without a clear word from the Lord. The study group, as a whole, was saddened that I had accepted Dr. Damadian's offer. Although many of them didn't have a good feeling about it, no one spoke up. They didn't want to selfishly hold us back.

Over the next four and a half months, I returned to Long Island twice more to prepare the groundwork for the new ministry. On my first trip back in November, I had the opportunity to meet Dr. Damadian's pastor, with whom I would be working closely. Although I couldn't put my finger on the exact reason for it, I felt very uncomfortable around this man. Our spirits did not connect. I discussed it with Sandy when I arrived back home. Not wanting to be judgmental, especially without cause, I soon dismissed the matter, chalking it up to different personalities. We proceeded to make preparations for the move. Firstly, I contacted the US

Government and started the preliminary immigration proceedings. Then, as instructed by Dr. Damadian, I obtained estimates from two accredited moving companies. Finally, we put our home up for sale, listing it with Royal LePage through our good friend Joanie Richter, who had originally found the house for us.

My third trip to Long Island, which was scheduled from January 25 to February 8, turned out to be my last one. In spite of the continual preparations that we were making for this total uprooting of our family, my spirit became more and more unsettled. Having no other real options at the time, I kept dismissing these feelings as probably a case of nerves and maybe a fear of the unknown. Sandy and I talked about it at length and once again submitted everything to the Lord. Two days before I was to leave for New York, I had a very unusual experience.

It was slightly after 11:00 p.m. on Wednesday evening, and Sandy and I had just crawled into bed. I wasn't feeling especially tired and was lying there on my back, when suddenly I found myself in the middle of a horrible dream. I was under water at the bottom of a swimming pool and about to run out of air. I knew that I had to reach the surface immediately or I would drown. With all the strength I possessed, I pushed off the bottom and swam frantically to the surface. Without any warning, my head struck a large object that prevented me from reaching the precious air. I immediately dove sideways to try to scramble around the object. I felt that my lungs were about to burst. After what seemed like a few seconds of paddling madly, my hands struck a concrete surface. Instantly I knew I had mistakenly swum the wrong direction and was back at the bottom of the pool again. I reacted immediately and flipped over into a crouching position. With every ounce of strength within me, I shoved off the concrete floor. In a flash, my body was out of the water and I was flying through the air, my feet landing softly on the pool deck.

At that point, I opened my eyes and looked straight at Sandy, who was lying on her back beside me, very much awake.

"Sandy," I blurted out, "I just had the most vivid dream, yet I don't think I was asleep."

"What do you mean?"

"Didn't we just get into bed?" I asked.

"Yeah."

"Well, I might have just had a vision then. I'm not really sure." After explaining the experience in detail, we prayed together, asking God to reveal the meaning to us, if there indeed was one. What came to my mind moments later was this: *"You are headed the wrong direction, and your spirit is feeling suffocated as a result. When you realize it and turn back you will be standing on solid ground again."*

Since we were not certain that my thoughts were from the Lord, Sandy and I discussed them for a few minutes and then felt that we should pray again. "Lord," I began, "We are not sure whether this was a vision from You or just from my own mind, therefore we submit this whole New York ministry and all that is involved to You once again. If this door of opportunity is not from You, Father, and is just a good idea, then we trust that You will close the door and not let us walk through it."

At this point, we both felt assured that I needed to stay with my present commitment and fly to New York one more time, believing that God would either confirm this ministry to me or somehow close it down. Two days later, as previously scheduled, I climbed aboard the Canadian Air flight to Toronto en route to New York's J.F.K. Airport. As requested by Dr. Damadian, I carried with me in my attaché case our preliminary immigration papers and the two moving company estimates for our future move. The flight was quiet and uneventful, that is until I checked in at US Customs in Toronto. What happened next was something I hadn't experienced before and haven't since: The moment I stepped up to the booth, the lady customs official demanded that I open my attaché case and place all of the contents on the counter.

The moment she saw the immigration papers and the moving estimates she came unglued. "So you have already set up shop in our country! You can't do that, Mister. In fact, once you begin immigration, you are not allowed into this country until everything is completed. Even though you are a minister, you still can't come in here and pass the hat around."

"No, I haven't moved to your country yet," I responded kindly. "I'm just taking these papers to a lawyer in New York, so he can complete my family's immigration proceedings."

"Not on your life, Bud," she snapped back at me. "You climb right back on your airplane and head for home. It's for sure you aren't getting into this country."

I was stunned. The door had been literally slammed in my face, and in my heart I knew that the Lord was behind it. We had asked God to clearly show us His will and to close the door if New York was not for us, but I didn't expect that it would happen so soon and be so obvious. In spite of my being refused entrance into the United States and having to return home, I felt relief and an amazing sense of peace. The Lord had made His will known, and there was no doubt in my mind that we were to stay in Kelowna.

Dr. Damadian had difficulty understanding my decision, and I felt saddened about that, but I had no other option but to turn down his wonderful and generous offer. The scary part was that I didn't have any other options at the time and had no idea from where or how our next dollar would come. However, Sandy and I were confident that God was leading us and that He would also provide our every need. The Lord had proven his faithfulness to our family, and we were learning to depend on Him more all the time.

The day after I arrived back home, I received a phone call from Phil Nordine, the pastor of Penticton Christian Centre. We had come to know Phil and his wife, Joan, through our ministry in the Okanagan Valley but hadn't seen or heard from them for many months. Phil was calling to invite Sandy and me to attend a special Sunday evening service at their church the next day. The two men that were to speak, Pastor Mel Davis and Pastor Dave Hubert from the West Coast, were both known to carry a prophetic anointing. Despite the short notice, Sandy and I agreed to attend. We both sensed that we were definitively supposed to be there. On the way to Penticton the next afternoon, we prayed specifically that the Lord would confirm His will to us. If He wanted us to start a church and pastor the little Bible study group in Kelowna, I would be willing, but it would have to be a clear confirmation.

The service that evening was excellent, from the worship led by Phil and Joan to the ministry of the two guest preachers. Sandy and I were enjoying ourselves immensely, sitting in the second row, when out of the blue Pastor Hubert looked directly at the two of us and said, "You two in the second row, the man in the blue jacket and the lady in the red dress—would you please stand up? I have a word from the Lord for you."

"Us?" I responded, pointing to myself as we slowly rose to our feet.

"Yes. I see a cloud above your heads. Written in the cloud is the word *DECISIONS*. You are at a crossroads, and you are wondering and asking the Lord what you are to do for Him. Written under the cloud, I see the word *SHEPHERD*. God wants me to tell you that He is calling you to *pastor*. I also see a crystal clear pool of water. If you don't obey God in this, that water will turn muddy and become polluted."

A little stunned, Sandy and I both sat back down.

Mixed emotions of excitement and apprehension swept over me. I was excited because God had spoken so clearly, yet I was concerned as to how our pastor, David Kalamen, would react to us leaving Kelowna Christian Centre and starting another work in the city. We had just witnessed a mass exodus of a few hundred people a few months earlier. Pastor David had been shaken by it all, and I didn't want to add more fuel to the fire.

About ten days later, my friend Herb handed me a book entitled *Tale of Three Kings*. It was a teaching on the lives of three Biblical kings, Saul, David, and David's son Absalom. The main message was that of submission to spiritual authority, which, it said, invokes the blessing of God. Conversely, it said, refusing to submit brings disastrous results.

After reading the book, I took the message to heart and waited for the Lord to release me from under Pastor David's authority. Nine months later, after much prayer and patience, Pastor David released me. I sensed the timing was right, and so did he. In fact, when I spoke to him about it, he said he already knew in his heart that I was leaving. He gave me the blessing I desired, and we left to start the new fellowship with full confidence that the Lord was calling us to pastor this young flock. The new work began the next Sunday morning, on December 6, 1988, with 17 people in our family room, and we named ourselves Resurrection Life Fellowship. A month later we moved to the French Cultural Centre in downtown Kelowna, where we remained for more than three years until the fellowship came to an end. The services averaged from 40 to 50 people on any given Sunday morning.

Resurrection Life Fellowship existed for exactly three and a half years to the day. During its short life span, it became known as a "spiritual hospital." Many spiritually wounded Christians who were floundering and who were not connected to any other church came and received some restoration and healing. Some of the restored saints moved on and found fellowship in other local churches. We closed the doors of RFL and stopped our services on June 6, 1991, after God spoke to my heart and confirmed His word to me three times in the one day. Our family returned to worship at Kelowna Christian Centre under Pastor Kalamen until the Lord called us back to Edmonton in March of 1992. The rest of the congregation moved on to various other fellowships in the Kelowna area.

Chapter 24

TAKE GOOD AIM

During my second to last year with the Eskimos, Sandy and I had spent a very interesting and divinely inspired evening in our home with our dear friend and spiritual mentor, Larry Kerychuk. At that time, Larry was the Director of Athletes In Action (AIA) Canada. He had been struggling for the past few months with his position in the ministry and shared his concerns quite openly with us. Larry, who is the son of Ukrainian Pentecostal Pastor Paul and Nida Kerychuk, had been baptized in the Holy Spirit in his formative years. The gifts of the Spirit had operated in his life in the past, but when he took on the duty and responsibility of the Director of AIA, he was asked to lay all those gifts aside, especially the gift of speaking in other tongues.

There was a lot of controversy in evangelical circles at that time concerning the charismatic gifts in the church. Larry told us that Campus Crusade for Christ, the parent ministry of A.I.A., wanting to avoid possible problems of disunity, required all their staff to sign an affidavit saying that they would not express any of these gifts, even in their private devotions. I believe that policy has since been changed, thank God, but that is where things were back in 1975. Larry had signed the paper, because he really felt that God had called him to this athletic ministry and the ministry had been very fruitful up to this point. However, after three years of spiritual struggle, he realized that he could not stay on as Director and continue to stifle the gifts with which God had graced him.

As we talked together that evening, Larry shared with us a vision he had for a charismatic, Pentecostal, athletic ministry which he believed should not have any of our human limitations placed on it, and where the gifts of the Holy Spirit would be free to operate. And as well, it would be a ministry where the Baptism of the Holy Spirit, with the evidence of speaking with other tongues, and the other eight gifts would be preached and encouraged. Sandy and I were in complete agreement with him, so the three of us brought our petition together before the Lord and specifically asked Him to raise up a ministry of this type in His perfect timing.

God heard our prayer and answered it, but it wasn't nearly as quick as we expected it would be. Athletes International Ministries (AIM) was birthed ten years later with the first Phoenix Prayer and Praise Conference in the spring of May 1985. Larry, the founder and director of AIM, was truly blessed to be united in spirit with one of the world's great modern day visionaries, Pastor Tommy Barnett of Phoenix First Assembly in Scottsdale, Arizona.

Tommy caught hold of the vision of reaching the world's youth through this anointed athletic platform and simply fanned the flame in Larry's heart. At the time, Larry was on staff at Phoenix First Assembly as an Associate Pastor. To this day, many thousands of athletes—amateur, professional, and retired professionals—have been reached and empowered through AIM. I was privileged to be one of the speakers at that first conference, and Sandy and I attended the next three as well. In 1988, we were able to attend once more, this time with the whole family. That conference in particular was mightily anointed of the Holy Spirit. Our son Brad was set on fire, and a passion to reach youth through his musical gift was ignited.

Numerous ministries have been birthed and anointed by the Holy Spirit at these conferences and have literally touched hundreds of thousands of lives. The most notable to date is the ministry of Promise Keepers. Coach Bill McCartney, the founder of Promise Keepers, came to the Phoenix Conference in June of 1989 and was baptized with the Holy Spirit in the first meeting. Later that same evening Dr. Edwin Lewis Cole spoke an anointed message entitled "Your Word is Your Bond." Following the meeting, Coach McCartney received a vision of football stadiums filled to capacity with men praising God, and the word "Promise Keeper" was planted into his spirit. The next morning he shared the vision with Larry, and the rest is history.

Promise Keepers has become, in my opinion, the greatest Christian men's movement of modern times, with over one million men gathering in Washington, D.C., in the fall of 1997. All across North America, hundreds of thousands of men are taking their God-given place of spiritual leadership in their homes, and the prophecy spoken through the prophet Malachi is being fulfilled before our very eyes: "And he shall turn the hearts of the fathers to the children and the hearts of the children to the fathers" (Malachi 4:6a). God's timing is always perfect.

I believe that Athletes International Ministries, along with many other athletic ministries, has been raised up to reach this generation of youth with the good news of the Gospel of Jesus Christ. Our young people need these positive role models more today than ever before. Athletes, due to their high profiles, are afforded many doors of opportunity to take the gospel to places where other ministries have not been permitted.

One cold Sunday morning in late February of 1990, while we were still living in Kelowna, an older brother in the Lord, Jim Stewart, approached me following our morning church service. As he walked up to me, he began to speak, trembling as he did.

"P-Pastor, I believe I have a word from God that I am supposed to give you. I've never done this before, and I'm not sure that it is really from the Lord, but it feels so strong in my spirit that I know I have to give it to you."

"Go right ahead and speak it out, Jim," I encouraged him. "If it doesn't witness to me, I'll just put it on the shelf. Who knows? It may be for the future. Please just share what's on your heart."

"Okay then, here it goes," he began. "It comes from the third chapter of the book of Revelation, starting in the seventh verse: 'These things says he who is holy, he that is true, he that has the key of David, he that opens and no man can shut, and shuts and no man can open. I know your works: behold I have set before you an open door and no man can shut it.' Pastor, all I know is that it has something to do with David and it has to do with God opening a new door of opportunity for you. That's all I have."

"Thank you, Jim, for obeying the Lord," I said. "It doesn't speak to me at the moment, but I will sure pray about it and see if the Lord speaks anything else to me along this line."

Later that afternoon, while sitting in my living room, I opened the scriptures to see if there was anything else that the Lord might speak to me. I read and re-read the seventh and eighth verses of Revelation chapter three, all the time asking God to speak to my heart if there was anything to this word Jim had given me. The fourth time through I continued on down the page. As I read, one individual word from the twelfth verse leaped off the page into my spirit. It was the word "pillar."

"Lord, what are you saying to me? Pillar . . . David . . . open door." I sensed the presence of the Lord with me, yet nothing came specifically to my heart and mind, so I continued to pray and commit it to God, trusting that He would show me what it meant in His good time. Five days later I received a telephone call from David Mainse in Toronto. He was coming out to Kelowna for some meetings the next week, and he asked me if I could take him skiing up at Big White. I agreed.

That afternoon on the ski lift, the word that Jim had given me was confirmed. As we sped up the mountain in the cool brisk air, David began to open up to me.

"Garry, there is a dual purpose in my asking you to come skiing this afternoon. I want to ask you to come back to work at Crossroads Christian Communications.

"We have been forced to move from our ministry headquarters, and we feel we have no other option but to build a Crossroads Centre. You know that I was content to stay where we were until Jesus comes, but we don't seem to have a choice. We have begun a capital campaign to raise the funds for the new building, and I would like you to consider helping us here in B.C. and Alberta. You could do it on a part-time basis and still pastor your church."

"Thank you, David, for the offer, and I will definitely pray about it," I said. "Perhaps the Lord will release me to help you with the campaign."

"That's great," David replied, and then added, "By the way, God gave me a theme for the campaign while I was in Israel last month. As I was looking at some old ruins in Capernaum, my attention was drawn to an ancient pillar. God showed me that the 100 Huntley Street Television Program was like an electronic umbrella over the nation of Canada, and that He would raise up pillars from coast to coast to help hold it up."

He didn't have to say any more. The moment he mentioned the word pillar, I knew that God had already prepared me, and I knew that my answer would have to be yes.

I worked with Crossroads on their capital campaign for the next two years on a part-time basis. It was exciting to work with David again and to be involved with 100 Huntley Street. In February of 1992 I was given the opportunity to move my family back to Edmonton to direct Huntley Street's Counselling Centre there. I don't know how many times I had said that I would never move my family back to cold Alberta winters. Yet, when I was offered the opportunity to take over the Centre there, I was excited. Sandy and the children were equally enthusiastic. In fact, as I broke the news to them all, Julie burst into tears and jumped for joy. When she finally settled down, she confessed that she had been secretly praying for the past nine months for God to move our family back to

Edmonton. God had been preparing all of us for the next chapter in our lives. The Lord is our Shepherd: He leads us, but never pushes us. He always works like a microwave oven, from the inside out, as He changes our hearts.

Completing the Circle

We arrived back in Edmonton on March 27, 1992, with all our belongings tightly packed in a large Rider rental truck. Brothers Blaine and Bob and a couple friends were there to help us unload our belongings. It was a beautiful warm day, not unlike the ones we had become accustomed to enjoying in the sunny Okanagan. As the day wore on, the temperature dropped noticeably to where it was quite cool. Just as the last box was unloaded and placed in the garage, a strong northwest wind blew up and a cold blanket of snow came down with a vengeance. I immediately turned to Sandy and jokingly said. "Welcome back to Alberta."

Julie's prayers had been answered and our family was back in our old stomping grounds. It felt good to be home, in spite of the weather. When you are where God has called you to be, the externals really don't seem to matter much. The home we were able to rent was a three-year-old bi-level near my old neighborhood on 53 Street and 152 Avenue, in the northeast area of the city. The house was smaller than we had become used to during our seven years in Kelowna, but it was spacious enough and suited us just fine. It was about a 35-minute drive to the Huntley Street Counselling Centre on 114 Steet and Jasper Avenue, but I didn't mind it at all. It gave me some time to meditate and reflect each morning on the way to the office.

I served as Counselling Director at the Centre until June of 1994 and enjoyed every minute of it. It was a joy and a privilege to work together with some of the dearest and most faithful saints in this world, the 100 Huntley Street volunteer counsellors. Most of them were retired women and men, with hearts of love, who sat for hours every day listening to people's problems and praying for God to intervene in their lives. The most blessed times of all were when the callers would ring back to give praise reports as to how God had answered the counsellors' prayers.

One afternoon in April of 1993, I received a phone call from my pastor, Tony Yakielashek. Our family had begun attending St. Albert

Christian Life Centre earlier that winter, and we had come to know and love Tony and his wife, Judy. Their vision of their fellowship that met in Bellerose Composite High School in St. Albert was so close to that of our little Resurrection Life Fellowship in Kelowna that it was scary. It was like Pastor Tony had been reading my sermon notes.

Our family had been traveling from northeast Edmonton to be a part of this church for a few months at the time this phone call came.

"Are you sitting down?" Tony began.

"Yes, I am. What's up?"

"I believe the Lord wants you and Sandy to own a home again, and I think He has shown me a way for it to be done."

"Tony, you can't be serious!" I exclaimed. "We don't have two nickels to rub together. How would we come up with a down payment?"

"You are not going to need one, if you are willing to throw in a few pounds of sweat. I've been talking with one of our congregation, Gerry Wigmore, a real estate agent, and he has a bank manager who is willing to swap 'sweat equity' in lieu of a down payment. I firmly believe that God wants you to have a home again, and we are going to help you get it. I have a friend who will do the excavating for free, and my brother David will help us pour the basement. My background is building, so I will help you all I can with the framing, and I am sure the Lord will send others to help as well."

"Pastor, I'm speechless," I replied, choking back the tears. "Sandy is going to come unglued."

"There are a lot of details to iron out yet," Tony cautioned, "but I am sure we can have it built by Christmas."

"Man, this is the greatest Christmas present we've ever received. The kids are going to be ecstatic."

When I arrived home with the good news, the whole family were overjoyed, especially Chéri. For months she had been confessing that God was going to move our family back to St. Albert. She must have known something in her heart that the rest of us were unaware of. God had planned this for us all along, and she somehow had got wind of it.

The construction of our new home was nothing short of a miracle. The bank manager gave us unbelievable favour and even tricked her computer with some misinformation so that our mortgage would pass. Stan Unger, the president of Carolina Homes in Calgary, gave us an interest-free loan of $10,000 to put down on the lot. We were able to pay it back from the first mortgage-draw a few months later. Pastor Tony helped me with the foundation, basement walls, framing, plumbing and numerous other things. My close friend Paul Collins, of Collins Industries, donated a steel beam and posts to carry the second story; as a result there were no bearing walls and we were able to put each wall wherever we pleased. My dear friend Larry Burden loaned us another $10,000, interest-free, at a critical time, as well as helping build our trusses on site. The Lord sent people to donate the drawings, electrical wiring, flooring, roofing, and much, much more. Bob Vanderwell, of Vanderwell Contractors in Slave Lake, donated every 2x6, 2x4 and 1x4 in the house, and saved us thousands of dollars. On top of all this, God gave us amazing deals on just about everything. When all was said and done, within nine months we moved into our three-bedroom, 2056-square-foot, two-storey home on March 1, 1994.

Our Home

One morning, while we were still in the construction phase, I was reading the Bible when I felt a prompting to turn to Psalms 127. I read: "Unless the Lord builds the house, its builders labour in vain."

Before the home was completed, God gave me a poem that expressed the miracle that took place.

"I'll build you a house," I heard the Lord say,

"But it won't be built in the conventional way.
I am preparing and anointing more than a few,
Who will come right on time and know just what to do."
From the planning to the framing to the finishing of each storey
We thank everyone, and we give God the glory."

A month after we moved into our beautiful home, Sandy surprised me with a very matter-of-fact comment. She was standing at the kitchen counter preparing dinner when I came in from work. She turned to me and said, "You know, of course, that your job at Huntley Street is only temporary and is about to come to an end."

"Why would you say that? What are you talking about?"

"I was praying for you this afternoon and sensed that God has given you this job, as a sabbatical. I know you love what you are doing, and this is a wonderful job, but you are definitely not being challenged. I believe the Lord has something else for us to do, just down the road. Don't you agree?"

"I don't disagree, Dear, but you're right: I am enjoying this rest from the front lines of battle."

"I trust God will show you what is next." Sandy reassured me.

"You're probably right, but I'm not going to concern myself with it now. That's the Lord's department. I love working with the counsellors at the centre, so if God has something else for me, He will surely tell me, when I need to know."

About a month later, I received a phone call from Phoenix, Arizona. It was Larry Kerychuk. "How's it going up there, you hockey puck?" he quipped. "Garry, the reason I am calling is to invite you to our 10th Annual Athletic Conference, which is going to be held here the last weekend of June. Our board feels very strongly that it is time for AIM to expand our borders. We would like to see the ministry come to Canada first before other countries. I think you are the man to launch AIM in Canada. Will you come to the conference with an open mind and take a look and see what the Lord says to you? A local Christian businessman who hails from Victoria, B.C., has offered to pay all your expenses, if you'll agree to come. What do you say?"

Without Larry saying another word, I already knew in my heart what my answer would be. This was what I had been prepared for during the last 22 years. I kept these thoughts to myself and responded to Larry's offer. "Yes Larry, I'll come on one condition. That is, if this gentleman will cover Sandy's expenses as well. If God is calling me, then she is being called too."

"Well, he didn't offer to pay for both of you, but I'll talk to him and get back to you by tomorrow."

I felt confident that Larry would come back with an affirmative, and he did. Sandy and I flew down to Phoenix on the 25th of June, and we flew back on the 31st with a vision for AIM Canada. At the publishing of this book, we have just completed our sixth year of operation with the Canadian Chapter of AIM. To date, we have held three great Canadian Conferences, one in Kelowna and two in Edmonton. We have witnessed hundreds of young people responding to the testimonies of athletes in numerous high school and youth outreach programs.

When God called us from the football wars to serve Him full time in the ministry at Circle Square Ranch, we thought it would be for the rest of our lives, or until Jesus returned, whichever came first. God in His wisdom didn't show us what He had for us down the road, or I most likely would have been reluctant to go. When I look back on the many mountain-top experiences and numerous valleys that the Lord has taken us through, I stand totally amazed.

I see now that each experience that He led us through was used for our spiritual development and training for the next stage of our spiritual journey. I am convinced that God's main concern for His children is that they "grow in grace" (mature spiritually) and develop in character. Our Heavenly Father is not so much interested in what we are doing for Him, but in what He is doing in us and, as a result, through us. Everything that we have encountered along our way has been an integral part of that learning process. When we finally came to understand this, the Word of God really began to come alive in our hearts. Scriptures like Romans 8:28, "And we know that in all things God works for the good of those who love him, who have been called according to his purpose," took on new meaning.

For our family, these last 29 years have been an exciting and often times challenging adventure. Through it all God has truly demonstrated His love and faithfulness to us. We have come to know him as Saviour, Healer, Provider, Protector, Comforter and Friend. Through these experiences and countless others not written in this book, He has shown us beyond any doubt that Jesus Christ is indeed Lord of all, and that He alone can satisfy the longings of the human heart. St. Augustine wrote, "Our hearts are restless, oh Lord, until they find their rest in thee."

Larry and Wendy Kerychuk

Epilogue

SIMPLY RECEIVE IT OR NOT

The purpose of this myriad of testimonies demonstrating God's divine intervention in the life of our family is to share with you, dear reader, the goodness of the Lord and to positively show that all of God's children are called to be the recipients of His matchless grace.

While I played as a wide receiver in the Canadian Football League for those eleven years, I learned how a receiver was supposed to perform in order to excel on the field. Unfortunately, I didn't always run the patterns or catch the ball as I should have, but in the process I did learn the principles of receiving, and I understood the reasons for my occasional failures. From that perspective, I was able to continually grow and improve as a player. In the football profession, like in any other, we call this experience or maturity.

The Christian walk is very similar in many ways, and the same principles hold true in life as they do on the football field. Basically, in order to develop into a good receiver, you must first make the team. A coach looks at your present ability, but he also considers your future potential. God looks at us in much the same way, and in His foreknowledge, He sees us perfected or matured in Christ. Many of us Christians stumble and make mistakes as we go through life, and although some may condemn us for dropping the ball or slipping on the turf, our gracious Heavenly Father never does. He lovingly forgives us, because His anger against sin was appeased at the Cross, when Jesus shed His precious blood. He simply encourages us to try again. Hopefully, we learn from our mistakes and grow a little more in His grace.

In the world of football, for a player to make the final cuts and be selected to the roster, he must prove to the coaching staff his ability to follow instructions; that is, he must study, understand, and submit to the coach's philosophy. In other words, he must know the playbook. God has a playbook for all of mankind. It is called the Bible. If we are going to make it on God's final roster, we are going to have to heed the instructions in the Book. One of the first and most important directives is given in John 1:12: "Yet to all who **received** him, to those who believed in his name, he gave the right to become children of God." In order for us to be a receiver on this eternal team, we must first make *The Ultimate*

Reception—that is, to receive Jesus Christ as our personal Lord and Saviour.

Anyone and everyone can receive the Lord into their life through a simple prayer of faith and surrender. Romans 10:10 says, "That if you confess (verbally agree) with your mouth, "Jesus is Lord," and believe in your heart that God raised him from the dead, you will be saved. For it is with your heartyhat you believe and are justified, and it is with your mouth that you confess and are saved." We believe with our hearts and we seal it with our lips.

The word *believe* here in scripture does not mean just intellectually assenting to a code of ethics or a philosophy, but the connotation has a much deeper sense of commitment. The definition of *believe* means *to commit to, to trust in, to rely upon, and to adhere or stick to like glue.* When we believe by God's definition, and declare our faith verbally, we truly have received Christ as our Lord and Saviour and have been accepted by God as an eternal team member—with a "no-cut" contract, I might add.

After we have received the Lord into our life, we have the right to receive from the Lord, which enables us to serve Him lovingly. The word *receive* occurs 128 times in 121 verses in the New Testament. We were created by God to be open receptacles of His blessings and grace, .i.e., divine favour. God has no favourite children, because His love for us all is unconditional and complete, and He certainly doesn't want to bless one more than any other. God has promised us in His Word soundness, healing, provision, preservation, and wholeness. That is what the word *salvation* actually means. All of these promises are found in Christ, so when we receive Jesus as Lord, we qualify for all the promises, simply because they are all found in Him.

"For no matter how many promises God has made, they are 'Yes' in Christ" (2 Corinthians 1:20).

Whether we receive of these blessings or not depends upon faith, which is the receiver that God has given us. "For it is by grace you have been saved, through faith—and this not from yourselves, it is the gift of God—not by works, so that no one can boast" (Ephesians 2:8,9). This gift of faith is given to those who repent of their sin and turn to God in humility. Jesus said to the religious leaders of His day, "Unless you repent, you cannot believe."

So then the gift of faith, *the power to believe*, is given by God to a repentant heart. To repent, by definition, is to make a 180-degree turn and head in the opposite direction. In other words, to repent is to have a "change of mind."

Trying to be good enough to be acceptable to God will never cut it. Isaiah the prophet wrote, "All our own righteousness is but filthy rags in the eyes of God." The only possible way to be acceptable or righteous before a Holy God is by faith—faith in the completed work of Christ's death and resurrection. We can add nothing to it by our own efforts, but must simply receive the truth and surrender our lives to Jesus, trusting Him to live His life in and through us by the Holy Spirit.

I want to pause here for a moment and ask you, dear reader, the most important question you will ever be asked: **HAVE YOU MADE THE ULTIMATE RECEPTION? HAVE YOU RECEIVED JESUS CHRIST AS YOUR PERSONAL LORD AND SAVIOUR?**

If you have never done that before, why don't you do it right now? Just simply pray this prayer from your heart and Jesus will come by His Spirit and enter into an eternal relationship with you. Jesus is patiently waiting for you to ask Him into your life and to receive God's forgiveness for your sins. The blood of Jesus will cleanse you of all sin and make you fit for this heavenly team.

The scriptures declare "that God was reconciling the world to himself in Christ, not counting men's sins against them. And he has committed to use the message of reconciliation." (2 Corinthians 5:19). The Gospel, or good news, is that God has already forgiven you for everything you have ever done wrong or ever will do. All that is left for you to do is to receive Jesus' incredible sacrifice on your behalf and to begin to live a life of thankfulness to God.

Go ahead and pray. God has been patiently waiting for you to accept His love, the love that He demonstrated to you at the Cross. It's not the exact words that God is concerned with, but the attitude and sincerity of heart. Go ahead. He is listening.

"Father, I thank you for sending Jesus to die on the cross for me. I thank you that His spotless blood totally paid for my sin. I humble myself before You and ask You to make me Your child. I will serve You in gratitude all the days of my life. Thank You, Lord, that I am a child of God. I am a new creation, just as you promised (2 Corinthians 5:17). *I surrender my whole life to you. Please come now, Holy Spirit, and begin to live Your life through me."*

If you just prayed that prayer from your heart, you have just made the greatest and most important decision of your life. I would encourage you to seek out other Christians and share your new-found faith with them. I strongly encourage you to look for a fellowship with a group of believers, where the Bible is taught and where you can begin to grow in the knowledge of God. The Apostle Peter wrote, "But grow in grace and knowledge of our Lord and Savior Jesus Christ." I would love to hear from you as well and would be delighted to recommend a church fellowship to you. Please write to the address below, or call me at either of the phone numbers listed. God bless you and keep you in His unfailing love.

Athletes International Ministries is a non-profit, registered charitable organization. Founded in 1995 by Garry and Sandy Lefebvre. Widely known as **AIM Canada** or just **AIM.**

For additional copies of **The Ultimate Reception**, *or to help support Aim's programs, please write or email us at the address below.*

Garry Lefebvre
157-Deer Ridge Drive
St. Albert, Alberta T8N 6G8
Ph. (780)-460-3943
Fax. (780)-460-9140
Email. aim_canada@shaw.ca

The Ultimate Reception

"Order Form for Additional Copies"

Name:_____

Address:_____

City:_____ Prov:_____ P.C.:_____

Phone: (_____) _____ Fax: (_____) _____

E-mail:_____

Method of Payment

Money Order _____ Cheque _____ VISA _____

VISA __ __ __ __ / __ __ __ __ / __ __ __ __ / __ __ __ __

EXP _____ / _____

Number of copies _____ x $20.00 $_____

Add $5.00 for shipping and handling $_____

                                        Total $_____

Please make payment payable to **Multiple Blessings Unlimited** and
send to **157 Deer Ridge Drive, St. Albert, AB T8N 6G8**.

**Multiple Blessings
    Unlimited**   **Aim Canada**